Linguistic Minimalism

"This deeply-informed study, drawing from a wide diversity of domains, provides a thoughtful perspective on how a minimalist program in linguistics emerges as a natural outcome of advances in understanding of the nature of language and its acquisition. It also outlines a course the program might take in seeking to identify the distinctive properties of human language, separating them from the effects of more general principles, which may reduce to laws of nature. To determine its special properties has been the goal of serious inquiry into language from its ancient origins. Such inquiry is now taking quite new forms, and, as Boeckx shows, is productively investigating questions that could scarcely have been formulated not long ago." **Noam Chomsky**, MIT

"An engaging, accessible, important exposition of Chomsky's pioneering Program, including its normal scientific evolution, the higher standards of explanation it imposes and the exciting new interdisciplinary linkages it has established." **Samuel David Epstein**, University of Michigan

"*Linguistic Minimalism: Origins, Methods, and Aims* is an insightful presentation of the conceptual underpinnings and internal logic of the Minimalist Program. It will show the curious why those of us pursuing this program are so excited by its prospects." **Howard Lasnik**, University of Maryland

"Cedric Boeckx has constructed an illuminating nontechnical exposition of the character, historical roots, new insights, and profound interdisciplinary reach of the Minimalist Program, which has for over a decade been moving the biolinguistic approach to the study of language and mind forward. For anyone who wants to learn (more) about the MP, this valuable overview is an excellent starting point." **Robert Freidin**, Princeton University

To Noam, for reasons that will be obvious
to anyone who reads this book
& above all
To Youngmi, for reasons that words cannot begin to express

Linguistic Minimalism

Origins, Concepts, Methods, and Aims

CEDRIC BOECKX

OXFORD

UNIVERSITY PRESS

OXFORD
UNIVERSITY PRESS

Great Clarendon Street, Oxford OX2 6DP

Oxford University Press is a department of the University of Oxford.
It furthers the University's objective of excellence in research, scholarship,
and education by publishing worldwide in

Oxford New York

Auckland Cape Town Dar es Salaam Hong Kong Karachi
Kuala Lumpur Madrid Melbourne Mexico City Nairobi
New Delhi Shanghai Taipei Toronto

With offices in

Argentina Austria Brazil Chile Czech Republic France Greece
Guatemala Hungary Italy Japan Poland Portugal Singapore
South Korea Switzerland Thailand Turkey Ukraine Vietnam

Oxford is a registered trade mark of Oxford University Press
in the UK and in certain other countries

Published in the United States
by Oxford University Press Inc., New York

© Cedric Boeckx 2006

British Library Cataloguing in Publication Data
Data available

Library of Congress Cataloguing in Publication Data
Data available

Typeset by SPI Publisher Services, Pondicherry, India
Printed in Great Britain
on acid-free paper by
Biddles Ltd., King's Lynn, Norfolk

ISBN 0-19-929757-6   978-0-19-929757-3 (Hbk.)
       0-19-929758-4   978-0-19-929758-0 (Pbk.)
1 3 5 7 9 10 8 6 4 2

Contents

Acknowledgements

Products of science are rarely the result of a single person's work. The present book is no exception. I benefited immensely from interactions with friends and colleagues in the process of conceiving and writing this essay, and it is a pleasure to acknowledge my indebtedness to them here.

First and foremost, I would like to thank Noam Chomsky, who has been extremely supportive of my work since I joined the field, and has encouraged me to write this book. Noam commented extensively on the manuscript, and always took time to meet with me to address various issues discussed in the following pages. It will be obvious to anyone who reads but a single page of this book that Noam's influence on me has been immense. His are shoulders of a true giant.

Next, I would like to acknowledge the constant support of three individuals who give meaning to the musketeers' dictum 'Un pour tous, tous pour un' in my scientific life: Norbert Hornstein, Massimo Piattelli-Palmarini, and Juan Uriagereka. Norbert has read virtually everything I have written on the minimalist program, has discussed the generative enterprise with me on what must come close to a daily basis, has provided much-needed laughs and intellectual support, and managed to make me think of something else when I needed a break. It is hard to imagine what I would do without him. Massimo has been a constant source of delightful scientific information and sound advice ever since we met in 2003. One-hour meetings with Massimo are worth decades of graduate education. His friendship is both an honor and a privilege. Juan has been a constant source of support and inspiration ever since we met and talked about Prigogine in 1997. Although our crazy lives have made it difficult for us to sit down and talk as much as we would like, the dialogue between us is something I treasure immensely. I don't think I would have thought about writing a book like this one if Juan hadn't first written *Rhyme and Reason*. To Norbert, Massimo, and Juan, thank you for making my understanding of the minimalist program much richer.

My teachers Željko Bošković and Howard Lasnik deserve special thanks for giving me an excellent introduction to minimalism, and the generative program as a whole. Howard, in particular, made me realize how rich the first chapter of *Aspects* is. More recently, Paul Pietroski has been a wonderful source of insights, and helped me understand what a genuine semantics for natural languages might look like. My colleague Marc Hauser raised many thoughtful questions that no doubt made the present book better. I wish many more cognitive scientists were as enthusiastic about the field of linguistics as he is, and invested as much time in understanding the enterprise as he does. Peter Galison, from the department of the history of science at Harvard, clarified notions like 'theory,' 'model', and 'program' and in so doing greatly facilitated the writing of Chapter 3. Steven Pinker, Ray Jackendoff, and Fritz Newmeyer took time to discuss what they regard as severe limitations of the program, and thereby helped me gauge which aspects of minimalism required special attention and further clarification. Fritz turned out to be one of the three reviewers of this book for Oxford University Press. His thorough comments, and those of the two anonymous reviewers, helped me greatly in organizing the material for publication.

A group of friends went over the pre-final draft and gave me invaluable comments: Kleanthes K. Grohmann, Adam Szczegielniak, Jairo Nunes, Cheryl Murphy, Dennis Ott, Martin Reitbauer, and Clemens Mayr. I cannot thank them enough for all the time they devoted to this project. Clemens Mayr went well beyond the call of duty as my research assistant, and considerably improved all aspects of the manuscript I gave him. Without his knowledge and expertise I wouldn't have been able to finish the book on time.

I also want to thank my students (Balka Öztürk, Ju-Eun Lee, Masa Kuno, Hiro Kasai, Taka Kato, So-One Hwang, Bridget Samuels, Beste Kamali, and Clemens Mayr) for listening to and commenting on some of the material that made it into this book, and my senior colleagues in the department of linguistics at Harvard, Jim Huang and Jay Jasanoff, for giving me much-valued freedom in designing courses and other projects, and more generally for creating an atmosphere in which I can thrive. In this context, I want to thank our department administrator, Cheryl Murphy, for greatly facilitating my research by making administrative duties (almost) a pleasure, and for providing good cheers.

Stephen Jay Gould can no longer read this book, but his influence on me will be obvious throughout the text. He is sorely missed.

For commenting on portions of the manuscript and/or taking time to talk about the meaning of the minimalist program with me, thanks go to (in no particular order): Sylvain Bromberger, Morris Halle, Lyle Jenkins, Justin Leiber, Andrea Moro, Jan-Wouter Zwart, Jean-Roger Vergnaud, Robert Chametzky, David Lightfoot, Sam Epstein, Richard Kayne, Naoki Fukui, Gary Marcus, and Luigi Rizzi. Thanks also to Lyndsey Rice, Sarah Barrett, and Chloe Plummer for expert editing.

I am grateful to my editor, John Davey, for his interest in the project, his constant encouragement, and his sound advice.

The writing of this book was made possible by various grants from Harvard University, which I gratefully acknowledge. I am also grateful to my colleagues at the Mind-Brain-Behavior Initiative and to Martin Nowak at the Program for Evolutionary Dynamics, for creating an environment conducive to the kind of interdisciplinary research that the study of language requires.

Pablo Picasso's *The Bull. State I–IV* (1945) is reproduced in Chapter 3 by kind permission of the Artists Rights Society.

Last, but not least, I want to thank my wife, Youngmi, for her help at all levels, her presence in all circumstances, and her constant encouragement in spite of the fact that my various projects are all too often synonymous with more time spent away from home. No words can adequately express what her love and her companionship in life mean to me. She is the stuff that dreams are made of.

Abbreviations

A	Adjective
AP	Adjectival Phrase
ECP	Empty Category Principle
EPP	Extended Projection Principle
GB	Government-Binding (model)
Infl	Inflection
InflP	Inflection Phrase
LCA	Linear Correspondence Axiom
LF	Logical Form
M	Modal (auxiliary)
MTC	Movement Theory of Control
N	Noun
NP	Noun Phrase
P	Preposition
P&P	Principles and Parameters (model)
PF	Phonetic Form
PLD	Primary Linguistic Data
POS	Poverty of Stimulus
PP	Prepositional Phrase
PS	Phrase Structure
S	Sentence
UG	Universal Grammar
V	Verb
VP	Verb Phrase

1

The Minimalist Gamble

The goal of the present volume is to synthesize and clarify ideas that may seem to some to be more imaginative or more outrageous than anything to be found in the pages of modern novels; ideas that at first sound, in the words of Bill Bryson, 'worryingly like the sort of thoughts that would make you edge away if conveyed to you by a stranger on a park bench'. The central idea to be discussed is that our human language capacity, our 'language instinct' as Pinker (1994) calls it, shows signs of optimal design and exquisite organization that may indicate the inner workings of very simple and general computational (physical and mathematical) laws in a mental organ. This idea was first formulated by Noam Chomsky in the early 1990s, and has been investigated systematically since then by linguists and other cognitive scientists under the rubric of the Minimalist Program. For now I want to refer to this enterprise as the minimalist gamble and tell you why a group of serious, professional, and well-informed scientists think their wild minimalist ideas have a chance of being true.

Scientists at all times make the standard gamble that the portion of the world they are investigating can be understood in a simple fashion, that the world is not as 'messy' as it looks, that it shows signs of organization, and that it is governed by laws of general applicability. Clearly, there must be more to the minimalist gamble than that. Otherwise, a book like the present one would have little reason to exist. Fortunately, there is more, much more to the minimalist gamble than the standard, universal search for simplicity in our quest for understanding. And it is that which makes the minimalist program in need of careful exposition and clarification.

1.1 Minimalism in a nutshell

So, what's special about the minimalist program? It will take me a whole book to tell you in detail, but let me try to formulate the essence of linguistic minimalism in a nutshell. For fifty years now, linguists have been involved in establishing the necessity of a specific component of our biological endowment to account for the remarkable (tacit) knowledge and ability we display when we produce and understand (spoken or signed) language. This inborn component has received various names. Among the most popular ones are the language faculty, the language organ, the language instinct, and Universal Grammar. Fifty years of intensive research have documented that the core properties of our linguistic capacity cannot be acquired by any naïve theory of learning that relies on reinforcement, correction, imitation, memorization, or brute instruction. Our ability to turn noise into sound and sound into meaning, our ability to extract words from the messy speech signal and organize them into meaningful units called phrases and to combine these phrases into sentences, our ability to expand any sentence into a longer sentence, our ability to perceive subtle but robust contrasts like *John is easy to please* (= 'it is easy to please John') vs. *John is eager to please* (= 'John is eager to please others'), and our ability to produce and understand utterances we have never encountered before—all these point to the need for an innate faculty of language. This much I take to be uncontroversial (Jerry Fodor would call it 'non-negotiable').[1]

Once the existence of an innate language faculty is granted, it is up to linguists and other scientists to determine its content. And here of course one expects controversy. Science is hard, the evidence

[1] The fact that I (and many others) take some innate component to support our linguistic ability to be necessary does not mean that everyone else does. I will not discuss this sad situation here, merely pointing that the arguments raised against an innate language faculty are extremely weak and very often incoherent (see e.g. Cowie 1999). For some discussion in the context of language, see Chomsky's work, Pinker (1994, 2002), Jackendoff (1994, 2002), Piattelli-Palmarini (1980), Crain and Pietroski (2001), and Fodor (2001).

is subject to multiple interpretations, and the theoretical options, though not infinite, are all too often numerous. Minimalism takes as its point of departure what many, myself included, consider our very best bet as to what the language faculty may contain.[2] I will refer to it here as the consensus view or the standard model.[3] Technically, it is known as the Principles and Parameters approach (P&P). I will have more to say about this approach in Chapter 2. For now, it suffices to say that the P&P approach provides the language learner with a fixed set of principles (rules of grammar, if you wish), valid for all languages. These principles come as a menu, a set of courses that the learner can combine in a limited number of ways (the 'para-meters') on the basis of well-defined properties of the linguistic input so as to match the language of her community. The linguist Mark Baker, in a general introduction to the P&P approach (Baker 2001), has likened principles to the list of atoms in the periodic table that may be combined in various ways (the 'parameters') to form molecules.

The general idea behind the P&P approach is clear enough (it's one of those ideas that once they are formulated, you can't stop wondering why nobody came up with it before—the tell-tale sign that the idea is right, according to Richard Feynman), and the model it gave rise to in the 1980s has been remarkably successful. It has allowed linguists to cover a truly impressive range of similarities and differences across the languages of the world like never before in the history of linguistics. The minimalist program grew out of the perceived success of the P&P approach. It took the

[2] I would even go further, and claim that the P&P view is the only serious bet we have at this point, and that it may be the only bet we can entertain given the dominant paradigm in cognitive science known as the computational-representational theory of the mind (see Pinker (1997) for a very accessible overview). But this is not the place to go into this issue.

[3] A note of caution for linguists: What I call the standard model is not to be confused with what is often referred to as the standard theory in generative grammar. The standard theory refers to a short-lived theory outlined in Chomsky (1965). Although the general remarks about language in Chomsky (1965) remain valid to this day, the specific linguistic theory sketched there was drastically modified in the early 1970s. For good overviews of this development, see Newmeyer (1996) and Freidin (1992).

principles-and-parameters shape of the language faculty for granted, and asked how much of this shape could be the direct result of optimal, computationally efficient design. This move in linguistic inquiry is far from trivial. Just imagine: barely fifteen years after formulating the first principles and parameters of Universal Grammar, linguists began to ask whether the principles they discovered could be understood in terms of higher standards of inquiry. Do linguistic principles display interesting symmetry, uniformity, economy? Why do we have these principles and not others? How much of these linguistic principles follow from the most basic assumptions/ axioms everyone has to make when they begin to investigate language (what Chomsky has called 'virtual conceptual necessity')? The last question gives meaning to the term 'minimalist.' The minimalist program for linguistic theory adopts as its working hypothesis the idea that Universal Grammar is 'perfectly' designed, that is, it contains nothing more than what follows from our best guesses regarding conceptual, biological, physical necessity. This hypothesis is probably too strong (Chomsky calls it the 'strong minimalist thesis'), but in practice scientists often adopt the strongest possible thesis as their working hypothesis. The strongest hypothesis then acts as a limiting case, enabling us to see more precisely where and when the hypothesis fails and how much of it may be true.

The strong minimalist thesis is indeed a wild idea. Even in the realm of physics, where understanding is so much more advanced than in an emerging science like linguistics, and where the evidence for beautiful regularity in nature is strongest, giants like Max Planck never failed to point out that 'we have no right to assume that any physical laws exist'. Einstein put it best when he wrote to his friend Solovine (30 March 1952): 'You find it surprising that I feel that the intelligibility of the world (as far as we are entitled to speak of such) is a mystery or eternal secret. Well, a priori, one should expect a chaotic world, which in no way could be comprehended by reasoning' (Einstein 1987). Eugene Wigner meant nothing else when he spoke of the 'unreasonable effectiveness of mathematics' in physics. The expectation that one will find not just order ('principles'), but deep, beautiful, minimalist order in the domain of language, a domain that has just been established as part of the purview of biology (the biology of mind, a.k.a. modern cognitive science), should indeed sound outrageous, wild, and completely unreasonable. And yet I will argue in the present book that the pursuit of the minimalist program makes eminent sense in the present context in cognitive science, on various grounds and at various levels: historical, philosophical, biological, and, most interestingly of all, empirical. I will investigate the nature of minimalism at all these levels in the following chapters, for I believe that it is the conjunction of various perspectives that strengthens and lends credence to minimalism in linguistics.

1.2 How to approach minimalism

I will begin by exploring minimalism in its historical dimension (Chapter 2). I will examine the origin of minimalist thought in the course of the development of the biolinguistic approach to language (often referred to as the 'generative enterprise') and show that a proper characterization of the history of the field supports the minimalist program, and that conversely, failure to appreciate past success may lead to too quick a rejection of the program as a whole. In much the same way as it is important to examine the nature of minimalism in its historical amplitude, it is equally important to emphasize the programmatic nature of the enterprise, and this is what I do in Chapter 3.

Chomsky never tires of pointing out in all his writings on minimalism that the minimalist program is, as its name suggests, just a 'program', a mode of investigation, and 'not a theory' (see e.g. Chomsky 2000a: 92, 2002: 96, and Fitch et al. 2004: appendix). By that, Chomsky means that minimalism asks questions and follows guidelines that are broad enough to be pursued in a great many directions. This flexibility, this room for alternative instantiations of minimalism, is what the term 'program' emphasizes.

From personal experience, I can say that the notion of a 'program' has been one of the most difficult to convey to colleagues in other fields who were eager to learn about minimalism. Invariably, they point out that if all Chomsky and others mean by 'program' is that there are no definite answers to minimalist questions yet, that if 'program' refers to the fact that minimalism is still a theory in the making, then minimalism is no different from any other scientific theory. There is, after all—they are quick to point out—nothing definite in science. Invariably, my reaction is to grant that my colleagues have a point, that maybe the programmatic character of minimalism is not all that different from the character of other theoretical investigation they have in mind, and that as long as we are clear about the fact that there is not yet any definite set of minimalist elements and principles of grammar, it does not matter much whether we call it a theory or a program. After all, a quick look at the literature on theory, theoretical models, programs, etc. reveals that philosophers of science, historians of science, and scientists themselves have not been consistent in their uses of these terms. But it is important not to lose sight of the fact (and this is all I want to stress by using the term 'program') that we are still far from having a fully-fledged minimalist theory of language. This fact has important repercussions for what it means to do research in the minimalist program. A program is open-ended, it may take a long time to mature, it allows researchers to make maximal use of their creativity as they try to move from minimalist guidelines to concrete principles, it makes room for multiple, not necessarily mutually consistent or compatible perspectives, and it cannot be evaluated in terms of true or false, but in terms of fecund or sterile.

The philosopher and historian of science Imre Lakatos (1970) proposed a model of the nature of scientific inquiry that transcended the difficulties inherent in Popper's and Kuhn's better-known approaches. Lakatos placed the term 'program' at the heart of his model, and claimed that programs encompass a maze or ocean of possible theories. Programs are characterized by a core which provides the essence of the program—the idea, or ideal, that persists beyond the fate of theories when they encounter facts. To ensure its survival, this core is protected by an envelope of auxiliary hypotheses. According to Lakatos, it is the presence of auxiliary hypotheses that allows the core of the program to survive even in the face of empirical falsification. If a given prediction fails, one need not abandon the program as a whole, as naïve falsificationists would have it. Rather, new auxiliary hypotheses have to be brought in to 'save the phenomena'. Lakatos clearly expressed the idea that programs are not disproved or falsified: they just give rise to positive or negative heuristics, fecund or sterile modes of discovery. If the program consistently fails to give rise to new predictions or to discovery of novel facts, or to a better understanding of previous discoveries, it progressively degenerates. It leads nowhere, and it is therefore abandoned.

In Chapter 3, I adopt Lakatos's characterization of research programs and attempt to define the core of the minimalist program in linguistic theory. That is, I try to enumerate that which every linguistic work written under the rubric of minimalism must endorse, either implicitly or explicitly. Since I think that the major thrust of minimalism is not technical in nature, it is possible to introduce key aspects of the program with relatively straightforward concepts and without too much jargon. It is my hope that the reader will thereby be able to get a sense of the motivations behind the current work in linguistics that tries to articulate the minimalist program. In so doing, I also try to go beyond the caricature of minimalism that can be found in numerous publications. Consider, for example, Radford (1997: 515), who in his lengthy and detailed textbook introduction to the minimalist program defines minimalism as 'a theory of grammar ... whose core assumption is that grammars should be described in terms of the minimal set of theoretical and descriptive apparatus necessary'. If this were the core assumption of minimalism, Occam would be the central figure in modern linguistics, and outsiders would see in the field little more than a formulation of responsible science. No one could rationally object to such a program—nor, I suppose, could anyone be expected to be particularly excited by it. Indeed, outsiders may reasonably wonder whether approaches to grammar before the minimalist program were doing real science. I think that what preceded the minimalist program was real science, and I think minimalism is particularly exciting, so the caricature just mentioned is just that: a gross oversimplification, one that must be corrected lest somebody be misled. One way of going beyond the caricature is to take the essence or core of the minimalist program and see what impact it would have, were it true. Chapter 4 does just that by putting minimalism into a broader intellectual, philosophical, and scientific context. In addition to examining the immediate sources of the minimalist program, it is indeed critical to highlight parallelisms between minimalism and the methodological foundations in better-developed sciences such as physics. Once established, such parallelisms (I will argue) help direct inquiry in linguistics and cognitive science/biology.

Recall that minimalism seeks to understand why the general conditions of grammar are of the sort the P&P system had roughly established. In particular, minimalism proposes investigating this question by asking how much of the P&P architecture follows from general properties of optimal, computationally efficient systems. Minimalism's *why*-questions are strongly reminiscent of general questions asked in modern theoretical physics: one may have a good theory, even the right theory, of what the universe is; still, one can worry about such issues as why the theory invokes the dimensions it appears to have (neither more nor less), why it presents the particular pockets of regularities that its various conservation laws define, or even why the universe it describes exists at all, as opposed to annihilating itself in perfect balance. These are not (just) philosophical questions: they are fundamental concerns that should lead to a better understanding of the universe, and which are uniformly considered essential items on the agenda of theoretical physicists.

As we will see, the minimalist program has a particularly strong commitment to the Galilean vision of natural phenomena and theory construction. That is, minimalists endorse the belief (held by all major proponents of modern science, from Kepler to Einstein) that nature is the realization of the simplest conceivable mathematical ideas, and the idea that a theory should be more highly valued if it 'give[s] us a sense that nothing could be changed, ... a sense of uniqueness, ... a sense that when we understand the final answer, we will see that it could not have been any other way' (Weinberg 2001: 39).

This minimalist/Galilean view on language is at odds with the general beliefs held by most majority of biologists to this day. As Fox-Keller (2002: 1) insightfully notes, whereas physicists 'seek to expand the boundaries of knowledge until nothing ... in the physical universe is left unexplained', 'the ambitions of biologists are manifestly less grandiose'. They don't 'seem to share [the same] concept of theory', of 'what counts as an explanation' (p. 3). (For similar remarks, see Gould 2002: 1207.) Throughout her book, Fox-Keller emphasizes the cultural divide between physicists and biologists, and notes the marginal role played within biology by figures like D'Arcy Thompson and Alan Turing, who devoted their energy to carrying out a Galilean program for biology, and who have figured prominently in Chomsky's general writings on minimalism.

Biologists are quick to point out that laws don't exist in biology, certainly not in evolutionary biology. Some contemporary giants like Richard Lewontin (2003: 39) go as far as asking questions like:

Can there be a theoretical biology? Is there a possibility of making sense of life? Is biology inevitably a story of different strokes for different folks, a collection of exquisitely detailed descriptions of the diverse forms and functions of organisms down to the molecular level, obtained by an unending history of experiment and observation? Or from this blooming, buzzing confusion can a biologist derive some general claims that are freed from the dirty particulars of each case, claims that while not of the universality of Newton's laws, at least characterize the properties of a very large part of the living world?

In evolutionary biology, and especially in modern cognitive science, increasingly grounded in (ultra) neo-Darwinism (see especially Pinker 1997, 2002, Barkow et al. 1992, and other proponents of evolutionary psychology), the general vision of language as a biological organ 'conforms not to the majestic Galilean perspective, but rather to a view, attributed to François Jacob, of biology as a "tinkerer"' (Culicover and Jackendoff 2005: 5).

To paraphrase: since Jackendoff and Culicover (and many others) assume that language is the product of adaptive pressures, language is expected to consist of a hodgepodge of loosely interacting computational tricks. If that were the case, the search for a restricted core of deep abstract principles of optimal design would be doomed from the start. Fortunately for minimalists, the view of nature as a tinkerer is being re-evaluated in biology, and the search for deep organizational motifs is slowly coming to fruition. One of the most fascinating aspects of the minimalist program is that if this program for linguistic theory turns out to be tenable, one will be able to draw 'conclusions of some significance, not only for the study of language itself' (Chomsky 2004a: 124) but for the biological and mental world at large.

As Chomsky has clearly stated in his most recent technical writings (2004a, 2005), the ambition—perhaps premature, although recent results are, I find, encouraging—of the minimalist program is clearly to delineate the three factors influencing language design: (i) genetic endowment, (ii) experience, and (iii) general properties of well-designed, optimal systems. These match point by point the loci of explanation that make up what Lewontin (2000), reviewing the future program of biological sciences, calls 'the triple helix': genes, environment, and organism. So, far from 'dissociat[ing] linguistics from biology' (Jackendoff 2002: 94), minimalism may well turn out to provide remarkable support for a silent revolution in biology (often called the Evo-Devo revolution; see Carroll (2005)). It is this very possibility that I want to emphasize in this work.

The proof of the pudding is in the eating. And so it goes with programs: the proof ultimately rests on how good the detailed products that result from taking the program's strictures seriously look and taste. Although minimalism has provided a platform for broader studies, with already promising results in related fields like acquisition, psycholinguistics, neurolinguistics (see the contributions collected in Jenkins (2004)), it is to be expected that the goods of the minimalist program are to be found in concrete analyses of linguistic phenomena.[4] These phenomena constitute

---

[4] Minimalism has also led to rapprochements between syntax and semantic theories like Categorial Grammar (see Berwick and Epstein 1995) and (neo-)Davidsonian views on linguistic meaning (see Pietroski 2005).

the bread and butter and the delight of linguists, but they are hard to appreciate for the non-initiated. But I think that they are so essential that they should figure in a book like the present one. However, I have decided to confine them to one chapter (Chapter 5), so that they can be less obtrusive for readers who do not rejoice in the intricacies of multiple *wh*-fronting, sluicing, control, and other technical matters. Abstraction and complexity are not signs that a given scientific direction is wrong, but they can make communication more difficult. I intend this book to be for every curious and intellectually engaged person, and I hope that outsiders to the field of linguistics will be brave enough to venture into the sections of Chapter 5. I have tried to make technical matters accessible to non-experts by providing useful background information and a glossary at the end of the book defining technical terms. Although simplification is always a double-edged sword, I hope that I have remained true to the spirit of the various analyses proposed by various authors. I would be delighted if the reader came away from reading Chapter 5 with a sense of the success and progress made possible by the minimalist program, and with a desire to learn more.[5]

1.3 Author's aims

By way of concluding my introduction, let me tell you why I decided to write this book. There are several reasons, and I want to make them clear to avoid any misunderstanding of the project. I do not intend this book to be a defense of the minimalist program against the critiques that have been leveled at it over the years. Although I address the main points of contention raised in the literature in the remaining chapters, I often do so in an indirect fashion (by way of

---

[5] If the reader indeed decides to learn more, I recommend Adger (2003), Poole (2002), and especially Haegeman (2005) for very good introductions to modern syntactic theory. For an excellent introduction to the central technical aspects of the minimalist program and how to 'do it', I refer the reader to Hornstein et al. (2006). For more advanced surveys of the minimalist program, see Lasnik et al. (2005) and Uriagereka (1998).

implication); or, to the extent that an objection is addressed explicitly, the discussion is confined to footnotes, and always appears only because it provides me with an opportunity to clarify or emphasize a property of the program.

My goal is to lay bare the logic of the program and let it speak for itself. (Here lies the reason for my using extensive quotes. The subject is so vexatious and confused that paraphrases would invariably fail to convey subtle distinctions. I hope that the reader will forgive me for sacrificing literate prose to proper documentation.)

Max Planck remarked in his autobiography that 'a new scientific truth does not triumph by convincing its opponents and making them see the light' (Planck 1949: 33). The perspective I adopt throughout is Darwin's, stated clearly at the end of *On the Origin of Species* (1964 [1859]: 481–2):

Although I am fully convinced of the truth of the views given in this volume . . . , I by no means expect to convince experienced naturalists whose minds are stocked with a multitude of facts all viewed, during a long course of years, from a point of view directly opposite to mine. . . . [B]ut I look forward with confidence to the future, to young and rising naturalists, who will be able to view both sides of the question with impartiality.

The main goal of this book is *not* to convince anyone that the minimalist program is the one and only correct scientific way of studying language and the mind, but rather to show that the program has unique insights to offer (Chapter 5 provides some empirical evidence to back this up). Minimalism is not more important, worthwhile, or interesting than other approaches to language, but it is unique, distinct, and equally important, worthwhile, and interesting.

There are highly individual reasons for adopting a research program. No single argument will convince a budding linguist to join forces with other minimalists. Examples abound in the history of science of research programs which, had they not been taken up quickly by a few individuals, might not have been able to develop sufficiently to attract the interest of the scientific community as a whole. As Kuhn (1962: 158) correctly notes,

The man who embraces a new paradigm at an early stage ... must have faith that the new paradigm will succeed with the many large problems that confront it, knowing only that the older paradigm has failed with a few. A decision of that kind can only be made on faith. ... Something must make at least a few scientists feel that the new proposal is on the right track, and sometimes it is only personal and inarticulate aesthetic considerations that can do that.

As Max Planck said, 'Anybody who has been seriously engaged in scientific work of any kind realizes that over the entrance to the gates of the temple of science are written the words: "Ye must have faith." It is a quality which the scientist cannot dispense with.'

For me, minimalism is worth pursuing because, to the extent that one can reach explanations by following minimalist guidelines, such explanations will have a deep and pleasing character. The pursuit of minimalism should also make eminent sense for those who are deeply committed to the goals of generative grammar laid out so clearly in Chomsky (1965: ch. 1), and who have participated in the development of the P&P model. For them, minimalism should be the obvious next step, for minimalism is an organic development of previous research. I am aware that very often scientists who take an interest in their subject's past often indulge in what Butterfield (1931) called 'the Whig interpretation of history', a self-serving tendency 'to praise revolutions provided they have been successful, to emphasize certain principles of progress in the past and to produce a story which is the ratification, if not the glorification of the present' (p. v). The historical reconstruction I attempt here does not just emphasize past successes; it also points out limitations of previous research. My only goal in retracing the roads previously taken is to locate minimalism within the larger map of linguistics. I cannot glorify minimalism, since it is a research program that in large part remains to be pursued. I hope to provide readers with promising signals from the results already obtained, but much of the work lies ahead. It will be for future historians to judge the program's ultimate success.

For all the conservative aspects of the minimalist program, the boldness of the minimalist conjecture and the open-ended character of the program provides another reason for pursuing it. Scientists come in two varieties, which Isaiah Berlin (1953), quoting the seventh-century BC Greek poet Archilochus, called foxes and hedgehogs. Foxes know many tricks, hedgehogs only one. Foxes are interested in everything, and move easily from one problem to another. Hedgehogs are interested only in a few problems which they consider fundamental, and stick with the same problems for decades. Most of the great discovery are made by hedgehogs, most of the little discoveries by foxes. Both types of discovery are needed to understand the universe. Science needs both hedgehogs and foxes for its healthy growth—hedgehogs to dig deep into the nature of things, foxes to explore the complicated details of our marvelous world. By its very programmatic nature, minimalism offers an opportunity for everyone to be a hedgehog. It is fair to say that in the past Chomsky has shown other linguists the way. We are now at a stage in linguistic theory where it is quite clear that there can be no privileged burrow dug by Chomsky or by any one else. Although Chomsky's contribution within minimalism remains invaluable, and his overall vision is extremely compelling, he has repeatedly pointed out that his articulation of the program is but one research path among many. Everyone should be encouraged to take part in an enterprise where most of the exciting problems remain to be solved.

Finally, I find minimalism worth pursuing because of the interdisciplinary perspectives it offers. By carrying out the program we will not fail to learn something about the properties of what are called the interfaces—the points of contact between language and other cognitive modules/organs—about evolution, and more; properties that would be harder to highlight, or easier to miss, by pursuing alternative approaches. Wouldn't it be nice if that turned out to be true?

2

The Minimalist Roots

In his masterful treatment of the structure of evolutionary theory from Darwin to the present, Stephen Jay Gould (2002: ch. 1) argues that a theory of range and power needs both history and essence. Gould was really talking about productive and comprehensive programs. In this chapter, I address the historical source, the context of emergence of minimalism, leaving a discussion of its essential features to the next chapter.

Describing the context of emergence of minimalism is an important part of my attempt to clarify what the minimalist program is, and why it makes eminent sense to try to articulate the said program, for at least two reasons. First, as Richard Feynman kept wondering (reported in Weinberg 2003: xv), it is never clear why people always want to know about the latest discoveries when they know nothing about the earlier discoveries that give meaning to the latest ones. An understanding of the past is an incredibly useful explanatory tool. Second, I suspect that a fair amount of the criticism aimed at minimalism in recent years came from a failure to appreciate the results that led to the formulation of minimalism.[1]

---

[1] See e.g. Postal (2003b: 4). Postal would take issue with much of the content of the present chapter by saying (as he does with reference to a claim similar to mine made by Epstein and Hornstein (1999: xi)) that '[t]he claim that GB has been a success is not backed up, and I claim could not be, by any citation of substantive factual results for the grammar of English, for example'. Here Postal makes reference to the so-called Government-Binding (GB) framework, the first incarnation of the P&P approach. Once the focus of the P&P approach is made clear, as I will do in this chapter, it is hard to see how anyone can fail to recognize the range and depth of research in this approach (and its specific GB instantiation), not only in the realm of pure syntax (see Baker 2001, Cinque and Kayne 2005) but also in related fields such as language

My point in this chapter is to show that minimalism rests on a firm scientific foundation: the Principles and Parameters (P&P) framework, the result of over thirty years of intensive research in generative grammar. In the following pages I intend to show how the P&P approach crystallized, and how it led to the formulation of the minimalist program. Although some of the material discussed below may be familiar to some readers, I want to be clear that everyone is 'on the same page', for the minimalist program does not make sense outside the P&P framework and the central goals and assumptions of generative grammar that led to it.

2.1 The birth of modern biolinguistics

It is very tempting to review the development of generative grammar by starting with Chomsky's first published work, *Syntactic Structures* (1957). Conceptually, however, it makes much more sense to start with Chomsky's review of Skinner's *Verbal Behavior* (Chomsky 1959) and the first chapter of *Aspects of the Theory of Syntax* (Chomsky 1965), along with Lenneberg's 1967 landmark on the *Biological Foundations of Language*. This is not to deny that *Syntactic Structures* initiated a revolution in linguistics. It clearly did. But the revolutionary character of that work, and of the work it was based on (*The logical structure of linguistic theory*, 1955), becomes even more significant once it is embedded in the psychological (mentalist) and biological setting that is made explicit in Chomsky (1959) and even more so in Chomsky (1965) and Lenneberg (1967).

Chomsky's 1959 review of Skinner's *Verbal Behavior* ushers linguistics into what Norbert Hornstein and I have called the cognitive era, setting the stage for the development of biolinguistics (see Boeckx and Hornstein forthcoming b). At the time, psychology was dominated by behaviorism, which saw language as a list of

acquisition (see e.g. Crain and Thornton 1998, Guasti 2002), language use/sentence processing (see e.g. Berwick and Weinberg 1984), and language change (see e.g. Lightfoot 1999, Kroch 2001). For accessible surveys of factual results for the grammar of English, see Radford (2004) and Haegeman and Guéron (1999).

behaviors acquired by some version of operant conditioning. According to behaviorists, any behavior could be understood in terms of a general learning schema of direct stimulus–response associations acquired after a period of repeated exposure, correction, and reward (reinforcement). Behaviorism left no room for internal mechanisms to play a role in the acquisition of behavior.

As Chomsky (1959) convincingly argued, no 'blank slate' theory relying solely on external input can account for the creative aspect of language use. Native speakers of any language are able to effortlessly produce and understand sentences in that language that they have never heard or produced before. Chomsky's rejection of any behaviorist account helped shape what came to be known as the 'cognitive revolution'—a mentalistic framework in which inborn ('innate') mechanisms played a central role in the acquisition and use of behavior.[2]

Following Chomsky's review of Skinner's book, 'it became increasingly clear that behavior is simply the evidence, not the subject matter of psychology', as psychologist George Miller put it when explaining the cognitive revolution that took place in the late 1950s (cited in Gazzaniga 1998: 17).

The subject matter of linguistics, as a branch of psychology, was made explicit in the first chapter of Chomsky's 1965 *Aspects of a Theory of Syntax*, which arguably remains to this day the clearest statement of the generative enterprise as a whole. There, Chomsky argues that the central problem of linguistics is how to account for children's acquisition of their native languages.

2.2 Levels of adequacy

To make the task of linguistics more precise, Chomsky described standards for evaluating grammatical proposals known as levels of adequacy. Building upon his 1955 work, Chomsky distinguished

---

[2] For a good overview of the demise of behaviorism and of the components of modern cognitive science, see Pinker (2002: part I). See also Chomsky (1968, 1975: Introduction).

three levels of adequacy for linguistic analysis: (i) observational adequacy; (ii) descriptive adequacy; and (iii) explanatory adequacy. Observational adequacy was deemed the minimum for empirical science:

The lowest level of success is achieved if the grammar presents the observed primary linguistic data [the linguistic input to the child] correctly. We will call this level the level of observational adequacy. (Chomsky 1962: 62).

The two higher levels of adequacy occupy center-stage in Chomsky (1965):

A grammar (regarded as a theory of a language) is *descriptively adequate* 'to the extent that it correctly describes the intrinsic competence of the idealized native speaker'. (p. 24)

The following quote clarifies this statement:

[The] distinctions that [the grammar] makes between well-formed and deviant, and so on ... correspond[s] to the linguistic intuition of the native speaker ... in a substantial and significant class of crucial cases. (p. 24)

Put differently, the grammar ought to describe correctly what a speaker (tacitly) knows in knowing a particular language. For example, speakers of English know that *John* is understood as the object of *please* in (1), but as the subject of *please* in (2).

(1)   John is easy to please (= it is easy to please John)
(2)   John is eager to please (= John has the desire to please others)

Note that grammars here are evaluated in abstract terms: whether they correctly describe a certain cognitive state, a native speaker's (tacit) knowledge of his native language.

  Explanatory adequacy is defined as follows.

To the extent that a linguistic theory succeeds in selecting a descriptively adequate grammar on the basis of primary linguistic data [*i.e. the information available to the child in the process of language acquisition*], we can say that it meets the condition of explanatory adequacy. (Chomsky 1965: 25)

In other words, linguistic theories will be evaluated in light of, and in terms of, the 'abstract problem' of constructing an 'acquisition model' for language (Chomsky 1965: 25).

Put differently, the central question of linguistics is as follows. How does the child go from primary linguistic data (PLD), i.e. well-formed, short sentences in the target language, to a grammar for that language, i.e. a procedure for generating a potentially infinite number of linguistic objects? For, indeed, children produce and understand sentences they have never heard before, and all such sentences display the property of being lengthened at will (think of *Mary said that Peter thought that Bill claimed that Sue believed that Ann said that John believed that Paul claimed that Amy thought that* ...).

A moment's reflection indicates that the problem facing the child looks formidable when considered from this perspective: it quickly becomes evident that the linguistic evidence available to the child in the period of language acquisition is simply too impoverished to account for how she generalizes from the small sample of cases she gets as input to a grammar that generates the infinite set of the well-formed sentences of the language (to say nothing of the truly amazing feat of being able to pick out some noise from the environment and categorize it as linguistic sounds put together into words). In light of this gap between linguistic input and linguistic knowledge, the broadest aim of linguistic theory is to discover the 'innate linguistic theory that provides the basis for language learning' (Chomsky 1965: 25). In other words, the aim of a theory of grammar is to outline the biologically given cognitive structure that enables human children so reliably and effortlessly to project grammars from the data they receive. The biologically given cognitive structure is what linguists call Universal Grammar.

It is extremely important for the reader to realize the magnitude of the problem faced by the child. Barring pathological cases, each and every human child in the course of a few years becomes a native speaker of at least one language, the language used around her. Often the language she will end up using will be that of her parents, but this need not be so, as generations of immigrants have shown. The child must be ready to learn any language in the world. In fact, as languages come and go in the world, disappearing or evolving into new idioms, the child must be ready to acquire any possible human languages. The child is thus faced with a vast array of possibilities. How can we explain why each and every child reliably and effortlessly converges on certain languages and not on others?

The answer cannot be so flexible as to rely completely on the fact that children build grammars to conform to the language they hear around them (although this is, of course, part of the answer) for, when looked at closely, there are too many ways for children to generalize from the linguistic input available to them to rules consistent with these inputs. Nonetheless, most of these logically possible options are not taken. Although children make mistakes, linguists working on language acquisition have established that those mistakes are far from random. The observed mistakes constitute but a small sets of the mistakes we may reasonably expect children to make. So what constrains the child?

2.3 The poverty of stimulus, and what must be done about it

Let me take one concrete example from the grammar of English.[3]

Consider how English forms *Yes/No* questions (questions which are answered by *Yes* or *No*).

(3) a. Is Mary at home? (Answer: Yes, Mary is at home)
    b. Can Bill sing? (Answer: Yes, Bill can sing)
    c. Will Mary be at the party tomorrow? (Answer: Yes, Mary will be at the party tomorrow)

The question seems to be related to its (affirmative) answer as follows.

(4) To form a Y[es]/N[o] question concerning some state of affairs described by a structure S, transform S as follows: Find the Auxiliary of S and put it at the front.

---

[3] This section is based on material taken from Boeckx and Hornstein (forthcoming c).

So, in (3a), the proposition of interest is described by the sentence 'Mary is at home'. The Auxiliary in this sentence is *is*. The rule says that one moves this to the front to derive the Y/N question: *Is Mary at home?* [4]

The procedure in (4) works fine for these simple cases, but it fails for more complex sentences like (5).

(5) Will Mary believe that Frank is here? (Yes, Mary will believe that Frank is here)

(5) is problematic because there is more than one Auxiliary (in this case, there are two, but there may be more), so the injunction to move *the* auxiliary is useless. We must specify which of the two auxiliaries gets moved. To accommodate (5) we can modify (4) in several ways. Here are several options:

(6) a. Move the main clause Aux to the front.
     b. Move the leftmost Aux to the front.
     c. Move any Aux to the front.

Each revision of (4) suffices to generate (5). However, with the exception of (6a), they all lead to unacceptable sentences as well. Consider how (6c) applies to the affirmative answer of (5). It can form the Y/N question depicted. However, it also can form the Y/N question (7) if the rule chooses to move *is*. In other words, (6c) overgenerates.

(7) *Is Mary will believe that Frank here?

(7) is English 'word salad' and will be judged highly unacceptable by virtually any native speaker. So, we know that native speakers of English do not use a rule like (6c). We are also confident that they do not use rules like (6b), based on sentences like (8).

---

[4] There are many additional factors to be taken into consideration to make the rule more adequate and complete. For example, not all sentences have overt auxiliaries. The details of the process were already discussed in *Syntactic Structures*, and the process of *do*-support was offered as a way of regularizing this process. For our purposes here, however, these additional details are of no moment. So I keep to simple cases like (3).

(8)   The man who is tall will leave now.

The Y/N question that corresponds to (8) is (9a), not (9b).

(9)   a. Will the man who is tall leave now?
      b. *Is the man who tall will leave now?

(6b) predicts just the opposite pattern. Thus, (6b) both over- and undergenerates.

(6a) runs into no similar difficulty. The main-clause Auxiliary is *will*. The Auxiliary *is* resides in an embedded clause and so will not be moved by (6a). So, it appears that we have evidence that the rule acquired by native speakers of English is roughly that in (4) as modified in (6a).

Now the typical question for linguists working under the guidelines of Chomsky (1965) is: how did adults come to internalize (6a)? There are two possible answers. First, the adults were once children and as children they surveyed the linguistic evidence and concluded that the right rule for forming Y/N questions is (6a). The other option is that humans are built so as to consider only rules like (6a) viable. The reason they converge on (6a) is not that they are led there by the linguistic data but because they never really consider any other option.

The second answer is generally considered the more exotic. Some still resist it. However, the logic that supports it is, I believe, impossible to resist.

Let us assume, for the sake of argument, that the correct rule, (6a), is learned. This means that children are driven to this rule on the basis of the available data, the PLD. A relevant question is: what does the PLD look like? In other words, what does the linguistic input that children use look like? What is the general character of the PLD? Here are some reasonable properties of the PLD. First, it is finite. Children can only use what they are exposed to and this will, of necessity, be finite. Second, the data that the children use will be well-formed bits of the target language, e.g. well-formed phrases, sentences. Note that this *excludes* ill-formed cases; the information that such cases are ill-formed (e.g. (7) and (9b) above) will *not* be part of the data that the child has access to in defining the Y/N rule, not part of its PLD for this rule). Third, the child uses relatively simple sentences. These will by and large be short, simple things like the sentences in (3). *If* this is the correct characterization of the PLD available to the child, then we can conclude that some version of the more exotic conclusion above is correct. In other words, it is not that the child learned the rule in the sense of using data to exclude *all* relevant alternatives. Rather, most of the 'wrong' alternatives were never really considered as admissible options in the first place.

How does one argue for this second conclusion? By arguing that the PLD is insufficient to guide the observed acquisition. Consider the case at hand. First, native speakers of English have in fact internalized a rule like (6a) as this rule correctly describes which Y/N questions they find acceptable and which they reject. Second, one presumably learns the rule for Y/N questions by being exposed to instances of Y/N questions, rather than, for example, seeing objects fall off tables or being hugged by one's mother. Say that the PLD relevant for this are simple well-formed instances of Y/N questions, sentences analogous to the examples in (3). On the basis of such examples, the child must fix on the correct rule, roughly something like (6a). The question now is: does the data in (3) suffice to drive the child to that rule? We already know that the answer is negative, as we have seen that the data in (3) is compatible with any of the rules in (6). Given that there is only a single auxiliary in these cases, the issue of which of several to move never arises. What of data like (5)? These cases involve several auxiliaries but once again all three options in (6) are compatible with both the data in (5) and the data in (3).

Is there any data that could decisively lead the child to (6a) (at least among the three alternatives)? There is. We noted that examples like (9a) argue against (6b) and that (9b) and (7) provide evidence against (6c). However, the child could not use these sorts of cases to converge on rule (6a) *if she only uses simple well-formed bits of the language as data.* In other words, if the PLD is roughly as described above, then sentences like (9b) and (7) are not part of the data available to the child. Examples (7) and (9b) are excluded from the PLD because they are unacceptable. If such 'bad' sentences are rarely uttered, or, if uttered, are rarely corrected, or, if corrected, are not attended to by children, then they will not form part of the PLD that the child uses in acquiring the Y/N question rule. Similarly, it is quite possible that examples like (9a), though well-formed, are too complex to be part of the PLD. If so, they too will not be of any help to the child. In short, though there *is* decisive linguistic evidence concerning what the correct rule is (i.e. (6a), not (6b) or (6c)), there need not be such evidence in the PLD, the evidence available to the child. And this would then imply that the child does not arrive at the right rule *solely* on the basis of the linguistic input of the target language. In other words, this implies that the acquisition is guided by some biological feature of children rather than by some property of the linguistic input. The conclusion, then, is that children have some biological endowment that allows them to converge on (6a) and not even consider (6b) or (6c) as viable options.

This is a brief example of what linguists call the Poverty of Stimulus (POS) argument: the linguistic input (stimulus) given to the child is not rich enough to account for what she (tacitly) knows. The logic of the POS argument is tight. If the acquisition does not track the contours of the linguistic environment, then the convergence to the correct rule requires a more endogenous, biological explanation.

Granted the premises, the conclusion is ineluctable. What then of the premises? For example, is it the case that children only have access to acceptable forms of the language (i.e. not cases like (7) or (9b))? Is it true that children do not use complex examples? Before considering these questions, let us reiterate that if the premises are granted, then the conclusion seems airtight.

For the PLD to be the main causal factor in choosing between the options in (6), we would, at the very least, expect the relevant data to be robust in the sense that *any* child learning English might be expected to encounter sufficient examples of the decisive data. Recall that virtually all native speakers of English act as if (6a) is the correct rule. So, the possibility that *some* children might be exposed to the decisive sentences is irrelevant, given that *all* speakers converge on the same rule. Moreover, the data must be robust in another sense. Not only must all speakers encounter the relevant data, they must do so a sufficient number of times. Any learning system will have to be supple enough to ignore what scientists would call 'noise' in the data. So, learning cannot be a single-example affair. There must be a sufficient number of sentences like (7) and (9b) in the PLD if such sentences are to be of any relevance.

It has sometimes been claimed that the PLD *does* contain examples like (9) (see, most recently, Pullum and Scholz 2002, Cowie 1999, and Sampson 1999). However, this is not (to repeat) the relevant point. What is required is that there be enough examples of the relevant sort; and we need to determine how much is enough. Legate and Yang (2002) and Yang (2002) address exactly this problem. Based on empirical findings in Yang (2002), they propose to 'quantify' the POS argument. To do that, they situate the issue at hand in a comparative setting and propose 'an independent yardstick to quantitatively relate the amount of relevant linguistic experience to the outcome of language acquisition' (Yang 2002: 111). The independent benchmark they propose is the well-studied use of null subjects in child language. They note that subject use reaches adult levels at around 3,0 (three years and zero months). This is comparable to the age of children tested by Crain and Nakayama (1987) for Y/N questions (youngest group: 3,2). The core examples which inform children that all English (finite) sentences require phonologically overt subjects are sentences involving pleonastic subjects (e.g. *there is a man here*). Such sentences amount to 1.2 per cent of the potential PLD (all sentences). Legate and Yang suggest, quite reasonably, that the PLD relevant to fixing the Y/N question rule should be of roughly comparable proportion. To be generous, let's say that even 0.5–1 per cent would suffice.

The best search one could do at the moment would be in something like the CHILDES database, a compendium of child–caretaker linguistic interactions (MacWhinney and Snow 1985). A search of this database reveals that sentences like (9) account for between 0.045 and 0.068 per cent of the sentences, well over an order of magnitude *less* than is required. In fact, as Legate and Yang observe, this number is so low that it is likely to be negligible in the sense of not being reliably available to every child. Just as interesting, of roughly 67,000 adult sentences surveyed in CHILDES (the kind of data that would be ideal for the child to use) there is not a single example of a Y/N question like (9).

In sum, if we take this survey of CHILDES as representative of the PLD available to the child (and there is no reason to think that it is not), it appears that the sorts of sentences that would provide evidence for choosing (6a) over (6b) are missing from the PLD. We can then conclude that the PLD is too poor to explain the facts concerning acquisition of the Y/N question rule in English. In short, the conclusion of the POS argument outlined above follows.

I have spent all this time on this issue as it is repeatedly advanced as a refutation of the nativist conclusion of the POS argument (i.e. the claim that some specific innate linguistic component must be posited). To be fair, however, I should point out that the discussion above is too generous to opponents of the POS. The discussion has concentrated on whether examples like (9a) occur in the PLD. Even if they did, it would not undermine the argument presented above. The presence of sentences like (9a) would simply tell us that the PLD *can* distinguish (6a) from (6b). It does not yet address how to avoid generalizing to (6c). This option must also be removed, or the nativist conclusions are once again required. However, (14a) does not bear on (6c) at all. It is (7) and (9b) that are relevant here. Such data, often called 'negative evidence', is what counts. Is negative evidence present in the PLD? If it is, how would it be manifest?

One way would be if adults made the relevant errors and corrected themselves somehow. However, nobody makes mistakes like (7) and (9b). Such sentences are even hard for native speakers to articulate. A second possibility would be that children make errors of the relevant sort and are corrected somehow. However, this too is virtually unattested. Children never make errors like those in (7) and (9b) even when strongly prompted to do so (see Crain and Nakayama 1987 for detailed discussion). If they do not make the errors, however, they cannot be corrected. Moreover, as has repeatedly been observed (see McNeill 1966, Jackendoff 1994, Pinker 1994), there is plenty of evidence that children are very resistant to correction. Thus, even when mistakes occur, children seem to ignore the best-intentioned efforts to help them grammatically. A third option is to build the negative evidence option into the learning process itself. For example, we might say that children are very conservative learners and will not consider as possible any structure of which they have not observed instances. (This is often referred to as 'indirect negative evidence.') The problem with this, however, is that it is difficult to state the restriction in a way that will not be obviously wrong. Recall that children are exposed to at most a finite number of sentences and, therefore, to at most a finite number of sentence patterns. Recall that it seems that a negligible number of sentences like (9a) even occur in the PLD, so if children were too conservative they would never form such questions. Moreover, mature native speakers can use and understand an unbounded number of sentences and sentence patterns. If children were conservative in the way hinted at above, they could never fully acquire language at all, as they would never be exposed to most of the patterns of the language. So, any simple-minded idea of conservativity will not do, and we must conclude that the assumption that children do not have access to negative data in the PLD is a reasonable one.

To get back to the main point: if what I have said above is correct, then why children do not opt for rules like (6c) is unaccounted for. Recall that only negative data tells against (6c) as the correct option, (6a), is simply a proper sub-case of (6c). It would seem, then, that both the logic and the premises of the POS argument are sufficient to lead us to conclude that language acquisition is not explicable *solely* on the basis of the linguistic input. More is needed. In particular, I follow Chomsky in asserting the need for some biological, human-specific mechanism for language acquisition.[5] This mechanism can be seen as an organ in the biological sense of the world (see Anderson and Lightfoot 2002: ch. 10).

Having established the need for a language organ, let me now turn to how to best characterize it.

---

[5] The term 'acquisition' is inappropriate in a generative setting. Unfortunately, it appears to have fossilized in the literature, so I will stick to the term here, noting that 'growth' or 'development' are more adequate.

2.4 Computational properties of the language organ

There is overwhelming evidence that organs of the mind are best understood in computational terms (see Gallistel 1990, 1998, 2000, 2001, 2005 for review and arguments). In the area of linguistics, the nature of computation is perhaps more advanced than in any other field of cognition (with the possible exception of navigation). Many of the insights in this domain go back to the earliest work in generative grammar.

2.4.1 *Early results*

Although the focus on language acquisition was 'not discussed in [Chomsky 1955], the issues lie in the immediate background of [that] work and [of *Syntactic Structures*]' (Chomsky 1975: 13).[6] The more immediate goal of these works was to develop rule systems that had the appropriate combinatorial/computational properties.

At the time, linguistic studies were the property of two schools of thought. On one hand were philosophical logic, philosophy of language, and mathematical logic, all of which are the result of a practice that goes back to Aristotle through the scholastics and that feeds, in the twentieth century, on the remarkable results of formal logic and mathematics; from this perspective, human language is a mere imperfection, reflecting logic through human limitations. On the other hand was structural linguistics, which wanted to separate the study of human language *as it is* from that of human thought, particularly in the form of logic, and was concerned both with the thousands of actual languages in the world and with methods for

---

[6] Lightfoot (2003) makes a similar observation in his introduction to the second edition of *Syntactic Structures* when he notes how easy the transition (or translation) was from Chomsky (1957) to Chomsky (1965), despite the absence of explicit discussion of 'cognitive' themes in *Syntactic Structures*. Lees's (1957) review of Chomsky (1957) contains the germs of such a transition.

describing them. Chomsky stressed the limitations of both of these traditions.

To understand the full potential of human language and, very specifically, the 'creative' aspect that had fascinated Descartes and Humboldt, it is very clear that one must go beyond the naive 'methodology' of structural linguistics, in principle incapable of providing an analysis of potentially infinite behavior via certainly finite means. Thus, the focus in Chomsky (1955, 1957) was on developing an explicit formalism adequate for representing linguistic phenomena and infinity in particular.

I will deal here with Chomsky's attempt in *Syntactic Structures* to compare the virtues and vices of alternative formalizations of natural language grammars.[7] First, Chomsky argues against the adequacy of finite state grammars as adequate models for natural language (see 1957: ch. 3).

2.4.1.1 *Finite-state machines*   Finite-state machines are very simple devices consisting of (i) an initial state, (ii) a finite number of states, (iii) a specification of transition from one state to another, (iv) a specification of a (finite number of) symbol(s) to be 'printed' when a particular transition obtains, and (v) a final state.

Let me briefly look at a few examples successfully handled by finite-state devices. Consider first a sentence like (10):

(10)   the tall man runs

This could be represented via a finite-state machine as:

(11)   1 the   2 tall   3 man   4 runs   5

The same machine can capture instances of infinite expressions like (12).

(12)   the (very very very very ...) tall man runs

All that needs to be added to (11) is a loop, as shown in (13).

---

[7] For a comprehensive coverage, see Lasnik (2000).

(13)

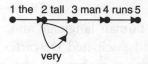

1 the 2 tall 3 man 4 runs 5

very

Although finite-state machines effectively capture infinite expressions, Chomsky quickly noted that they run into problems in a number of circumstances. In particular, he showed that finite-state machines are formally incapable of modeling 'languages' that display certain non-local dependencies between expressions in a string, e.g. languages that have n occurrences of a followed by n occurrences of b. For example, imagine a language that looks like (14).

(14)   ab
       aabb
       aaabbb
       aaaabbbb

This language can be described as consisting of sentences with any number of as followed by exactly the same number of bs as long as that number is greater than 0. More compactly: $a^n b^n$, $n > 0$.

Finite-state machines fail to capture the 'exactly the same number' property of the language in (14). The best they can do is represented in (15).

(15)

1

a   b

This machine can generate an infinite number of as followed by an infinite number of bs, but cannot make sure that there will be an equal number of as and bs. It may turn out that the machine hits upon the same number for a and b, but this would be pure coincidence. The reason for this limitation of finite-state machines is easy to identify. Such machines only have access to one type of information: the state they are in, what state they can get to from there, and what symbol they will be printing. But they have no memory. They do not know what states they used to be in or how many times they have been in that state. They have no way to connect the 'print-b state' with the 'print-a state'. Once they reached the 'b-state', it is as if they start all over again. Of course, the next question that immediately arises in the face of this limitation of finite-state machines is whether this limitation has any bad effect on capturing real linguistic examples, and not just invented languages like (14).

Examples that are hard for finite-state machines to handle abound in natural languages. I will limit myself to one.[8]

Consider the term *anti-missile missile*. Setting aside technological limits, we can imagine *anti-anti-missile missile missile*, *anti-anti-anti-missile missile missile missile*, etc. and so on. The pattern is quite clear, and is captured in the schema in (16).

(16)   anti^{n}missile^{n+1} (*n* occurrences of the word *anti* followed by $n + 1$ occurrences of the word *missile*)

Finite-state grammars fail to capture (16), as they are unable to keep track of the number of *anti*s in order to make the number of *missiles* greater by one.

As I said, cases of real-life linguistic examples that are problematic for finite-state machines are ubiquitous. Because finite-state grammars cannot generate *all* the grammatical sequences of English, they are inadequate formal models of grammar. (This does not mean that they may not underlie some linguistic processes (see Uriagereka forthcoming). It just means that something extra is needed.)

2.4.1.2 *Phrase structure grammars*   The next kind of grammar Chomsky considers is a Context-Free Phrase Structure Grammar (or rewrite-rule system). These consist of a designated initial symbol (Σ) and rewrite rules (F), which consist of one symbol to the left, followed by an arrow, followed by at least one symbol (A $\rightarrow$ B) (the arrow stands for 'rewrite as' or 'consist of'). They also contain a procedure for moving from one step to the next known as a

[8] I owe this example to Howard Lasnik, my first syntax teacher, who in turns owes it to Morris Halle, his first linguistics teacher and one of the founders of generative phonology.

derivation, where exactly one symbol is being rewritten as another (sequence of) symbol(s) per step.

Phrase structure grammars in addition distinguish between terminal (lower-case) symbols and non-terminal (capital) symbols. The grammar stops when all non-terminal symbols have been rewritten as terminal symbols.

As we did for finite-state machines, let us take one example and see how phrase structure grammars work. Consider (17).

(17)   a. Σ: S
        b. S $\rightarrow$ aSb

Take S to be the designated initial symbol, an abstract, non-terminal symbol that will not be part of the sentence (it will have to be rewritten as a (sequence of) terminal symbol(s)).

The derivation proceeds as follows:

(18)   Step 1: S   (according to (17a))
        Step 2: aSb   (according to (17b))
        Step 3: aaSbb   (by reapplying (17b) to Step 2)
        Step 4: aaaSbbb (by reapplying (17b) to Step 3)

It is easy to see that we could go on for ever, caught in a loop, by reapplying (17b) to the preceding step. We need one more rule to turn off the machine. Let us add the following rule to (17).

(19)   S $\rightarrow$ ab

With (19), the grammar in (17) now generates ab, aabb, aaabbb, etc.

The device consisting of reintroducing non-terminal symbols into the derivation (reapplying (17b)) effectively captures infinity, just as the loop in a finite-state machine did. But this time we found a way to keep track of the number of *a*s and *b*s by introducing them into the derivation simultaneously. This is the key difference between phrase structure grammars and finite-state machines: the former, unlike the latter, can keep track of and pair up elements that are infinitely far apart (so-called unbounded discontinuous dependencies). The trick lies in the use of non-terminal symbols.

Phrase structure grammars are now regarded as the foundation of human languages. The reason *John* and *the man that I met on Friday* behave the same in language, though they look wildly different on the surface (as terminal symbols), is because both are instances of the same non-terminal symbol (called 'Noun Phrase' in the case at hand).

To give you an example of a phrase structure grammar for a simplified human language, consider (20).

(20)   a.   Σ: S (imagine S stands for 'Sentence')
       b.   F:
            S → NP VP   (NP = 'Noun Phrase'; VP = 'Verb Phrase')
            NP → N
            VP → V
            N → John
            N → Mary
            V → sings
            V → laughs
            V → thinks

A derivation for (20) will run as follows (replacing one non-terminal symbol at a time).

(21)   Step 1: S
       Step 2: NP VP   (via S → NP VP)
       Step 3: N VP   (via NP → N)
       Step 4: Mary VP   (via N → Mary)
       Step 5: Mary V   (via VP → V)
       Step 6: Mary laughs   (via V → laughs)
       STOP

Phrase structure grammars like (20) don't capture infinity. All we need to add for them to do so is a rule that will reintroduce S. For example: VP → V S. This will give rise to derivations like:

(22)   Step 1: S
       Step 2: NP VP   (via S → NP VP)
       Step 3: N VP   (via NP → N)
       Step 4: Mary VP   (via N → Mary)
       Step 5: Mary V S   (via VP → V S)
       Step 6: Mary thinks S   (via V → thinks)
       Step 7: Mary thinks NP VP (via S → NP VP)
       Step 8: Mary thinks N VP   (via NP → N)
       Step 9: Mary thinks John VP (via N → John)

Step 10: Mary thinks John V   (via VP → V)
Step 11: Mary thinks John laughs   (via V → laughs)

Phrase Structure Grammars are wonderful at capturing the pattern of embedding in languages, the type of Russian-doll effect that gives rise to sentences within sentences within sentences:

(23)

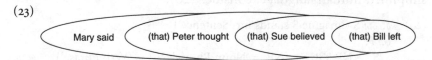

Derivations of phrase structure grammar can also be represented via graphs known as tree diagrams. For example, (22) can be represented as (24).

(24)

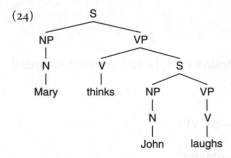

Trees of this sort are ubiquitous in the linguistics literature. The same information can be represented in a so-called labeled bracketing format, as in (25):

(25)   [s [NP [N Mary]] [VP [V thinks] [S [NP [N John]] [VP [V laughs]]]]]

I will go back and forth between tree representations and labeled brackets in the pages that follow (trees are more visual, but brackets can save a lot of space and word-processing trouble). Whenever I do so, remember that these are just short-cuts for phrase structure grammar derivations like the ones I have just discussed.

2.4.1.3 *Transformations*   Although phrase structure grammars are very good at capturing unbounded discontinuous dependencies, Chomsky argues in *Syntactic Structures* that PS grammars fail to be *fully* adequate because the grammars constructed exclusively in phrase structure terms will sometimes be 'extremely complex, *ad hoc*, and "unrevealing"' (1957: 34). To put this another way, grammars restricted to PS formats will be incapable of expressing some obvious, significant generalizations displayed by natural languages in an interesting way. Note that the claim here is *not* that these grammars cannot capture all the grammatical and ungrammatical sentences of a language. Rather, the claim is that they cannot do so in a way that cleaves to the generalizations that the language reveals, i.e. that they do so clumsily, without, as it were, cutting the language neatly at the joints.

The type of relation that PS grammars fail to capture neatly is known as a cross-serial discontinuous dependency. The discontinuous dependencies we have looked at so far have a nested pattern:

(26)

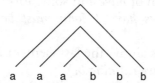

a   a   a   b   b   b

Crossing dependencies look like (27).

(27)

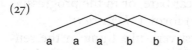

a   a   a   b   b   b

The clearest and most famous example of cross-serial dependencies in language comes from Chomsky's justly famous discussion of the English auxiliary system in chapter 7 of *Syntactic Structures*. (I know of quite a few people who were won over to generative grammar by Chomsky's analysis of the English auxiliary system.) Lasnik (2000) offers a detailed explication of this argument. I will limit myself to offering a taste of Chomsky's reasoning.

In addition to main verbs in sentences like *John sings, John laughed*, English makes use of auxiliary verbs that give rise to sentences like *John has sung, John will sing, John must run, John is running*, etc. There are basically three types of auxiliary in English: modals (*can, must, may, will*, etc.), *have*, and *be*. They can be combined into sentences like *John will have left, John will be running, John has been running, John may have been running,* etc. Chomsky's genius was to uncover significant generalizations when auxiliaries are combined, and express them in a compact, equation-like formula. The generalizations are the following: (For each generalization I will provide an example sentence that violates it, which I will indicate by a * symbol)

Generalization A: When a sentence contains a modal auxiliary (call it M), it is always the first thing after the subject in a declarative sentence. (**John has must be running*)

Generalization B: In the presence of M, no verbal element (auxiliary or main verb) bears agreement morphology that cross-references the subject (subject–verb agreement). (**John must has been running*)

Generalization C: When some form of *have* and some form of *be* cooccur, *be* immediately follows *have*. (**John must be have running*)

Generalization D: The main verb is always the last element of the verbal sequence. (**John must have running be*)

Generalization E: If the main verb is the first verb-like thing in the sentence, then it is inflected for tense (present/past), and for subject agreement. It cannot appear bare, or in the progressive (*-ing* form) or perfect (participle) form. (**John run*)

Generalization E′: If *have* is the first verb-like thing in the sentence, then it is inflected for tense (present/past), and for subject agreement. It cannot appear bare, or in the progressive (*-ing* form) or perfect (participle) form. (**John have run*)

Generalization E″: If *be* is the first verb-like thing in the sentence, then it is inflected for tense (present/past), and for subject agreement. It cannot appear bare, or in the progressive (*-ing* form) or perfect (participle) form. (**John be running*)

Generalization E‴: If M(odal) is the first verb-like thing in the sentence, then it is inflected for tense (present/past: e.g. *will/would*), but cannot appear bare, or in the progressive (*-ing* form) or perfect (participle) form. (**John musting have been run*)

Generalization E+: Whatever verb-like thing is first in a sentence, it will be inflected for tense (present/past), and for subject agreement. It cannot appear bare, or in the progressive (-*ing* form) or perfect (participle) form. (*John run/*John running*)

Generalization F: When a sentence has two verb-like things and the first is some form of *have*, the second appears in the perfect form. (**John has being run*)

Generalization G:[9] When a sentence has two verb-like things and the first is some form of *be*, the second appears in the progressive (*ing*) form. (*John is run)

Generalization H: When a sentence has two verb-like things and the first is an M, the second appears in the bare form. (**John must having been run*)

You may not be aware of all these generalizations about English verbal morphology, but all native speakers of English (unconsciously) rely on them when producing sentences.

Chomsky captured all of them in the following rule:[10]

(28)   Aux → Inflection (M) (have en) (be ing)

Chomsky proposed that the Verb must combine with Aux in all sentences. The brackets around the elements in (28) indicate optionality.

As it stands, the PS rule in (28) will lead to gibberish sentences like *John Inflection may have en be ing kiss Mary*, when Aux is rewritten as 'Inflection modal have en be ing'. It is clear what the problem is: some of the elements in (28) are not in their proper place. Although it is true that perfect -*en* and *have*, and progressive -*ing* and *be*, go together (and this is what (28) expresses), they are not pronounced as a unit. -*en* goes on the verb-like thing immediately following *have*, and -*ing* goes on the verb-like element immediately following *be*:

(29)
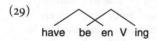
have   be   en   V   ing

(29) represents the cross-serial dependencies PS grammars cannot capture. PS grammars capture cooccurrence restrictions, but can't

---

[9] This generalization ignores passive forms like *John is arrested/*arresting*, which I do not consider here.

[10] I have changed the notation slightly, using I for Inflection (past/present) instead of Chomsky's 'C'. *En* next to *have* stands for the morphological ending of the perfect.

achieve the right word order. To remedy this problem, Chomsky argues that PS grammars must be supplemented with transformations, a device that moves elements around.[11]

Taking (30) as a point of departure, transformations will yield (31).

(30)   John Inflection may have en be ing kiss Mary
(31)   John Inflection may have en be ing kiss Mary

= John may have been kissing Mary

The device of transformations allowed linguists to relate sentences like active and passive, declarative and interrogative, etc.[12] For example, switching the order of the subject and the first verb-like thing in a declarative sentence like *John can swim* yields *can John swim?* (Chomsky managed to formulate the relevant transformation so as to cover pairs like *John swam/Did John swim?*—a significant achievement, as native speakers feel the pair *John swam/Did John swim?* is related in the same way as the pair *John can swim/can John swim?*). Likewise, by changing the shape of the verb and the auxiliary and switching the subject and the object of a declarative sentence like *John arrested Peter*, one gets *Peter was arrested by John*.[13] The need for PS grammars and transformations have remained part of the theory of generative grammar up to the present, and it remains a significant focus of the minimalist program, as we will see in Chapter 3.

---

[11] I leave the notion of transformation at this intuitive level, as this suffices for my purposes here. For formalization, see Chomsky (1955, 1957) and Lasnik (2000).

[12] Chomsky's teacher, Zellig Harris, introduced the notion of transformation; but, as has been well documented (see Chomsky 1975), Harris's conception of transformation was very different from Chomsky's. For Harris, transformations expressed relations between pairs of sentences (e.g. active and passive). For Chomsky, transformations were rules of grammar applying within a sentence, specifically mapping a string of words (technically known as 'terminals') onto another. That is, for Chomsky, both active and passive sentences are the result of transformations.

[13] I am simplifying here, ignoring the fact that the subject of the active sentence is preceded by a preposition in the corresponding passive sentence, for example. I just want to keep the workings of transformations at an intuitive level.

2.4.2 *Later developments*

After Chomsky's initial discovery regarding the computational properties of human languages, linguists focused on three major areas.

(1) What is the relationship between structure and meaning?
(2) Can we refine our understanding of the nature of PS grammars and transformations? Can we deduce some of their properties?
(3) How does the child select the correct combinations of transformations and PS rules for her target language?

I think it is important to retrace some of the history of how these questions have been addressed, as it will allow me to shed light on central aspects of the minimalist program.

Issue 1 was investigated under the rubric of level of representation.

2.4.2.1 *Levels of representation*   The notion of level of representation was formalized in Chomsky (1955). I will not go into all its intricate details,[14] but will focus on those aspects that are essential for understanding some of the works in the minimalist program, where the issue of level of representation is all-important.

Every introduction to modern linguistics starts with examples that show the need for distinct levels of analysis or representation (another appropriate term may be 'level of structure'). An analysis of word combination in terms of linear order alone would fail to represent the ambiguity of sentences like *John hit the man with the umbrella* or *Flying planes can be dangerous*. It also seems necessary to analyze different aspects of sentences differently: word structure (the purview of morphology), sound combination, syllable structure (the domain of phonology), the structure of phrases (syntax), etc. Each level appears to require its own set of axioms, primitive symbols, and rules of combination (e.g. syllable structure appears to be irrelevant to the syntax of phrases). Determining which levels of structure are needed, and what their characteristics are, is a central task of modern linguistics.

---

[14] For an excellent overview, see Lasnik (2005b).

Within syntax, linguists over the years have made a strong case for distinguishing at least two levels of structure: one that will interface with the morphology and the phonology of the language to yield the surface form of sentences, and another that will interface with other conceptual components of the mind to yield the meaning of sentences. Notice that there is nothing logically necessary about this. One may imagine a system where the very same level of structure can be read appropriately on both the sound side and the meaning side. But biologically, human languages seem different. Even if we set aside the irreducible fact that different languages have different ways of expressing the same meaning (different words for the same concept), they also appear to have different ways of combining words to achieve the same sentence meaning. For example, English speakers must start sentences with question words like *who, what, where*, etc. (these are called *wh*-words because they all start with *wh*-, with the exception of *how*) to ask questions. Chinese speakers, on the other hand, do not require a different syntax (word combination) for interrogative sentences. They use the same word order they use in declarative sentences.

(32) Ni mai-le   shenme?
      You buy-past what
      'What did you buy?'
(33) (compare: Ni mai-le   yiben shu
                You buy-past one   book
                'You bought a book')

To the non-linguist there appear to be countless modes of combinations to achieve the same meaning across the languages of the world. (This position was also popular among linguists in the first half of the twentieth century, to the extent that Joos could write in his 1957 survey of linguistics that 'languages can differ from one another without limit and in arbitrary ways'.) Although linguists have discovered that there is only a finite way of combining words and phrases (a topic I will discuss below), they have not been able to reduce the gap between different word orders yielding the same meaning. This seems to be a fact about how language is built.

Once it is established that languages require two levels of structure, we must find a point, a step in the PS grammar derivation, where different surface forms are represented in the same ways. Once we find that point, we can say that it is here that the conceptual component looks at the syntax and determines meaning.

It took thirty years for linguists to reach some consensus about what that point, that level of structure is.[15] Today, it is called Logical Form (LF). But this was not always so. At first (see Katz and Postal 1964, Chomsky 1965), linguists claimed that the point where structure and meaning interface is 'Deep Structure'. Deep Structure was defined as the level of structure obtained before any transformations apply. This was far from being a crazy idea.

The Deep Structure hypothesis readily allowed one to express the fact that by and large active and passive sentences mean the same. They sounded different, but that was due to transformations. Before transformations, *John arrested Bill* and *Bill was arrested by John* look roughly like *John (Past tense) arrest Bill*. The Deep Structure hypothesis was modified because (among other things) it is only by and large that active and passive sentences mean the same thing. *Beavers build dams* and *Dams are built by beavers* express different things (the second sentence, unlike the first, strongly suggests that all dams are built by beavers). Likewise, *Everyone in this room speaks at least two languages* means something quite different from *At least two languages are spoken by everyone in this room* (the second sentence, unlike the first, strongly suggests that it is the very same two languages that everyone speaks).

Of course, as my students invariably say, 'it all depends on what you mean by meaning'. And that's true: the sentences just mentioned express different relations, but not completely different relations: both *Beavers build dams* and *Damns are built by beavers* are about

---

[15] It was a hard-won battle, often referred to as the 'linguistic wars', during which generative grammar lost many gifted linguists who went off in various research directions. For comprehensive coverage of this period, see Harris (1993) and especially Huck and Goldsmith (1996).

beavers building something, the action of building, and dams being
built. To capture this significant similarity, linguists decided to cling
to the Deep Structure hypothesis as one point of contact between
the syntax and the semantics. It wasn't the only point of contact, but
it was the point where meaningful relations pertaining to what they
call theta-roles (agent-of, patient-of, event-of, goal-of, etc.) are
determined. What Deep Structure cannot capture is everything
that linguists call scope, a term borrowed from logic and that has
to do with relations between elements (known as quantifiers) like *a,
no, some, every*. These scope relations seem to be affected by transformations. So, reasonably enough, linguists claimed that the level
of structure reached after all transformations are done, which they
called Surface Structure, is the point where the conceptual systems
concerned with scope access the syntax. It so happens that Surface
Structure is also the point which is accessed by the sound side. So
the model of grammar we ended up with was like the following:

(34)

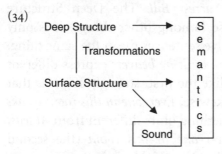

This was different from the very first model of grammar, which
looked like this:

(35)

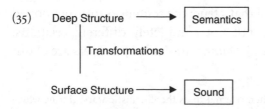

Things are never that easy. Soon after they proposed the model in
(34), linguists noted two things that pointed to the fact that Surface

Structure was not the right level to capture scope relations.[16] First, a sentence like *Every girl kissed some boy* has only one Surface Structure—there is only one way of pronouncing this sentence (setting intonation aside). But it has two scope readings. It can either mean that all the girls kissed one and the same boy, or that each girl (of a relevant set established in discourse) kissed a different boy. Which level of Structure can express this difference? It cannot be Deep Structure, since we have established that scope is affected by transformations, and it cannot be Surface Structure. Scientists are always creative in such paradoxical situations, and linguists are no exception. They came up with an extra level of representation, which they called Logical Form, where the relevant scope facts can be expressed. The question is where Logical Form could be located in a model like (34). Here is something you may not have been expecting: linguists claimed that Logical Form is the level of representation that is reached after some *unpronounced, invisible* transformations have taken place. Linguists noted that if you take the problematic sentence *Every girl kissed some boy* and you front *some boy* to the beginning of the sentence (a transformation not too different from switching the order of the subject and the verb in a question like *John can swim/can John swim?*), as in *Some boy, every girl kissed*, all of a sudden, the sentence is no longer ambiguous. It only refers to a situation where it's the same (lucky) boy that got kissed by all the girls. Linguists were inspired by this and claimed that this fronting transformation may happen 'silently', rearranging the order of the words in Surface Structure after it has been passed onto the sound side. The model they came up with is shown in (36).

---

[16] Many of these scope facts were originally discussed by Lakoff (1971), who tried to account for them at the level of Deep Structure by means of rules that many saw as an undesirable enrichment of the power of the grammar.

(36)

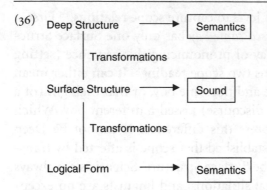

Linguists took advantage of Logical Form to capture the similarity between English and Chinese questions. As we saw above, the two languages have different ways of asking the same thing. Logicians tell us that the meaning of questions boils down to establishing the right scope relations. Suppose they are right. This means that the Chinese/ English contrast is a case where different word orders give rise to the same scope relations. So we must find a level of representation where this scope similarity is captured. It cannot be Deep Structure, which is inadequate for scope relations. It cannot be Surface Structure, since this is also the point of access to the sound side, and the Chinese and English structures sound different. So linguists concluded that it must be Logical Form. That is, they claimed that Chinese question words front to the beginning of the sentence as they do in English, but that this fronting is not pronounced.

Interestingly enough, this hypothesized fronting was found to take place in Chinese, as in (38), which reinforced linguists' intuition about the hypothesized invisible movement.

(37)   OK: Zhangsan mai-le   shenme?
           Zhangsan buy-past what
           'What did Zhangsan buy?'

(38)   Also OK: Shenme Zhangsan mai-le?
               What   Zhangsan buy-past
               'What did Zhangsan buy?'

All in all, cases of 'different scope readings, but same surface form' and 'same scope readings, but different surface forms' appear to be handled rather well by the extra level of representation known as Logical Form.

The model of grammar linguists thus ended up with in the late 1970s is as in (39), the so-called (inverted) Y-model.

(39)

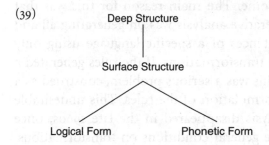

Deep Structure

Surface Structure

Logical Form   Phonetic Form

Details aside, (39) is the model of grammar that was the point of departure for the minimalist program in the early 1990s. And I will come back to it in the following chapters when I describe what changes minimalism wants to bring to it. For now, I hope that the reader has a sense of how linguists got there.

The next area of intense investigation that I want to discuss concerns the nature of PS grammars and transformations.

2.4.2.2 *Conditions on transformations*   In many ways the early models of transformational generative grammar looked a lot like very good traditional grammars of specific languages. In some ways, of course, they were different. In particular, generative grammars were meant to provide explicit[17] rules for processes that were often left implicit in traditional grammar books because the effects of these processes were taken for granted by grammarians, since they referred to unconscious, tacit knowledge (hence, hard to detect if it is not the focus of enquiry, as is the case for traditional grammars, aimed primarily at non-native speakers). However, the end results of generative studies often looked like a catalog of ever more elaborate transformations that mirrored the discussion of construction-specific rules in traditional grammars: rules for passive-, question-,

---

[17] That is what Chomsky intended the term 'generative' to mean when he borrowed it from the field of mathematics.

negative-formation found their counterparts in transformations. (This is very clear from works like Stockwell et al. 1973.)

As generative grammarians sought to achieve greater empirical coverage, transformational analyses, unsurprisingly, grew more complicated and cumbersome. The main reason for this was that the emphasis of early generative analysis was on generating all and only the grammatical sentences of a specific language using only phrase structure rules and transformations. If the rules generated a deviant expression, then this was a serious problem, construed as a direct refutation of that formulation of the rules. This undesirable feature of generative analysis disappeared in the late 1960s, once linguists began to propose general conditions on transformations. Under the influence of Noam Chomsky and John R. Ross, linguists began to limit the power of the apparatus available for the description of particular languages by factoring out individual grammars and transformations principles, conditions, conventions, and concepts that are necessary in all grammars and transformations. The advent of general principles (some of which I will discuss shortly) allowed rule mechanisms (transformations, for example) to mis-generate structures and then filter out the bad cases by appealing to some general constraint.

I think it is no overstatement to say that much of the history of generative grammar since the end of the 1960s boils down to the detailed articulation of a system of general principles/conditions on syntactic processes. Very soon, Chomsky and others realized that such principles of great generality had the salutary effect of dramatically simplifying the formulation of rules. As we will see later, minimalism is an integral part of this research agenda, and it certainly builds on the successful simplification of grammars made possible under a principle-based approach.

Some of the first and, in many ways, most accurate general conditions on rules ever formulated, go back to John R. Ross's 1967 seminal doctoral dissertation 'Constraints on Variables in Syntax'. To illustrate some of these ideas, I shall briefly summarize how early transformational accounts dealt with *wh*-questions.

They assumed that *wh*-questions resulted from a fronting trans-formation (called *wh*-movement) which takes a *wh*-word to the front of the sentence. The point of origin of *wh*-movement is equated with the position occupied by the word providing the answer to the question in the corresponding declarative sentence. (In many languages, interrogative words like *who* and *what* look a lot like indefinite nouns like *someone* and *something*.) For example, sentence (40) is the result of fronting the *wh*-word *what* from the position occupied by something in (41). (For now, ignore the word *did* and the tense difference between *buy* and *bought*. Such factors play no role in the point I want to make.)

(40) What did John buy
(41) John bought something

(42)   John bought ⟶ what
       └──────────────────┘

With this background we can now examine some of Ross's findings. The bulk of Ross's thesis was devoted to discovering constraints on processes like *wh*-movement. For example, Ross observed that it is not possible to front a *wh*-word from within a structure where the *wh*-word is conjoined with some other element. That is, you cannot turn the sentence in (43) into the sentence in (44).

(43) John ate cheese and something (else)
(44) *What did John eat cheese and

Similarly, Ross observed that you cannot front a *wh*-word from within a relative clause (a clause modifying a noun). The following contrast illustrates this.

(45) John met the woman that gave something to Bill
(46) *What did John meet the woman that gave to Bill

Another constraint Ross discovered pertains to subjects that look like full sentences, as in (47).

(47) That John kissed someone surprised everybody at the party

Ross noted that you cannot front a *wh*-word from such sentential subjects:

(48)   *Who did that John kissed surprise everybody at the party

Although I do not have space to illustrate this here, one of the most significant contributions of Ross's thesis is that it documented that no transformation (i.e. not just *wh*-movement) could front anything from within a conjoined phrase, relative clause, or sentential subject. Ross's conclusion is that it would be massively redundant and cumbersome to list these constraints, which he memorably called Islands,[18] as part of the formulation of each and every transformation. Instead, it is much simpler to let the transformations be formulated maximally simply, and filter out the bad outputs by appealing to general constraints.

Chomsky, who had been the first to hint at general constraints on transformations in a 1964 paper, emphatically put the investigation of such general constraints on the agenda of generative grammar in his famous 1973 paper aptly called 'Conditions on Transformations'. And it has remained on linguists' favorite list of phenomena since.

Let me mention a few more constraints on transformations that continue to play a central role in the minimalist program. Chomsky observed that a sentence like *Someone bought something* can be turned into a question like *Who bought what?* The presence of two *wh*-words doesn't affect the status of the sentence: *Who bought what?* is a good sentence in English. But Chomsky noted that the order of the *wh*-words matters. *Who bought what?* is good, but *What did who buy?* is not. Somehow, the order of the *wh*-words must mirror that of the corresponding answer-words (*someone, something*), a constraint Chomsky calls superiority.

An additional constraint on *wh*-words, known as the *wh*-island constraint, emerges from the following paradigm. Whereas it is possible to turn a sentence like *John said that Bill bought something* into a *wh*-question like *What did John say that Bill bought?*, you cannot do the same with a sentence like *John asked whether Bill bought something*: *what did John ask whether Bill bought?*

---

[18] The idea behind the term 'Island' is that this a domain that separates you from the mainland (the main part of the sentence) and from which you can't escape.

Chomsky and others were quick to note that *wh*-questions are always blocked if the *wh*-word is fronted across another *wh*-word:

(49) *what did John ask *where* Bill bought (cf. *John asked where Bill bought something*)

(50) *what did John ask *who* bought (cf. *John asked who bought something*)

(51) *what did John asked to *whom* Peter gave (cf. *John asked to whom Peter gave something*)

(52) *what did John asked *why* Bill bought (cf. *John asked why Bill bought something*)

The investigation of the *wh*-island constraint led to the discovery of another central condition on transformations known as (strict) cyclicity.

Chomsky noted that if the *wh*-island refers to a situation where a *wh*-word is fronted across another *wh*-word, one wants to avoid a situation where the crossing could be 'concealed' (thereby allowing a bad transformation). The situation Chomsky had in mind was something like this.

Consider again a sentence like *what did John asked to whom Peter gave*. This sentence is not quite derived from the affirmative sentence *John asked to whom Peter gave something*, which I put in brackets in (51). It is derived from something like *John asked a question: Peter gave something to somebody?* The derivation of our target sentence proceeds in several steps. First, front the *wh*-word corresponding to *somebody* to the front of the sentence *Peter gave something to somebody*, which results in *to whom Peter gave something*. This is the question John asked: 'To whom did Peter give something?'

Replace the *a question* with its corresponding *wh*-sentence, and you obtain: *John asked to whom Peter gave something*. After uniting the two clauses into one, front the *wh*-word corresponding to *something*. A bad sentence results, since *what* crosses another *wh*-word:

(53) Basis: John asked a question: Peter gave something to somebody?
      Step 1: John asked a question: Peter gave ~~something~~ → what to somebody?
      Step 2: John asked a question: what Peter gave to some
      Step 3: John asked what Peter gave to ~~somebody~~ → whom

Notice that for the crossing situation to arise, the steps in the derivation just sketched must take place in the particular order I gave. But it is not the only conceivable order. You could imagine an alternative derivation along the following lines: start with *John asked a question: Peter gave something to somebody.* Front the *wh*-word corresponding to *something* to the front of the whole sentence. (Notice that at this point, no crossing of *wh*-words happens.) After fronting of *what*, front the *wh*-word corresponding to *someone* to the front of the clause starting with *Peter gave*, then replace *a question* with *to whom Peter gave.* The end result is just the same as the one we obtained when we followed the other derivation: *what did John ask to whom Peter gave.* But this time the sentence should be good, because no crossing of *wh*-words took place. Since we want the sentence to be bad, we must find a way to force the crossing of *wh*-words. Chomsky formulated the principle of (strict) cyclicity to do just that. Roughly put, the principle forces you first to do all the transformations you want in the most deeply embedded sentence (the smallest Russian doll) before you integrate that sentence into a bigger one. The alternative derivation we considered (which avoided crossing) was one in which we first took an element from the most deeply embedded sentence and fronted it to the beginning of the bigger sentence, and then went back to the most deeply embedded clause and did something internal to it (fronting of *to whom*). Strict cyclicity forbids such 'going back'. Today, strict cyclicity is still assumed, along with superiority, the *wh*-island, and other islands. Hundreds of unrelated languages have been shown to abide by them. And they constitute a major area of research in the minimalist program, for reasons I will return to in later chapters.

At the same time as people investigated conditions on transformations, they also tried to understand similarities in the workings of distinct transformations.

2.4.2.3 *Uniformity*   For example, just as the passive transformation fronts a noun like *Mary* from a postverbal position to a preverbal position, the so-called raising transformation does the same, even though it does not involve any passive verbal morphology or any other feature of passives.

(54) John arrested Mary → Mary was arrested by John
(55) It seems that Mary is sick → Mary seems to be sick

Chomsky and others formulated the idea that transformations like passivization may be decomposed into more primitive transformations like 'noun phrase preposing', which would make it easier to relate (54) and (55). It also avoided problems like the categorization of sentences such as (56).

(56) John was believed by Sue to be sick

As is immediately obvious, (56) shares properties of both *Sue believes that John was sick* and *It was believed by Sue that John was sick*. In the early days of transformational generative grammar this was a problem, because (56) was supposed to be the result of either the passive-transformation or the raising-transformation. But it couldn't be both. As soon as one recognizes a more abstract level of analysis in terms of 'noun phrase preposing', the categorization problem disappears. (56) above is neither quite passive or raising; it is the result of noun-phrase preposing, an operation that also underlies passive and raising sentences.

The trend of decomposing transformations into more primitive operations went on unabated. Very soon people realized that the transformations from the early days of generative grammar were just taxonomic devices, best understood as the conspiracy of the workings of several more general and primitive processes that were very different from what traditional grammars had described.

This was just another reflection of the tendency to factor out from transformations general principles and constraints/filters, a tendency crucial to the elaboration of the P&P approach, from which the minimalist program emerged. Instead of construction-specific rules, linguists focused on general principles. This, as we will see, allowed them to isolate better what is universal and what is language-specific, a crucial step in the characterization of Universal Grammar and its contribution to language acquisition.

Before I elaborate on the P&P approach, let me mention another important strand of research in generative linguistics in the 1970s: the discovery of representational invariance across phrases.

The similarity between *The enemy's destruction of the city* and *The enemy destroyed the city*, or between *The city's destruction by the enemy* and *The city was destroyed by the enemy*, led Chomsky in 1970 to claim that noun phrases and sentences really have the same structural representation. In other words, they offer the same structural space within which transformations like passivization can apply.

The structural representation Chomsky assigned to both sentences (verb phrases for him) and noun phrases was roughly as in (57) below.

(57) a.

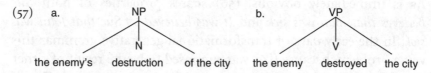

Chomsky further observed that nominal groups like [*John's portrait of Saskia*] and verbal groups like [*John portrayed Saskia*] were not all that different from adjectival groups like [*very fond of Saskia*] and prepositional groups like [*right above Saskia*].

In each case, Chomsky noticed, there is a key element which gives its identity to the whole phrase: the noun for noun phrases, the verb for verb phrases, the adjective for adjectival phrases, and the preposition for preposition phrases. Chomsky called this key element the 'head,' and the identity of the whole phrase the 'label' of the phrase, which is projected (or copied) from the head. The head can be modified by material to its left and to its right. Chomsky noted that the material to the left of the head in English can more easily be omitted than the material to the right of the head. For example, most prepositions need to be followed by some material (*for __; *of __; etc.), but none needs to be modified by elements like *right*, as in (*right*) *above Saskia*. For this reason Chomsky claimed that the material to the right of the head, which he called the complement, is more tightly connected to the head, and forms a sub-unit (a sub-phrase, if you like) to the exclusion of the material to the left of the head, which Chomsky called the specifier. Chomsky called the sub-unit consisting of the head and the complement the bar-level category. Putting all this information together, the structures for noun phrases (NPs), verb phrases (VPs), adjectival phrases (APs), and prepositional phrases (PPs) are given in (58).

(58)

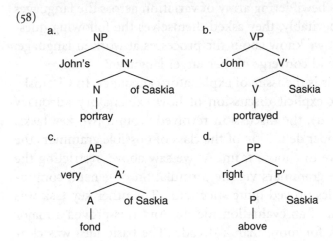

Chomsky hypothesized that all four phrases are the reflexes of a more abstract category he called X (a variable varying over {N, V, A, P}).

Since Chomsky wrote his seminal X-bar paper in 1970, numerous elements have been found to function as heads and project phrases. As I write, many linguists working in the generative tradition believe that simple declarative sentences consist of about fifty phrases, all embedded inside one another (see especially Cinque 1999). Crucially, all of them have been found to project in accordance to the X-bar schema. This abstract representation of invariance[19] was the very first thing that convinced me (and no doubt many others) that something deep was at work at the very foundation of our language faculty. It certainly was a first step in the formulation of a minimalist program for linguistic theory, as we will see in Chapter 3.

2.4.3 *Parameters*

In addition to work on levels of representation and on general principles in syntax, linguists in the 1970s focused more and more

---

[19] In the context of representational invariance, I want to note that the work of Joseph Emonds, especially Emonds (1970), stands out as a landmark.

on the syntax of languages other than English. Invariably they faced the tension between more and more general principles of Universal Grammar and a bewildering array of variation across the languages of the world. Inevitably, they asked themselves the following question: given what we know about the processes at work in language, how does the child converge on her target language?

Recall that this is the issue of explanatory adequacy. In Chomsky (1965) (the first explicit discussion of how explanatory adequacy could be achieved), the discussion revolved around two key tasks. One was the proper definition of the class of possible grammars the child would have to choose from. As we saw above, restricting the class of possible grammars via the formulation of general computational principles proved quite successful. The other key task was the specification of an evaluation metric. And this proved a major stumbling block for more than a decade. The basic idea was clear enough. The evaluation metric arrays the class of possible grammars in a descending order of 'desirability'. The task, then, is for the child to take the data she receives as input and find the 'best' grammar (i.e. highest ranked by the evaluation metric) that fits or matches it. Although this characterization is abstractly correct, it proved hard to implement. There just seemed to be no good way to rank grammars in terms of desirability. Put differently, although the problem was clearly identified in Chomsky (1965) and the general form of a solution sketched out, a *workable and usable* proposal was not. Put bluntly, nobody quite knew how to specify the evaluation metric. But for a long time, an evaluation procedure was thought to be an indispensable element of the theory. Chomsky expresses this very clearly in (1965: 36–7):

To acquire language, a child must devise a hypothesis compatible with presented data—he must select from the store of potential grammars a specific one that is appropriate to the data available to him. It is logically possible that the data might be sufficiently rich and the class of potential grammars sufficiently limited so that no more than a single permitted grammar will be compatible with the available data at the moment of successful language acquisition, in our idealized 'instantaneous' model. In this case, no evaluation procedure will be necessary as a part of linguistic theory—that is, as an innate property of an organism or a device capable of language acquisition. It is rather difficult to imagine how in detail this logical possibility might be realized, and all concrete attempts to formulate an empirically adequate linguistic theory certainly leave ample room for mutually inconsistent grammars, all compatible with primary data of any conceivable sort. All such theories therefore require supplementation by an evaluation measure if language acquisition is to be accounted for and selection of specific grammars is to be justified; and I shall continue to assume tentatively, as heretofore, that this is an empirical fact about the innate human *faculté de langage* and consequently about general linguistic theory as well.

Put succinctly, early work on generative grammar assumed that linguistic theory would not be able to restrict the generative power of the grammar so as to have only one grammar compatible with the data, and therefore concluded that only the weaker requirement of providing an evaluation procedure for grammars was attainable.

However, with the development of the P&P framework during the past decade and a half an evaluation measure for grammars has become essentially superfluous. With the reduction of the transformational component to a set of general principles that are part of Universal Grammar (UG), it became possible to entertain the idea that linguistic theory allows only a severely limited number of grammars—perhaps only one for each given language.

At the end of the 1970s, Chomsky conceived of the language faculty as follows (see Chomsky (1981) for a comprehensive treatment, and Baker (2001) for an accessible overview). Children come equipped with a set of principles of grammar construction (i.e. UG). Among the principles of UG are some with open parameters.[20] Specific grammars arise once values for these open parameters are specified. Parameter values are determined on the basis of the linguistic input the child receives. A language-specific grammar, then, is simply a specification of the values that the principles of UG leave open. This conceives of the acquisition process as sensitive to the details of the environmental input (as well as the level of development of other cognitive capacities), as it is the linguistic input to the child that provides the relevant information for setting

---

[20] The idea of parameters was first formulated explicitly in Rizzi (1978).

the parameter values correctly. However, the shape of the knowledge attained (the structure of the acquired grammar) is not limited to information that can be gleaned from the linguistic data, since the latter exercises its influence against the rich principles that UG makes available.

Much of the work since the mid-1970s, especially the countless studies inspired by Kayne (1975), can be seen in retrospect as demonstrating the viability of this conception. At the beginning of the 1980s, there was an explosion of comparative grammatical research that exploited this combination of fixed principles and varying parametric values, showing that languages, despite apparent surface diversity, could be seen as patterns with a common fixed core. A couple of examples should be enough to provide a flavor of this research.

Consider first the placement of adverbs in English and French.[21] In English, an adverb may not intervene between the verb and the direct object, in contrast with French.

(59)　a.　*John eats quickly an apple
　　　b.　Jean mange rapidement une pomme
　　　c.　John quickly eats an apple
　　　d.　*Jean rapidement mange une pomme

The paradigm in (59) appears to be the result of a parametric variation between the grammar of English and that of French. In both languages, the clause has a structure roughly as in (60).

(60)　[$_S$ Subject [Inflection [Adverb [$_{VP}$ Verb Object]]]]

What makes a sentence finite are features in the Inflection position. These must be added to the verb in both languages (call this the 'Inflection-Attachment' Principle). The languages differ, however, in how this happens (call this the 'Inflection-Attachment' Parameter). In English, Inflection lowers onto the verb, whereas in French the verb raises to Inflection. The difference is illustrated in (61).

---

[21] This example is based on groundbreaking work by Emonds (1978) and Pollock (1989).

(61)

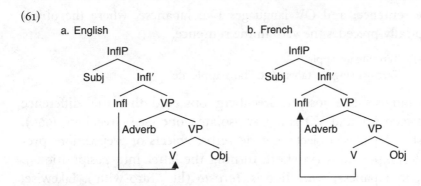

Note that this one difference explains the data in (59). In English, since the Verb doesn't raise, and the adverb is assumed to stay put, the adverb will be to the left, but not the right, of the finite verb (61a), whereas in French the opposite holds, due to V-movement across the adverb (61b).

Note, crucially, that we keep the basic clausal structure the *same* in the two languages. Likewise, the demand that Inflection be attached to the verb remains constant. What changes is how this attachment takes place.

Another popular example comes from Huang's (1982) treatment of questions in Chinese. As we have already seen, Chinese interrogative words, unlike English ones, are not pronounced at the beginning of the sentence. Huang proposed a very simple parameter that almost trivializes the difference between English and Chinese. He assumed the general principle that, for purposes of interpretation (scope), *wh*-words must move to a position very high in the syntactic tree. This can be done overtly (before reaching Surface Structure) or covertly (after Surface Structure, in the syntactic component leading to Logical Form). Note that at the point the sentence is being interpreted for scope (Logical Form), Chinese and English questions have identical representations.

A third example comes from X-bar theory. It is an old observation by typologists that close to 90 per cent of the world's languages divide into two broad classes: so-called V(erb)O(bject) languages like English, where the object of the verb typically follows the verb in the sentence, and OV languages like Japanese, where the object typically precedes the verb in the sentence.

(62)   Taro ate an apple
        Taro-ga ringo-o tabeta (lit. 'Taro apple ate')

Typologists like Joseph Greenberg observed that this difference between OV and VO is not an isolated one (see Greenberg 1966). Just as Japanese objects precede verbs, objects of prepositions precede prepositions (in effect, turning the latter into *post*positions). So, in Japanese, *with Taro* is *Taro-to* (lit. 'Taro-with'). Likewise, objects of nouns (*portrait of Taro*) precede nouns in Japanese: *Taro-no shasin* (lit. 'Taro-of portrait'). And similarly for objects of adjectives: *kind to Taro* is *Taro-ni shinsetu(-da)* (lit. 'Taro-to kind').

Generative grammarians soon came up with a simple parameter to characterize OV and VO languages. They claim that, while it is a principle of X-bar theory that every phrase must have a head, it is a matter of parametric variation whether the complement of the head precedes or follows the head. If the language picks the 'precede' option, it will be like Japanese. If the language picks the 'follow' option, it will be like English. Notice that the parameter applies to all phrases. What is true of Verb Phrases is true of Noun Phrases, Prepositional Phrases, Adjectival Phrases, etc. So X-bar trees for Japanese look like inverted X-bar trees for English:

(63)

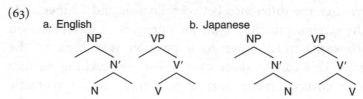

As Baker (2001) clearly demonstrated, this sort of account can be multiplied to accommodate all sorts of difference across languages. Simple parameters, located in the right points in the tree, can have massive consequences for the principles they interact with such that it is possible to capture the idea that really all languages are alike even if they look and sound vastly different. Linguists went as far as to say that apart from lexical differences, there is basically one human language (call it 'Human'). The languages we speak and hear around us are just dialects of it. Like Darwin, Chomsky is fond of asking what a Martian would say about differences on Earth. In the case of human languages, if the P&P approach is right, the Martian may well not be able to tell our languages apart, since deep down they are so similar.

A good part of research in the 1980s involved exactly these sorts of analysis. It proved to be extremely successful, and very insightful, so much so that grammarians came to the conclusion that something like a P&P account of the language faculty was essentially correct. Note that this does *not* say which of the many possible principles and parameters theories is the right one. It only says that the right theory should have this general architecture: a combination of some principles and some parameters.

In particular, the P&P proposal has three great virtues. (a) It accommodates the fact that the language a person ends up speaking is closely related to the one that s/he is exposed to; (b) it accommodates the fact that acquisition takes place despite a significant poverty of the linguistic stimulus by having the linguistic input to the child act against a fixed backdrop of invariant principles; and (c) it is immediately applicable in day-to-day grammatical research. In particular, in contrast to the vagaries of the evaluation metric, the parameter-setting model has been widely used to account for grammatical variation. These three facts have led to a general consensus among linguists that the language faculty has a P&P architecture. I feel justified in saying that it is our standard model.

This consensus invites a new question: granted that the language faculty has a P&P character, which of the many possible P&P models is the right one? Minimalism is nothing more, and nothing less, than an attempt, a program, to answer this question.

2.5 Conclusion

In the brief historical sketch in this chapter I have ignored many details, and historical twists and turns, but I have tracked the major historical developments and shifts of emphasis fairly closely. This chapter was intended to convey two important features that constitute the foundation of the minimalist program for linguistic theory. First and foremost, the program—and indeed the generative enterprise as a whole—sits firmly in a broader cognitive, ultimately biological, context, one that, starting with *Aspects* and culminating in the P&P model, successfully frames a general kind of solution to the central problem of language acquisition. Second, the enterprise is committed to developing adequate formal tools for the study of natural language grammars. This is what gave the approach its name, *generative* grammar, by which Chomsky meant 'formally explicit'. This is also what gave the approach its 'Galilean' character a commitment, shared by all modern scientific enterprises, that the book of nature 'is written in the mathematical language, and the symbols are triangles, circles and other geometrical figures, without whose help it is humanly impossible to comprehend a single word of it, and without which one wanders in vain through a dark labyrinth' (Galilei 1960 [1623]: 183–4). Galileo here is expressing the fundamental idea that the world is a system in which everything can be understood in terms of mathematically specifiable laws of motion. To reach this level of mathematization (i.e. intelligibility), Galileo taught the world of science that one must judiciously select the things one observes. Only once phenomena have been artificially isolated will one find that the purified, idealized experiments of nature result in physical laws which can be described in precise mathematical terms. These abstract mathematical models of the universe are then given a higher degree of reality than is accorded to the ordinary world of sensation. I will return to the Galilean style of science in Chapter 4, because almost invariably in the history of science it has led to the discovery not just of mathematical patterns in the world, but *beautiful* mathematical patterns, that are then taken by the scientist to be too good/beautiful not to be true. This attitude, I will argue, is very helpful in clarifying and refining the minimalist program.

3

The Minimalist Core

The historical development discussed in the previous chapter high-lighted the fact that until well into the 1980s, solving the acquisition problem was the paramount measure of theoretical success in linguistics. Once, however, this problem is taken as essentially understood, then the question is *not* how to solve it but how to solve it *best*. By its nature, this question abstracts away from the Poverty of Stimulus problem and points towards other criteria of adequacy (that is, going 'beyond explanatory adequacy', to use a popular phrase in the minimalist literature). Seen in this context, Minimalism emerges from the success of the Principles and Parameters (P&P) program. Because the P&P approach 'solves' the logical problem of language acquisition, more methodological criteria of theory evaluation can become more prominent. Such criteria revolve around simplicity, elegance, and other notions that are hard to quantify but, as we will see in Chapter 4, are extremely important. I cannot overstate the fact that minimalism presupposes the major findings from the early P&P period. In many ways, minimalism is but an attempt to find ways of gaining a better grasp of the same model. In this chapter I will examine the ingredients that were extracted from the P&P approach and show how these constitute the core of the minimalist program. This will allow me to discuss the nature of scientific programs as a whole.

3.1 The Government-Binding model

If, as I have argued, P&P provides the context of emergence for minimalism, the specific and best-worked-out version of the P&P

approach known as Government-Binding theory (GB) provides specific (technical) principles ('details') from which minimalist guidelines—what I will define as the conceptual core of minimalism—could be extracted.

3.1.1 *Why take Government-Binding as a starting point?*

The GB theory is a very well-developed version of the P&P theory, with wide empirical coverage and an interesting deductive structure. It thus provides both a foundation and a foil for methodological reflection, a starting point for explanatory refinement. This is nicely expressed by Hornstein (2001: 14):

> Methodological concerns such as parsimony get their bite when pairs of possibilities are played off against one another. Theories are neither simple nor complex, neither parsimonious nor profligate simpliciter. They must be as complex and intricate as required. [*Einstein once said that 'theories should be simple, but not too simple'*—CB.] Thus, when accounts are considered singly evaluations of methodological economy are moot. It is only in the context of theory *comparison* that such notions find a foothold. As such, it always pays to have a competing companion account for purposes of comparison. Absent this, methodological considerations quickly lose their grip and utility.
> GB accounts admirably fit the role of straight man to the minimalist kibbitzer. One way of fruitfully launching a minimalist research program is to simplify, naturalize, and economize earlier GB accounts. These are always good places to begin and provide solid benchmarks against which to measure putative progress.

At the end of the 1980s, after a decade of research of unmatched intensity and scope in the linguistic sciences, GB had several important features that I wish to highlight here. (See Chomsky and Lasnik (1993), Culicover (1997), Haegeman (1994), Ouhalla (1994), and Roberts (1996) for extensive discussion and illustration of these.)

GB was highly *modular*. UG-specific modules included a Phrase Structure module, a binding module, a control module, a case module, and a locality module. (Don't worry about the specific names of the module; they are just listed for the sake of exposition. For brief discussion, see the glossary.) Such modules, each associated with principles and parameters, may be conceived of as sub-theories dealing with a well-defined set of data. These sub-theories interacted with one another and produced the constructional complexity, the various constructions specific to each language, that traditional grammars and early transformational models of generative grammar had identified.

For example, a central tenet of GB was that noun phrases could only occur in specific, well-defined positions in the sentence. These positions were called case-positions, following an insight by Jean-Roger Vergnaud. Vergnaud pointed out in 1977, in a famous letter to Noam Chomsky and Howard Lasnik, that many transformational rules could be simplified if the grammar made use of the traditional notion of case (visible in English on pronouns only, e.g. *he* vs. *him*, but much more pervasive in many languages of the world). The idea was that noun phrases are licit only in those positions where they can be assigned a case (nominative, accusative, genitive, etc.). Specifically, Vergnaud proposed a principle which he called the Case Filter. The Case Filter expresses the requirement that all noun phrases must bear a case (i.e. must be in a position where case is assigned) by Surface Structure.

Vergnaud and many others went on to define precisely those positions where case was available. They claimed that the complement position of a verb bearing a passive morpheme, unlike the complement position of a verb without such a morpheme, is not a case-licensing position. Accordingly, no noun phrase can be licensed in that position (cf. *John was arrested Mary*). If a noun phrase shows up in this position at Deep Structure (as it must to express such thematic information as the fact that the arrest of somebody took place—a requirement of the theta module), it cannot stay in that position. It must be displaced by Surface Structure to a position where case is available. At this point the locality module kicks in. Its role is to identify the range of positions available for displacement from the complement position of any verb (among all the positions in the sentence created by the Phrase Structure module). Some such positions are case-assigning positions, some positions are not. In the passive situation under discussion, the relevant noun (phrase) will be looking for a case-assigning position (a requirement imposed by the case module). The position right before the auxiliary verb (call it the 'subject' position) is such a case position (as determined again by the case module in conjunction with the phrase structure module). But that position is occupied by the subject of the corresponding active sentence (*John arrested Mary*) (a requirement imposed by the theta module).¹ To make it vacant and allow *Mary* to get case, we'll put *John* at the end of the sentence (a position made available by the phrase structure module and rendered accessible by the locality module). Now, *Mary* can be displaced, and gets case-licensed. The final step consists in saving the postposed noun *John*, which by vacating the subject position is no longer in the right case position. In this situation, the case module determines that the addition of a preposition (*by*) (which is assumed to assign case to its object/complement) can be used as a last resort. The end result is *Mary was arrested by John*, where both nouns are case-licensed by Surface Structure.

As I tried to show with this example, what used to be called the passive transformation—which, for simplicity's sake,² can be said to turn what looks like active sentences into passive sentences by post-posing the subject, preposing the object, and changing the morph-ology of the verb (see Chomsky 1957; see also Chapter 2)—can now be seen as the end result of a complex interaction among simple modules. The Phrase Structure module creates all possible positions in the tree. The theta module places noun phrases in the right positions to be interpreted thematically as agents, patients, etc. of the event expressed by the verb. The case module makes sure noun phrases end up in case-assigning positions. If these do not corres-pond to the positions imposed by the theta module, the locality module displaces the noun phrases to the right kinds of position.

---

¹ I here set aside the fact that in many analyses of the passives in the P&P era, the subject of active sentences does not occupy the surface subject position in correspond-ing passive derivations (specifier of the inflection/tense phrase), but instead occupies a predicate-internal position (the so-called VP-internal subject hypothesis). This refine-ment does not affect the depiction of modular interaction I want to give in the text.

² I am simplifying here. Technically, *both* active and passive sentences are derived from a common Deep Structure representation (recall n. 12 in Ch. 2).

So instead of building all the specificity of English passives into a rule, the P&P approach claims that modules conspire to yield it:

(1)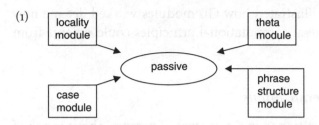

I think that the reason why the GB model was so successful at capturing many significant facts about hundreds of languages is largely due to its modular structure. Modules allow scientists to isolate or dissect phenomena artificially and find out more about their component parts. There is nothing specific to linguistics about this. As I will discuss in Chapter 4, the considerable success of biology in the 1950s is largely due to the fact that it entered into what Piattelli-Palmarini (1981) aptly called the 'age of specificity', with a multiplication of micromodules that are fit for intense study. François Jacob (1982: 10) characterizes the modular method thus:

It is probably a need of the human brain to have a representation of the world that is unified and coherent. A lack of unity and coherence frequently results in anxiety and schizophrenia. It seems only fair to say that, as far as coherence and unity are concerned, mythical explanation often does better than scientific explanation. For science does not aim at reaching a complete and definitive explanation of the whole universe. It proceeds by detailed experimentation on limited areas of nature. It looks for partial and provisional answers for certain phenomena that can be isolated and well defined.

The success of modularization does not mean that one need not look for principles of great generality, for laws of nature. But it does mean that in many cases such laws can only be unveiled after a period of intense specificity and modularization. This is certainly what the (short) history of the field of linguistics reveals. The advent of the minimalist program, the search for general guidelines of computation, etc. was made possible by the intense modularization witnessed in the GB era.

Having briefly illustrated how GB modules worked, let me now illustrate how general computational principles could emerge from these modules.

3.1.2 *Some Generalizations*

The Case Filter mentioned in the context of passives above is one of the important *axioms*, principles that had to be met, according to the GB model.[3] As the workings of these principles became clear, GB practitioners uncovered a list of non-trivial empirical *generalizations*, hypotheses, and 'big facts' that many now take to be fundamental to the working of UG.[4]

3.1.2.1 *Last resort*   Among the generalizations arrived at was one that proved instrumental in the development of the minimalist program. Chomsky (1986a: 199) interpreted the unacceptability of sentences like *John seems is ill* (compare *John seems to be ill*) as indicating that an element could not be displaced twice to a case position (preverbal position triggering subject agreement on the verb movement). Put differently, displacement of a noun phrase may happen until that noun phrase reaches a case-assigning position. But once it has reached that position, it is stuck there. From this, Chomsky concluded that movement to a preverbal subject position

---

[3] For linguists: in addition to the Case Filter, the Theta Criterion, the Empty Category Principle (ECP), the Minimality Principle, the PRO theorem, and Conditions A, B, and C of the Binding Theory deserve mention. I return to some of these in detail in Ch. 5. For brief discussion, see the glossary.

[4] Among these, I would mention (for experts) Burzio's Generalization (see Reuland 2000), the VP-internal subject hypothesis (alternatively, the distributed character of the notion 'subject' and, by hypothesis, other grammatical relations like subject-of, object-of, etc.; see McCloskey 1997, Haegeman 2005), the great usefulness of Functional Projections (leading to Cinque's (1999) hierarchy), a rich parametric structure (cf. Baker's (2001) Parameter Hierarchy), and the successive cyclic nature of long-distance movement (see Ch. 5 and Boeckx forthcoming a).

was 'a last resort operation'. In more general terms, he claimed that, once an operation has taken place, it must not happen again, as nothing is gained by performing a second instance of the same operation.

It was not the first time that the Last Resort character of syntactic operations had been highlighted. At around the same time Chomsky was writing, Koopman and Sportiche (1986: 362, 366) were able to state:

> it is *an often made observation* that languages seem to adopt 'minimalist strategies' as unmarked strategies when possible; licensing processes are invoked only when necessary. [*emphasis mine*]

Two fairly straightforward examples of extra steps taken just in case less complex strategies fail come from the literature of *do*-support and resumption.

The basic take on question formation ever since Chomsky (1955, 1957) has been that the crucial step consists of fronting the auxiliary material over the subject ('subject–auxiliary' inversion), as can be seen in examples like *John can swim* → *Can John swim?* The process is transparent in the event the auxiliary is a modal, some variant of *have* (*John has left* → *Has John left?*), or some variant of *be* (*John is leaving* → *Is John leaving?*). But there is no obvious declarative sentence corresponding to *Did John leave?* except *John left.* Unlike the other cases just mentioned, the form *Did John leave?* appears to require the use of some variant of *do*, which has no corresponding element in the declarative form.[5] Chomsky's insight to handle such cases was to resort to the claim that the auxiliary in the absence of a modal, *have*, or *be* is an affix, a piece of a word that cannot stand alone. It must be attached to some verbal form. In the normal case (declarative sentence), this affixal auxiliary will attach to the main verb, combining with it to form an inflected verb. But if the affixal auxiliary is fronted (as in the case in question), the affix will be separated from its regular host, the main verb, by the subject, as represented in (2).

---

[5] The sentence *John did leave* is bad, unless *did* is stressed, which Chomsky (1957) (and virtually everyone else after him) treated as a special case.

(2)

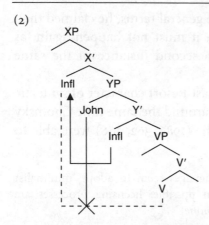

To satisfy the requirement that an affix must be properly attached to a host, languages like English will introduce a dummy, meaning-less verb like *do* that will act as a proxy host for the affix, resulting in the use of so-called *do*-support in questions. This marked strategy is only used if the affix would otherwise be left unattached to anything at Surface Structure. If the affix can attach to the main verb (as in declaratives, where the subject does not intervene between the affixal auxiliary and the verb), or if the auxiliary is not affixal (modal, *have*, or *be*), *do*-support need not take place, and therefore—following minimalist requirements of least effort—cannot take place.

The other example I want to use to illustrate the idea behind Koopman and Sportiche's assertion comes from the realm of re-sumption. As discussed in the previous chapter, Ross discovered islands, domains out of which fronting cannot take place, as illus-trated in (3):

(3)   *This is the woman that I am not sure whether ___ met Bill

Although many linguists interpreted Ross's findings as indicating that fronting out of islands was completely forbidden, this was not quite Ross's claim. Instead, his claim was that fronting out of islands is bad unless the original site of movement is filled by a so-called resumptive pronoun, a pronoun that directly refers back to the fronted element. Witness the improvement of (3) in (4).

(4)   This is the woman that I am not sure whether *she* met Bill

Subsequent studies have revealed that resumption is a last-resort strategy (pretty much like *do*-support) consisting of the insertion of a dummy pronoun that acts as a stand-in for the fronted material (see Shlonsky 1992, Pesetsky 1998, Boeckx 2003a). This strategy is only used if the fronting is otherwise illicit, as in the case of islands. Thus, we expect resumption to lead to unacceptability if fronting is otherwise possible.

(5) This is the woman that John met
(6) *This is the woman that John met *her*

Both resumption and *do*-support indeed suggest that some strategies are only used in languages as last-resort strategies, when repair is needed.

In a similar vein, at the end of the 1980s Chomsky and others began to reinterpret some generalizations and principles in terms of least-effort strategies. Arguably the clearest example of this development revolves around analyses of sentences like (7) and (8) (the superiority phenomenon mentioned in Chapter 2).

(7) Guess who bought what?
(8) *Guess what who bought?

All native speakers of English consider (7) acceptable, and most consider (8) unacceptable. Every native speaker perceives it as sharply less well-formed than (7). The general line of research (see Chomsky 1986b) to explain a variety of such phenomena was in terms of complex licensing mechanisms. Since the details don't matter here, I won't go over them. What is more interesting and relevant for our present purposes is Chomsky and Lasnik's (1993) reinterpretation of groundbreaking work by Luigi Rizzi (1990) in terms of least effort.

Chomsky and Lasnik's basic idea is very clear. In situations where you have the option of fronting either of two elements, pick the one that would have to move less; that is, pick the one that is closer to the position it ends up with after fronting. In other words, minimize the distance traveled by the moving element. In their terms, '[t]he basic intuition is that the operation [of movement] should always try to construct "the shortest link"' (p. 89).

Chomsky and Lasnik went on to elevate this shortest principle to a 'general principle of economy of derivation' (p. 90). Since then, considerations of economy have been the major focus of research in syntactic theory. Indeed, they constituted the concrete cases on which minimalist logic was based.

3.1.2.2 *Economy*   Following Chomsky and Lasnik's reinterpretation of Rizzi's work, several principles of grammar were reinterpreted in terms of economy (least effort). Take, for example, the Minimal Distance Principle. Rosenbaum formulated this principle in 1970 to deal with instances of so-called control.

'Control' is a cover term for the mechanism that lies behind the way we interpret sentences like *John tried to leave* as indicating that *John* is both the agent of 'trying' and of 'leaving'. That is, we interpret the sentence *John tried to leave* as meaning that John did something that would make it possible for him (and not somebody else) to leave. Control is also at work in sentences like *John persuaded Mary to leave*. The control module in this case dictates that this sentence be understood as meaning that the leaver is Mary, not John. Rosenbaum's Minimal Distance Principle expresses the idea that the element understood as the subject of the infinitival clause (*to leave* in our examples) is the element that is closest to that infinitival clause. This, too, has the flavor of an economy/least effort condition.[6]

From the early 1990s onward, Least Effort and Last Resort principles became a cornerstone of syntactic theorizing. Indeed, I think that the very 'first act' toward the formulation of the minimalist program was to elevate the Last Resort character of movement identified in Chomsky (1986a) to a principle that all derivations must meet. That step was taken in Chomsky (1991). The next step, taken in Chomsky (1993), was to ask why languages should be organized around principles that legislate against superfluous steps in derivations and superfluous elements in representations.

---

[6] For linguists: Principles like the A-over-A condition (Chomsky 1964) and the Minimal Binding Requirement (Aoun and Li 1993) can also be seen as reflexes of more general least effort conditions.

Before turning to other essential steps toward the formulation of a minimalist program for linguistic theory, I think it is useful at this point to note that of course linguists did not wait until the 1990s to look for redundancies, superfluous steps, etc. and seek to eliminate them. Early generative grammar was good natural philosophy (i.e. science), which Hume (1948[1779]: 40) characterized thus: 'To multiply causes, without necessity, is indeed contrary to true philosophy.'

As Freidin and Vergnaud (2001: 641) have observed, Chomsky's earliest writings on generative grammar (Chomsky 1951, 1955) already contain allusions to simplicity. Freidin and Vergnaud (2001: 641 n. 2) point out that Chomsky's (1951) notion of simplicity bears some general similarity to the more current discussions of economy.

For the formulation of any relative precise notion of simplicity, it is necessary that the general structure of the grammar be more or less fixed, as well as the notations by means of which it is constructed. We want the notion of simplicity to be broad enough to comprehend all those aspects of simplicity of grammar which enter into consideration when linguistic elements are set up. Thus we want the reduction of the number of elements and statements, any generalizations, and, to generalize the notion of generalization itself, any similarity in the form of non-identical statements, to increase the total simplicity of the grammar. As a first approximation to the notion of simplicity, we will here consider shortness of grammar as a measure of simplicity, and will use such notations as will permit similar statements to be coalesced. (Chomsky 1951: 5)

To avoid circularity, the notation must be fixed in advance and neutral to any particular grammar.

Given the fixed notation, the criteria of simplicity governing the ordering of statements are as follows: that the shorter grammar is the simpler, and that among equally short grammars, the simplest is that in which the average length of derivation of sentences is least. (Chomsky 1951: 6)

Similarly, in Chomsky (1955), an entire chapter (chapter 4) is devoted to 'simplicity and the form of grammar'.

Although minimalist themes resonate with Chomsky's earliest writings (we shall discuss some minimalist themes in Chomsky 1965 in Chapter 4), such themes could not be systematically investigated before the 1990s because there was a more pressing goal: understanding how the child acquires the language of her environment given the poverty of stimulus. It was only after the P&P approach was found adequate in solving the language acquisition problem, in separating the universal from the language-specific, and the principles from the parameters, that the shape of principles, the deeper *why*-questions, could begin to be asked. (For observations along similar lines, see Chomsky 2005.[7])

3.1.2.3 *Virtual conceptual necessity*   In addition to economy guidelines Chomsky developed the concept of 'virtual conceptual necessity', which has come to occupy center stage in the minimalist literature. The clearest application of the concept has been in the realm of levels of representation.

3.1.2.3.1 *Levels of representation*   Recall that the standard (Y-)model sketched in Chapter 2 included four levels of representation: Deep Structure, Surface Structure, Phonetic Form, and Logical Form.

---

[7] Newmeyer (2005: 36) appears to miss this important point when he cites the following passage from Chomsky (1972: 67–8): 'Notice that it is often a step forward, then, when linguistic theory becomes complex, more articulated and refined—a point that has been noted repeatedly. ... Thus it is misleading to say that a better theory is one with a more limited conceptual structure, and that we prefer the minimal conceptual elaboration, the least theoretical apparatus. Insofar as this notion is comprehensible, it is not in general correct.' Chomsky was reacting to Postal's 1972 paper on 'The Best Theory', where Postal admonished linguists to opt for the framework of Generative Semantics because of its a priori logical and conceptual properties. Postal claimed that because of such properties, Generative Semantics 'should be abandoned, if at all, only under the strongest pressures of empirical disconfirmation' (Postal 1972: 135).

Newmeyer 2005 writes that Chomsky at the time dismissed claims such as Postal's as misguided. What Chomsky stressed was not a conceptually simple organization for a theory, but rather a rich internal structure, capable of narrowing down the class of possible grammars. Newmeyer goes on to note (as Pullum 1996 has done) that ironically, the Chomsky of the twenty-first century reads like a reincarnation of the Postal of the twentieth. This seems incorrect to me, for the context of writing is very different. In the 1970s the main goal was not minimalist in nature, and could not have been, since the issue of explanatory adequacy was far more pressing. To solve it, a rich UG had to be assumed. With hindsight, we can say that the search for conceptual simplicity in the 1970s was premature.

(9)

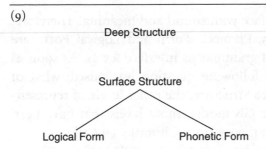

Chomsky (1993) remarked that one way of making the minimalist program concrete is to start off with the big facts we know about language (studied from a biolinguistic perspective and encoded in the P&P model). These are: (i) sentences are the basic linguistic units; (ii) sentences are pairings of sounds and meanings; (iii) sentences are potentially infinite; (iv) sentences are made up of phrases; (v) the diversity of languages are the result of interactions among principles and parameters; (vi) sentences exhibit displacement properties (in the sense that some elements, like the subject of a passive sentence, appear to be interpreted in a position different from which they are pronounced (it is interpreted as the logical object of the predicate)).

Such big facts are, to the best of our understanding, essential, unavoidable features of human languages (for discussion of these big facts, see Hornstein et al. (2006: ch. 1)). They thus define a domain of virtual conceptual necessity. That is, to the extent that they are true (and there is every reason to think they are, but in science we must always be ready to be proven wrong, which is why Chomsky used the modifier 'virtual'[8]), they must somehow be captured by linguistic theory.

Chomsky's bold claim in (1993) is that the minimal apparatus required to capture these facts is enough to capture everything else in language. This is a very strong claim, and Chomsky made it concrete in the context of levels of representations. Since sentences are pairings of sounds and meaning, the grammar must, by virtual

[8] Chomsky (1995: 186) is very clear about this, stressing that 'the (virtual) conceptual necessities [hold] within th[e] general [generative] approach'. Postal (2003a, 2003b) and Seuren (2004) appear to miss this point completely.

conceptual necessity, interface with sound and meaning. Therefore, Chomsky claimed in 1993, Phonetic Form and Logical Form are forced upon any model of grammar as interface levels. As soon as this claim was made, the following question was raised: what of Deep Structure and Surface Structure, the other levels of representation that are part of the GB model, those levels that have been essential ingredients of the theory since Chomsky (1965)?

Chomsky 1993 rightly pointed out that Deep Structure and Surface Structure are more theory-internal than LF and PF.

As such, they must carry a heavier burden of proof than those levels that follow from virtual conceptual necessity.

Accordingly, one of the central tasks of the minimalist program is to show that the role of both Deep Structure and Surface Structure, the grammatical principles they were responsible for, the conditions which had to be met at these levels in the GB model, were either superfluous (i.e. they can be eliminated entirely from the grammar) or else can be recast in a sparer representational vocabulary (i.e. in terms of LF and PF). The first steps towards the elimination of Deep Structure and Surface Structure have been well documented in the technical minimalist literature, especially at the introductory level (see e.g. Lasnik et al. 2005, Hornstein et al. 2006, Hornstein 2001: ch. 1, Marantz 1995). I will not repeat them here because they presuppose technical aspects which I have found unnecessary to introduce here.

The gist of this development is that, in retrospect, it becomes clear that, although both Deep Structure and Surface Structure captured some real properties of grammar (thematic relations, bifurcation point between PF and LF), these properties had been coded in conditions that had fossilized into levels of representation. Upon closer scrutiny, it became obvious that alternative conceptions of these properties no longer necessitated levels of representation. The latter were historical residues (of the type one finds everywhere in scientific theories) that proved to be no obstacles for the formulation of the minimalist program.

Before turning to other features of minimalism, I want to clarify the notion of virtual conceptual necessity. The latter forces us to claim that, barring strong evidence to the contrary, there are no narrow syntax-internal levels of representations. It crucially does not specify how many levels there are. Even though the standard minimalist approach assumed that only two levels of representation (LF and PF) were needed, virtual conceptual necessity demands that only those levels that are necessary for relating sound/sign and meaning be assumed.

Virtual conceptual necessity leaves the door open for the possibility (admittedly unlikely, at this stage of our knowledge about language) that the nature of sound and meaning is such that it requires sixteen levels of representation (see Williams 2003 for a multi-level framework in a minimalist setting). So long as these levels are all interface levels (i.e. none of them are internal to narrow syntax in the way Deep Structure and Surface Structure were), their existence would fit snugly into the minimalist program.

It is important to emphasize the fact that the nature of sound and meaning is an empirical matter. Whatever complexity needs to be assumed in the sound or meaning systems, narrow syntax will retain its minimalist character if no syntax-internal level of representation needs to be posited.

The point bears emphasis, as appeal to virtual conceptual necessity has been criticized in the literature (see in particular Postal 2003a, 2003b, Seuren 2004), due, in my view, to a misunderstanding of the concept.

As Chomsky (2001: 1) stresses, the emphasis on ' "[g]ood design" conditions are in part a matter of empirical discovery'. Virtual conceptual necessity refers to what appears to be necessary at the present stage of understanding (everything we now know is subject to change; this is what makes minimalism an empirical science: all its theoretical constructs are subject to empirical falsification). In Chomsky's words (1995: 222–3):

We do not know enough about the 'external' systems at the interface to draw firm conclusions about the conditions they impose. ... The problems are nevertheless empirical, and we can hope to resolve them by learning more about the language faculty and the systems with which it interacts. We proceed in the only possible way: by making tentative assumptions about the external systems and proceeding from there.

Elsewhere (Chomsky 2004c: 396), he notes:

The external systems are not very well understood, and in fact, progress in understanding them goes hand-in-hand with progress in understanding the language system that interacts with them. So we face the daunting task of simultaneously setting the conditions of the problem and trying to satisfy them, with the conditions changing as we learn more about how we satisfy them. But that is what we expect in trying to understand the nature of a complex system.

Virtual conceptual necessity applied to levels of representation leaves room for the existence of only one interface level, i.e. the very same representations would be accessed by both sound and meaning. The 'single-output syntax model' advocated by Brody (1995), Bobaljik (1995, 2002), Pesetsky (2000a), Groat and O'Neil (1996), Chomsky (2000a), and Nissenbaum (2000), schematized in (10), makes exactly that claim.

(10)

LF-PF

Similarly, virtual conceptual necessity leaves room for the absence of *any* level of representation. That is, we may be misled into thinking that sound and meaning systems require levels of representation (fully-fledged structures) to work on. All they need may be chunks of structure (LF and PF snapshots). This too has been explored in the recent minimalist literature, under headings such as strictly derivational models of syntax (Epstein et al. 1998, Epstein and Seely 2006), multiple spell-out models (Uriagereka 1999, 2003, Grohmann 2003, forthcoming), or phase-based computations (Chomsky 2000a, 2001, 2004a, 2005, forthcoming).

Such models argue that semantic and phonological interpretation need not operate on the output phrase-structure representation (i.e. *at* a specific level of representation) created by the syntactic derivation. Instead, they argue that interpretation is computed derivationally, by interpreting a derivation step by step. Such models, schematized in (11), are in effect level-free. ('pf' and 'lf' are in lower case to indicate that these do not refer to levels of representation, but only to partial, incomplete, bits and pieces of structure.)

(11)

   I am highlighting these possibilities here to show how far one can depart from the original, standard minimalist model (Chomsky 1993, 1995) while still formulating hypotheses that fall within the range of minimalist theorizing.

   As I will emphasize below, this range of possibility illustrated here in the context of levels of representation and virtual conceptual necessity is what it means for minimalism to be a program, not a theory. We do not yet know which model among the two-level, single-level, or level-free models mentioned here will turn out to be the correct one (the one that will be part of the theory). The minimalist program offers a space that encompasses them all and allows exploration of their distinct or convergent empirical predictions.

   In addition to the domain of levels of representation, Chomsky and others have applied the concept of virtual conceptual necessity to the other big facts about language mentioned above.

3.1.2.3.2 Merge (and Move)   The fact that sentences are made up of a potentially infinite number of distinct phrases has been taken to force upon linguistic theory a grouping operation which combines at least two elements forming a labeled set. This is the operation Chomsky calls Merge. Sharpening the use of virtual conceptual necessity, Chomsky claimed that since *at least* two elements must be the input of Merge, we must say that *at most* two elements must be the input of Merge. This means that if we want to combine three elements into a set (phrase), two steps are required. A first step that puts two elements together, and a second step that takes the group just formed and joins the third element to it.[9] This in effect yields Kayne's (1984) binary branching requirement representations of the type posited under X-bar theory:

(12) a.   XP   b.   XP

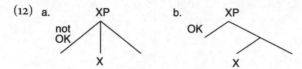

The deduction of this piece of GB syntax (Kayne's binary branching requirement) from virtual conceptual necessity was later strengthened when Chomsky (2005) claimed that binary branching trees are computationally more efficient/economical than other kinds of representations. If true, this convergence of virtual conceptual necessity and computational economy/efficiency is the type of result that scientists would regard as strongly suggesting that the minimalist program is on the right track.

Imposing no upper bound on the number of applications on Merge yields recursion, and thus captures the fact that sentences

---

[9] By hypothesis, every labeled set is taken to be an atom. Any element introduced into the derivation will be added on top of the labeled set, not inside it. This is referred to as the Extension Condition or the No-Tampering condition in the minimalist literature:

NOT OK:

(i)

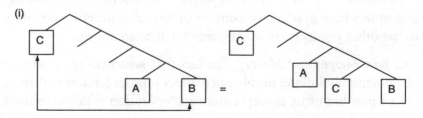

are potentially infinite. Likewise, allowing Merge to recombine members of the sets it forms—what Chomsky recently called Internal Merge (Epstein et al. (1998) call it Remerge)—yields a version of transformation (displacement).[10]

(13) External Merge

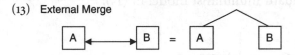

(14) Internal Merge

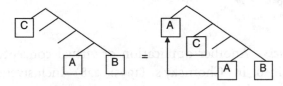

Note that no additional condition is needed to allow displacement. In fact, as Chomsky (2004a, 2005) points out, it would take an extra condition to disallow it.

3.1.2.3.3 Spell-Out   Finally, the fact that sentences are in effect finite in length (though they are potentially unbounded) means that at some arbitrary point the syntactic computation must bifurcate to LF and PF (in the standard two-level minimalist model). Chomsky calls this arbitrary point of transfer the Spell-Out point. Notice that

---

[10] In some versions of the minimalist program, several investigators have pursued the idea that merge applies in parallel, targeting two separate subtrees (this has come to be known as sideward movement or parallel merge (a.k.a multi-dominance structure); see e.g. Nunes (2004), Citko (2005), Svenonius (2005), Starke (2001), Gärtner (2001), Hornstein (2001).

(i)

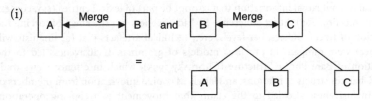

Spell-Out is distinct from Surface Structure. Although it captures the basic function of Surface Structure as a dividing line between PF and LF, Spell-Out is not a level of representation. No conditions, principles, etc. can be forced to apply *at that point.*

This yields the standard minimalist model in (15):

(15)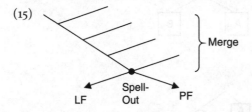

3.1.2.3.4 *Inclusiveness*   Another application of virtual conceptual necessity is contained in Chomsky's (1995: 228) Inclusiveness Condition.

(16) Inclusiveness Condition
      Any structure formed by the computation is constituted of elements already present in the lexical items selected for N; no new objects are added in the course of the computation apart from the rearrangement of lexical properties

It is a fact that lexical information must be available to the syntax (one must know that *pumpkin* is a noun, *eat* a verb, etc.). Inclusiveness makes the strong claim that no other information is needed in the syntax.[11]

3.1.2.3.5 *Parameters*   Finally, Chomsky and others suggested we extend the action of virtual conceptual necessity to principles and parameters. For parameters, Chomsky followed Borer (1984), who

---

[11] Inclusiveness goes beyond defining a domain of autonomy for syntax, as it rules out appeal to contextual information that cannot be part of lexical entries (say, context of communication etc.). Strict adherence to Inclusiveness has the effect of forcing the elimination of traces, indices, bar-levels, etc., technical artefacts that (as linguists will remember) were rampant in previous models of grammar. Inclusiveness led to the formulation of Bare Phrase Structure (Chomsky 1995), which in essence views traditional X-bar constructs as relations, and labels as copied information from members of merge. Inclusiveness also led to the claim that movement is a copying operation. I return to copying and Bare Phrase Structure in Ch. 5.

proposed that parameters be restricted to lexical properties of lexical items. In the early days of the P&P model, this was far from true. In addition to the most basic points of variation across languages (different words, with different properties technically called 'features'), it was assumed that languages could vary along much more controversial dimensions, such as X-bar theory. The so-called configurationality parameter (Hale 1983), for example, originally stated that some languages had binary branching structures, other 'flat structures' giving rise to less rigid word order possibilities. However, as our knowledge of languages grew, such non-lexical parameters were discarded; the possibility that all parametric differences reduce to lexical properties (a virtual necessity) gained some plausibility, and is now part of the standard minimalist model. (In the context of the non-configurationality parameter, so-called 'free word order' languages exhibited binary branching structures as much as languages with more rigid word order did; see Saito and Hoji (1983), Miyagawa (2003)).[12]

3.1.2.4 *Unity and symmetry*   Virtual conceptual necessity also led linguists to try to unify various phenomena and reduce them to conditions that are arguably more basic. The clearest example of this strand of research in my opinion comes from Hornstein's 2001 attempt to reduce all rules of construal (control phenomena, binding relationships such as the relation holding between *John* and *himself* in *John likes himself*; cf. **John likes him (meaning: John likes himself)*; **John likes herself*) to movement rules (see also Kayne 2002).[13] The

---

[12] Some non-lexical parameters remain, though. For example, some of the macro-parameters discussed in Baker (2001) have not yet been successfully reduced to properties of lexical items. This is clearly a difficult task ahead for minimalists. Kayne (1994, 2005) offers some optimism for thinking that the task may not be impossible. But I will not pursue this complicated matter here.

[13] Another example of symmetry in syntax would be the reduction of all case-assigning configurations to one. The first step in this direction was taken by Chomsky in (1993), where he argued that all case-assigning configurations reduce to the specifier positions of dedicated projections (so-called agreement phrases), which he took to be basic (in the sense of virtually conceptually necessary) configurations. Subsequent theoretical developments (retraced in Boeckx (2003b, 2004, 2006b)) led to the claim that all case configurations instead reduce to head–complement relations (the so-called

details are far from trivial, and so I will refrain from discussing them here (see Chapter 5 for some discussion; see also Hornstein's own work). But the logic is very clear. If construal rules have properties that follow movement properties closely (say they are subject to islands or least effort), of course one should try to reduce one to the other. We don't need minimalism to tell us that. Occam's razor or Hume's principle of true philosophy quoted above fit the bill.[14] Minimalism comes into the picture by giving us the direction of reduction: reduction should go in the direction of what appears more conceptually necessary (better motivated conceptually, biologically, physically). In this case, as Hornstein argues (persuasively in my opinion), the reduction should go in the direction of (internal) merge (a virtual conceptual necessity, as mentioned above).

This unification of rules under the banner of virtual conceptual necessity gives to the theory a certain degree of harmony and symmetry—features that scientists since time immemorial have taken to be constitutive of beautiful or optimal design. Just like the convergence of virtual conceptual necessity and computational economy that I pointed out in the context of binary branching, the convergence of beautiful design and empirical pay-offs (if several rules are reduced to one, the empirical scope of the more basic rule is thereby enhanced) achieved under reductionism is one of those things that scientists invariably interpret as signs of significant progress.

Agree operation; see Chomsky (2000a)) on grounds of computational economy. See Ch. 5 for some discussion.

[14] Not surprisingly, one finds intriguing instances of symmetry-seeking endeavors in earlier phases of generative grammar. Among these, Chomsky's (1973) attempt to find a single locality condition for all instances of displacement, Koster's (1978, 1987) attempt to reduce movement to construal rules (in many ways the opposite of Hornstein's approach discussed in the text), and the desire to fill in all the slots within a symmetrical chart of phonetically empty elements in syntax, leading up to the discovery of PRO: a [+anaphor; +pronominal] element involved in control constructions, posited by trying to fill up the space defined by features like [+anaphor], [+pronominal] (see Lasnik and Uriagereka 1988: 67–8 and Haegeman 1994: 235 for detailed accounts of this episode in theoretical syntax).

3.2 Taking stock

The emergence of economy conditions on derivations and representations, the consequences of virtual conceptual necessity, and the
search for unity and symmetry in syntactic operations and representations represent the three pillars on which the minimalist program
rests—the program's essence and core.

Minimalism can thus be conceived of as a tripod, resting on a
firm Principles and Parameters (conceptual and empirical) foundation. The image of the tripod is borrowed from Gould (2002) to
capture the notion of essences as 'minimal sets of propositions so
crucial to the basic function of a system that their falsification must
undermine the entire structure, and also so necessary as an ensemble
of mutual implication that all essential components must work in
concert to set the theory's mechanism into smooth operation as a
generator and explanation of nature's order' (p. 11).

The legs of the tripod (economy, virtual conceptual necessity, and
symmetry) stand for the most 'minimal list of defining attributes'
(Gould 2002: 10) that must be present in any given proposal for that
proposal to be deemed minimalist. (Of course, authors may choose
to focus on one or the other attribute. What I mean is that the three
attributes must all be part of the (spirit of the) analysis.)

All three attributes are already present in the first explicitly
minimalist paper (Chomsky 1993) and they tend to reinforce
one another. Just to give the reader an abstract idea, take symmetry.
Given that symmetry underlies the fact that a is identical to b under
some operation c, the more symmetry one finds in a system (say,
$x = y$), the fewer devices will be needed to generate x and y, since x
$= y$. In other words, the more symmetry one finds, the fewer distinct
processes one needs to generate a wide array of forms (i.e. the more
economical the system is), and the greater the likelihood that the
remaining processes follow from virtual conceptual necessity.

As I have tried to show, economy, virtual conceptual necessity,
and symmetry are concepts that are general and flexible enough to
leave room for innovation and originality. This is what lends minimalism its distinctive programmatic character.

Let me now expand on the notion of program and see how it affects the minimalist enterprise. Hornstein (2001: 21) captures the spirit of what I want to express in this section when he says (paraphrasing Chomsky):

Minimalism is a program, not a theory. The program, if successful, will prompt the creation of various minimalist models of grammar each of which gains inspiration from the sorts of considerations outlined above. These models will differ in (at least) ... how they weigh the broader [minimalist] concerns and how they implement them in particular analyses.

As a research program, minimalism provides a conceptual framework that guides the development of a given linguistic theory. More specifically, it identifies a number of preoccupations and predilections that facilitate the complex decision-making process that is an inevitable aspect of theory construction. In particular, it is essential to note that as a program (as opposed to a theory) minimalism does not aim at providing specific solutions to known technical problems, and it does not in itself provide exhaustive explanations for observed linguistic phenomena. On the contrary, a program like minimalism merely outlines a number of research goals which guide the development of a given theory. Of course, a theory developed under the auspices of minimalism may provide specific solutions for particular problems, but this goes beyond the inherent capacity of the minimalist program. This is what Chomsky (2000a: 92) means when he points out that 'there are minimalist questions, but not minimalist answers'.

3.3 The notion of 'program' and how it applies to minimalism

To make sure that the notion of program is clear, let me examine the notion of 'program' in science more closely. I begin with the contrast between program vs. theory. As stated in Chapter 1, the distinction, though real and significant, is rarely made in a consistent fashion in scientific writings. Of the two notions, it is perhaps the more common notion of 'theory' that is harder to define.

3.3.1 *Program vs. theory*

Take James Clerk Maxwell's theory of the electromagnetic field. The theory is generally acknowledged as one of the most out-standing intellectual achievements of the nineteenth century—indeed, of any century. (Richard Feynman once remarked (1965b: 2: 1.11) that from a long view of the history of mankind, Maxwell's discovery of the laws of electrodynamics will be judged as the most significant event of the nineteenth century; everything else will 'pale into provincial significance.') By the mid-1890s four equations, later to be known as 'Maxwell's equations', were recognized as the foundation of one of the strongest and most successful theories in all of physics; they were up there with Newton's laws of mechanics. And yet the fullest statement Maxwell gave of his theory, his 1873 *Treatise on Electricity and Magnetism*, does not contain the four famous equations, nor does it even hint at how electromagnetic waves might be produced or detected. As beauti-fully recounted in Hunt (1991), these and other aspects of the theory were quite thoroughly hidden in the version of it given by Maxwell himself. In the words of Oliver Heaviside, 'they were "latent" in the theory, but hardly "patent".' The task of formulating Maxwell's theory was undertaken by subsequent Maxwellians (FitzGerald, Lodge, Heaviside, and Hertz). It is they who transformed the rich raw material of Maxwell's *Treatise* into a fully-fledged, concise theory as we know it today. It is through their works that the theory acquired its reputation and its breadth of application. As Heaviside declared, 'Maxwell was only ½ a Maxwellian.' As Hunt notes:

The evolution of 'Maxwell's theory' provides a striking example of a process quite common in science. Scientific theories rarely spring fully formed from the mind of a person; a theory is likely to be so refined and reinterpreted by later thinkers that by the time it is codified and passes into general circulation, it often bears little resemblance to the form in which it was first propounded. (Hunt 1991: 2)

I have chosen 'Maxwell's theory' as an example because of Hunt's unusually detailed account of the development and coming into being of that theory, and also because in my search for scientific programs I found a reference to Einstein's characterizing his own work as the 'Maxwellian Program' (see Holton 1998: 1). But similar examples abound. For example, Feyerabend (1993: 191) comments on quantum mechanics:

> There may not exist a single theory, one 'quantum theory,' that is used in the same way by all physicists. The difference between Bohr, Dirac, Feynman and von Neumann suggests that this is more than a distant possibility. ... quantum theoreticians differ from each other as widely as do Catholics and the various types of Protestants: they may use the same texts (though even that is doubtful—just compare Dirac with von Neumann), but they sure are doing different things with them.

The term 'program' is rarely used in the physics literature (a literature I always turn to first when theoretical issues arise, as physics provides the richest examples of what (successful) theoretical endeavors can offer).[15] It is more commonly used in the mathematics literature. The best-known example (where the term 'program' has been explicitly used) is probably Hilbert's Program.[16] In the early 1920s the great German mathematician David Hilbert put forward a new proposal for the foundation of classical mechanics which has come to be known as Hilbert's Program. It was like a rallying call for a formalization of all of mathematics in axiomatic form, together with a proof that this axiomatization of mathematics is consistent. (The consistency proof was to be carried out using only what Hilbert called 'finitary' methods.) The specific elements of Hilbert's Program need not concern us here. What is important is the abstract nature of the

---

[15] I think that Einstein had something like 'program' in mind when he corrected I. Bernard Cohen in the last interview he gave (1955). After Cohen had asked him a question about his 'theory of photons', Einstein said: 'No, not a theory. Not a *theory* of photons.' As Cohen (1955 [2005]: 222) notes, Einstein's 1905 paper on photons (for which he was awarded the Nobel prize) did not contain the word 'theory' in the title, but instead referred to considerations from a 'heuristic viewpoint'.

[16] Descartes's *Mathesis Universalis* may be the most comprehensive research program to date.

program (and, I will argue, of programs as a whole). Hilbert proposed a set of guidelines, sketched a project and imposed boundary conditions that had to be met for the program to be judged successful. More than the task of a single individual, it was like a manifesto, a call for papers, a large-scale project that was on the horizon at the time, coupled with a conjecture, a 'gut feeling' of the type scientists crucially rely on, that the program could be carried out.

Although Hilbert proposed his program only in 1921, various facets of it are rooted in foundational work of his going back to 1900. Programs do not arise from nowhere; they are rooted in previous work that the researcher judged successful or promising enough to move forward. Work on the program progressed significantly in the 1920s with contributions from various logicians, including von Neumann, and further restrictions and guidelines given by Hilbert in 1928. Hilbert's Program also exerted a great influence on Kurt Gödel, whose work on the incompleteness theorems were motivated by Hilbert's Program. Gödel's work is generally taken to prove that Hilbert's Program cannot be carried out. It has nevertheless continued to be an influential position in the philosophy of mathematics, and work on so-called Relativized Hilbert Programs have been central to the development of proof theory.

Gödel's proof that Hilbert's optimism was undue (note that this does not entail that the program ceased to inspire important work) is not an aspect of programs one is likely to find outside mathematics. Almost by definition such *coups de grâce* fall outside the realm of possibilities in empirical science, where nothing can be proven once and for all; and, as we will see shortly, refutation is a much more complicated affair than Popper's popular version of falsificationism (1959) would have it. But refutation aside, the core aspects of Hilbert's program are constitutive of all scientific programs.

3.3.2 *Lakatos on research programs*

The philosopher of science Imre Lakatos developed a methodology of scientific research programs (see especially Lakatos 1970), where he identified a set of properties that I find very useful to bear in mind when we consider the nature of minimalism in linguistic theory. In an attempt to solve problems which the more popular philosophical accounts of scientific practice like Popper's failed to solve, Lakatos argued that the 'typical descriptive unit of great scientific achievements' is not an isolated hypothesis (or theory), but rather a research program.[17]

3.3.2.1 *Core*   A research program is made up of a core (Maxwell's four equations, Newton's laws of mechanics and his law of gravitation). For Lakatos, the core of a research program has a logico-empirical character, as opposed to, say, an aesthetic character. But I think that it is important to recognize and admit as part of the core of any program some elements like Holton's 1973 themata that are 'irrational' only in the sense that they escape method, as Feyerabend would say.[18] Themata are biases, prejudices, Baconian idols, tastes, beliefs, conscious or unconscious presuppositions, motifs, and motivating aids that undeniably[19] guide scientific discovery.[20]

---

[17] There are interesting points of convergence between Lakatos's notion of research program and Kuhn's 1962 better-known notion of paradigm, or period of normal science. But there are non-trivial differences, as discussed in Lakatos (1970) and Suppe (1977: 659ff.). I will not go over them here, as Kuhn's vision seems to me to be directed largely at public or social aspects of science, as opposed to the constitutive aspects of an individual's research program, which I want to focus on here.

[18] Einstein captures the spirit of this 'irrational' aspect of research well when he says that he had 'no better term than the term "religious" for this trust that reality is rational and at least somewhat accessible to human reasons. Where this feeling is absent, science degenerates into mindless empiricism' (Einstein 1987: 118). He is right to say that 'while it is true that scientific results are entirely independent from religious or moral considerations, those individuals to whom we owe the great creative achievements of science were all of them imbued with the truly religious conviction that this universe of ours is something perfect and susceptible to the rational striving for knowledge' (Einstein 1954: 61).

[19] Even Popper (1959) recognized the existence of 'metaphysical aids [that show] the way' (p. xxiii). He clearly recognized that 'every discovery contains "an irrational element" or a "creative intuition"' (p. 8), and was willing to 'recognize its value for empirical science' (p. 16), but he set such elements aside in his search for a logical characterization of the growth of scientific knowledge.

[20] Themata may also underlie what appeared to Kuhn as irrational paradigm shifts, although I will not discuss this possibility any further here.

At any rate, whatever the constitutive elements of a program's core may be, that core is rightly characterized by Lakatos as 'irrefutable', and 'stubbornly defended'. Wittgenstein would have called it 'unassailable and definitive'. The core is tenaciously protected from refutation by a vast protective belt of auxiliary hypotheses. A research program also has a heuristic, a powerful problem-solving machinery which digests anomalies and even turns them into positive evidence.[21] As Lakatos rightly observes, all theories are born refuted and die refuted. As Feyerabend (1993: 50) puts it, 'there is not a single theory that is not in some trouble or other'. For many non-scientists, the naïve falsificationism advocated by Popper has become what Francis Bacon called an idol of the theatre, an illusionary or fairytale account of reality that obscures our understanding of the latter (in this case, our understanding of scientific discovery and practice).

If refutation is not the name of the game, a research program, Lakatos correctly pointed out, cannot be distinguished in terms of right or wrong. Instead, programs are fecund or sterile—in Lakatos's words, 'progressive' or 'degenerating'. According to Lakatos, a program is degenerating if the theories it spawns are fabricated only in order to accommodate known facts.[22] By contrast, progressive

[21] Lakatos notes here that if, for instance, a planet does not move exactly as it should, the Newtonian scientist checks his conjectures concerning atmospheric refraction, concerning propagation of light in magnetic storms, and hundreds of other conjectures which are all part of the program. He may even invent an hitherto unknown planet and calculate its position, mass, and velocity in order to explain the anomaly. Feynman (1965a: 156f.) makes a similar point when he says, 'If [your guess] disagrees with experiment, it is wrong. ... When I say if it disagrees with experiment it is wrong, I mean after the experiment has been checked, the calculations have been checked, and the thing has been rubbed back and forth a few times to make sure that the consequences are logical consequences from the guess, and that in fact it disagrees with a very carefully checked experiment.' Einstein was more forceful when he said to his assistant, Ilse Rosenthal-Schneider, who asked what he would have done if Sir Arthur Eddington's famous 1919 gravitational lensing experiment, which confirmed relativity, had instead disproved it: 'Then I would have felt sorry for the dear Lord. The theory is correct.'

[22] Norbert Hornstein made me realize that the end of the GB era exhibited such a degenerated character. New facts were accommodated in an ad hoc fashion, often by revising definitions of central relations (like *government*) on a case by case basis, with no great sense of unity.

programs, according to Lakatos, characteristically make dramatic, stunning, unexpected predictions. They predict 'novel' facts, which Lakatos (quoting his student Elie Zahar) defined as follows:

A fact will be considered novel not just if it is temporarily novel, but with respect to a given research program, if it did not belong to the problem situation which governed the construction of the research program or of the hypothesis in question. (Lakatos and Feyerabend 1999: 108)

Thus, novel facts can be old facts seen in a new light, a 'switch in visual gestalt', as Kuhn (1962: 111) rightly stressed: 'what were ducks in the scientist's world before the revolution are rabbits afterwards.'[23] I will offer examples of such novel facts and predictions in the context of minimalism in Chapter 5 (see especially the sections on control and sluicing).

In addition to new facts, progressive programs generate new families of questions, create new problems and conflicts, which they may not solve, but which might have gone unnoticed without the crucial change in perspective which programs typically generate. (For some discussion of this in the context of minimalism, see below.) To this I would add that progressive paradigms create new coherence, neater, simpler views of the world, or of those portions of it that are of interest to the scientist. This aspect is particularly relevant to the minimalist program, as I try to illustrate in this book.

In closing this section, let me point out two further aspects of research programs identified by Lakatos. Closely following Kuhn's notion of paradigm shifts following periods of normal science,

---

[23] Kuhn is here referring to images like those shown in (i).

(i)

rabbit/duck   goose/eagle

Lakatos assumes that scientific revolutions come about once scientists join a progressive program at the expense of a degenerating competing one. But Lakatos notes that, while it is a matter of intellectual honesty to keep the record public, it is not dishonest or irrational to stick to a degenerating program and try to turn it into a progressive one. As Lakatos points out, one must treat budding programs leniently: programs may take decades before they take off and become empirically progressive. As Lakatos observes, 'criticism is not a Popperian quick kill, by refutation. Important criticism is always constructive: there is no refutation without a better theory.'

Feyerabend (1993: 118) stresses this point when he points out that 'propaganda is of the essence, because interest must be created at a time when the usual methodological prescriptions have no point of attack; *and because this interest must be maintained, perhaps for centuries, until new reasons* [evidence in favor of one's position—CB] *arrive*' (emphasis mine).

He goes on to say: 'It is also clear that such reasons, i.e. the appropriate auxiliary sciences, need not at once turn up in full formal splendor. They may at first be quite inarticulate, and may even conflict with the existing evidence. ... Partial agreement ... is all that is needed at the beginning.'

Feyerabend here raises two important issues that touch on the nature of programs. Programs take time to mature, and rigor cannot be required in the beginning.[24]

3.3.2.2 *Rigor and maturation*   As Plato said in *Theaitetos* (184c), 'To use words and phrases in an easy going way without scrutinizing them too curiously is not, in general, a mark of ill breeding; on the contrary, there is something low bred in being too precise...'. The clearest example of the advantage of skirting rigor in the beginning stages of a program comes from mathematics, the field which we associate with rigor and

---

[24] I am raising these points because much of the criticism directed at the minimalist program has ignored them, demanding too much too soon.

precision. Consider, as Kitcher (1983: 307f.) has done in a very clear fashion, the different research strategies/programs pursued by British and Continental mathematicians in the years after the well-known priority dispute between Newton and Leibniz over the invention of the calculus.[25] A portion of Kitcher's discussion is worth quoting in full:

Leibnizians confidently set about using new algebraic techniques, vastly increased the set of problems in analysis, and postponed the task of attempting to provide a rigorous account of their concepts and reasonings. Their attitude is not only made explicit in Leibniz's exhortations to his followers to extend the scope of his methods, without worrying too much about what the more mysterious algebraic maneuvers might mean, but also in the acceptance of results about infinite series sums that their successors would abandon as wrongheaded. Insofar as they were concerned to articulate the foundations of the new mathematics, the Leibnizians seem to have thought that the proper way to clarify their concepts and reasonings would emerge from the vigorous pursuit of the new techniques. In retrospect, we can say that their confidence was justified.

By contrast, Newton's successors were deeply worried about the significance of the symbols that they employed in solving geometric and kinematic problems. They refused to admit into their mathematical work questions or modes of reasoning that could not be construed in geometric terms, and they lavished attention on the problem of giving clear and convincing demonstrations of elementary rules.

Both research strategies are rational. Each is gambling. What is significant in the present context is that the less rigorous approach of the Leibnizians achieved solutions to problems that even the Newtonians also viewed as significant.

As Feyerabend (1993: 159) notes in retracing the history of another chapter of science, 'one of the assets of the Copenhagen School [*of physics led by Niels Bohr*] was its ability to avoid premature precision.'

I am highlighting such remarks here because, as Steven Weinberg (2004) pointed out in his historical sketch of the Standard Model in

---

[25] I am grateful to Robert Chametzky for drawing my attention to Kitcher's work in the present context.

particle physics, it is important to emphasize times of confusion and frustration. In Weinberg's words, 'it is important to show that it took a long time before we realized what these ideas were good for partly because I want to encourage today's string theorists, who I think also have good ideas that are taking a long time to mature' (p. 6). Likewise, I want to encourage the pursuit of the minimalist program even if some of its ideas are taking a long time to mature.

I conclude this discussion on rigor, precision, and slow maturation of research programs by quoting Piattelli-Palmarini (2005: 1):

The Italian physicist Gabriele Veneziano is acknowledged to have been the first inventor/discoverer of the core idea behind string theory. ... Veneziano had not realized, back in 1968, where his idea was leading. Initially, his 'dual resonance models' were only an elegant way of summarizing several apparently scattered facts and hypotheses and of solving some inconsistencies of the standard theory.

In the fullness of time, it turned out that the consequence of that initial idea, and of the mathematical formalism used to express it, was that the world of elementary particles is the projection onto our 4-dimensional space of modes of vibration and oscillation of microscopic uni-dimensional strings in a space with 11 dimensions. String theory is, for the moment at least, so many steps removed from experimental observation that its partial success has to be gauged by indirect confirmations of some of its secondary predictions. This is, understandably, far from deterring physicists, and work in string theory is in full swing.

One lesson here is that good scientists may well embark into intellectual ventures whose nature, conceptual contents, boundaries and interpretations are only dimly perceptible to them at the very start. The hairsplitting conceptual analysis onto which certain philosophers so eagerly embark can often be an exercise in futility.

Only the full unfolding of a scientific enterprise will reveal what the meaning of certain scientific concepts is. Modern physics has taught us that, even when conceptual analysis manages to lay bare some hidden inconsistencies, the remedy consists in improving and radicalizing the theory, possibly making of these inconsistencies a virtue, not in freezing all inquiry until those concepts are duly sanitized under a shower of educated commonsense.

3.3.2.3 *Beyond the core: openness and flexibility*   Let me now return to important features of research programs that will prove important for our understanding of minimalism. As Lakatos stressed, programs are more than a core. They consist of auxiliary hypotheses that may vary from one researcher to the next, and they have a heuristic, a plan for addressing problems.

Regarding the latter, Chomsky has been very clear in his writings. For example:

> The minimalist goal of discovering how perfect/well-designed language is will inevitably meet with obstacles. Language seems to be full of imperfections, properties that do not seem to follow from economy, virtual conceptual necessity, or symmetry. When faced with some apparent property P of language, the way to proceed is to find out whether:
> (i) P is real, and an imperfection (i.e., a real problem for minimalism)
> (ii) P is not real, contrary to what had been supposed
> (iii) P is real, but not an imperfection; [upon closer examination, P can be shown to be] part of a best way to meet design specifications. (Chomsky 2000a: 112)

As for auxiliary hypotheses, their existence simply indicates that there are various ways of articulating and defending a given research program. One can think of a research program as a recipe. The core specifies the basic ingredients to be used, but, as all chefs know, the final product is more than the basic ingredients. Different quantities and extra ingredients can lead to quite different results. The same is true of programs in general, and of minimalism in particular. Programs allow researchers to try different combinations of the basic tenets, and to develop them with different emphases, vantage points, and ways of directing attention. The core will remain as a nucleus for observations and reflections, but beyond that there is great freedom and flexibility.

Richard Feynman was acutely aware of this remarkable feature of programs, as he remarked (1965a: 50):

> A very strange [thing] that is interesting in the relation of mathematics to physics is the fact that by mathematical arguments you can show that it is possible to start from many apparently different starting points, and yet come to the same thing. That is pretty clear. If you have axioms, you can instead use some of the theorems; but actually the physical laws are so delicately constructed that the different but equivalent statements of them have such qualitatively different characters, and this makes them very interesting.

Different auxiliary hypotheses, or different arrangements of the elements of a program's core, may lead to radically different questions, empirical problems, solutions, etc. Logically, the resulting models or budding theories may be equivalent, but *psycho*-logically, and from there, empirically, when one is trying to guess new laws, they may turn out to be very different.

I find this feature that minimalism has by virtue of being a program remarkably liberating. As I said in Chapter 1, it allows every researcher to act like a hedgehog, to consider and reconsider the entire architecture of the language faculty by simply starting from different corners of the map.

Among various ways of pursuing minimalism and exploring programs in general are two that are often contrasted, though they are in fact complementary and equally useful. The two methods are often referred to as the top-down and the bottom-up methods.[26] The top-down method starts with very rigid axioms and sees what theorems can be squeezed out of them. The best example of such a method we have comes to us from the ancient Greeks. The Greeks simplified all construction in geometry to figures that could be drawn with only two tools, the unmarked straight-edge and the compass—the simplest tools they could conceive of and ones that they believed should suffice to construct any geometrical figure one could imagine or need. Their research program could be phrased as follows: given the two simplest tools that exist, show that all figures can be drawn.

Chomsky often starts off his minimalist inquiries in a similar fashion (increasingly so in recent years). His current general strategy is something like: 'Given the barest conditions imposed on the

[26] The two approaches are reminiscent of the two methods of research identified by Dirac in 1968. One method consists of removing the inconsistencies, 'pinpointing the faults in [the theory] and then tr[ying] to remove them, ... without destroying the very great successes of the existing theory'. The other method consists in unifying theories that were previously disjoint. Boeckx and Hornstein (forthcoming b) refer to the first method as the vertical, reductionist method (digging out inconsistencies, and reducing some properties to other, more fundamental properties) and the second as the horizontal, or expansionist method (embracing disjoint set of phenomena and laws, encompassing more phenomena). Together these form the axes of scientific research, trying to deepen understanding, and both can be seen at work within the minimalist program for linguistic theory.

sound and meaning sides and the most basic properties of lexical items and modes of combination (merge), show that all of syntax that is needed can be derived.' Chomsky then concludes that, if successful, the program will warrant the conclusion that language is the result of optimal design.

One of the most interesting expressions of the top-down method is the so-called map problem, which can be formulated as follows: how many distinct colors are needed to fill in any map so that neighboring countries are always colored differently. (As conjectured in the nineteenth century, only four colors are needed; see Wilson (2004) for a very good discussion of how this was proved.)

In linguistics the map problem is a little more complicated, hence more interesting. In linguistics (as in all fields of empirical science), you discover the boundary conditions, the terrains, the maps along the way; they are a matter of empirical discovery. As Chomsky (2001: 1–2) notes,

Good design conditions are in part a matter of empirical discovery ... a familiar feature of rational inquiry. ... Even the most extreme proponents of deductive reasoning from first principles, Descartes, for example, held that experiment was critically necessary to discover which of the reasonable options was instantiated in the actual world.

The bottom-up strategy works differently. It is best illustrated on the basis of Picasso's series of bull-paintings (see Figure 1).

A top-down researcher would start by asking: how many lines do I need to draw a minimal(ist) picture of a bull? The bottom-up researcher starts off from the fully-fledged bull and proceeds by eliminative refinements to arrive at the minimal(ist) bull. Notice that (in the ideal case) the top-down and bottom-up strategies converge on the minimalist bulls. But their paths of discovery are very different. They have to ask radically different questions, the answers to which can lead to interesting consequences that would be inaccessible if the starting point had been different. In the context of the minimalist program, the bottom-up method amounts to taking the set of well-entrenched GB results, and take this to be the fully-fledged bull. From there, the bottom-up minimalist will progres-

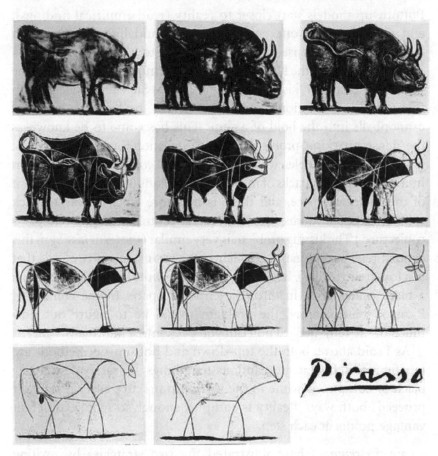

FIGURE 1. © Pablo Picasso. *The Bull*. State I–IV 1945. Lithography. The Museum of Modern Arts, New York, NY, USA.

sively refine and discard GB assumptions and ultimately reach a minimalist conception of language. I have tried to proceed in this fashion in Boeckx (2003a), on the nature of locality conditions. Norbert Hornstein has often proceeded in the same fashion in his work on rules of construal (see Hornstein 2001). Both Hornstein and I find GB a very good sketch from which to proceed.[27]

---

[27] Not surprisingly, the best textbook on minimalism (Hornstein et al. 2006) starts with examining the lie of the GB land.

Bottom-up models start closer to reality (read empirical findings), and may therefore offer more concrete guidelines and research questions. In that sense, they may be easier to handle.

In mathematics, the bottom-up problem finds its equivalent in the 'densest-packing' or 'kissing' problems. It was Sir Walter Raleigh who first posed the question: how do you cram the largest number of cannonballs into the hold of a ship? This has come to be known as the 'densest packing' problem. Raleigh's question found its way to the great astronomer Kepler, who replied that you could not do better than imitate the grocer's stacks of melons. The melons take up 74.05 per cent of their allotted space, and there is no more efficient way to pack spheres of equal radius. (It took several centuries to prove Kepler's conjecture.) The kissing problem is very similar (the term *kissing* in this context refers to the game of billiards, where it signifies two balls that just touch each other). It is about how many white billiard balls can kiss a black billiard ball in three-dimensional space. In the context of Picasso's bull-painting, the problem would be to figure out how much of the fully-fledged bull can you pack into a minimalist one.

As I said above, both the top-down and bottom-up methods are terrific research strategies; and, as few things are rarely completely black or completely white in the world, in practice every researcher proceeds both ways. Reality is complex enough to require different vantage points at each step.

3.3.2.4 *Extrema*   I have illustrated the two strategies by relating them to problems of extrema in mathematics (simplest tools from the Greek mathematicians, densest packing, least number of colors for maps), in part because I think they capture the spirit of the point I want to make better than long and confused definitions, but also because by its very nature the minimalist program searches for an extremum: optimal/best design for language.

Almost inevitably in such cases, many different possibilities of reaching the desired result come to mind. As Descartes clearly expressed in his *Discourse on Method* (1965 [1637]: 52):

I must confess that the power of nature is so ample and so vast, and these principles [the theoretical principles he had developed for his mechanical universe] so simple and so general, that I almost never notice any particular effect such that I do not see right away that it can [be made to conform to these principles] in many different ways.

In this, Descartes was not alone, as the development of economy principles in physics reveals.[28] It is a long-held observation that economy principles seem to be at work in laws of nature. Hero, a Greek mathematician in the first century, already asserted that the actual path of a ray of light traveling from point A to point B reflecting at point P is the shortest possible one. Pierre de Fermat in 1657 claimed that this and other phenomena were better captured by a principle of least time. Finally, Maupertius argued in 1744 that the principle of economy of nature is best satisfied not by time of transit, but by a scalar quantity that he called action, and so went on to propose a principle of last action, a principle that was made precise by Euler and Lagrange using the calculus of variation.

It is just a fact about Nature that she has different ways of breaking symmetry (the leopard's spots, the zebra's stripes),[29] of regulating the action of master-control genes to generate exquisite visual forms, and, more generally, of optimizing the functions of the limited number of elements she has at her disposal. There is no knowing in advance which method nature resorted to in the case of language. So, minimalism, deeply grounded in empirical consider-ations as it is, cannot fail to be a program. It must offer enough space to consider all the conceivable optimization paths. As Chomsky (2001: 3) correctly points out, 'Note the indefinite article: *an* optimal solution [in the strongest formulation of the minimalist thesis, which holds that language is an optimal solution to interface conditions].'

Notice that it took centuries for mathematicians and physicists to make the economy at work in nature precise. The intuition was there right from the beginning, but different perspectives were needed to

[28] See Fukui (1996) for a linguist's perspective on this development and the lessons we can draw from it for language. See also Uriagereka (1998).

[29] For delightful discussions, see Stewart (1999), Ball (1999), and Goodwin (1994).

hit upon the right formulation. The same process has already taken place in the short history of the minimalist program in linguistics (a fact that I interpret as indicating how even vague intuitions can lead to tangible progress, although it has been interpreted by some as a sign of failure for the program as a whole).

From the very beginning of the minimalist program, economy was recognized as a central feature. Prefigured in Chomsky (1991), it featured prominently in Chomsky (1993) and (1995). But, as hasn't gone unnoticed, 'Chomsky barely alludes to economy principles in [*Chomsky 2002 and other recent publications*], despite the fact that they were the centerpiece of his minimalist theorizing in the 1990s' (Newmeyer 2003: 586 n. 5). This has been taken to indicate failure of the entire program, or a lack of continuity in minimalist theorizing. However, I take the gradual abandonment of *explicit* economy *principles* (axioms) in favor of principles that yield economy *effects* (theorems) to be a significant achievement of minimalism, a result that should reinforce the minimalist thesis. After all, there was nothing dogmatic about explicit economy principles or axioms, and economy considerations explored in the first minimalist papers (so-called 'global economy', as it demands the comparisons of entire sets of derivations as opposed to the comparison of local points within a single derivation) were but one specific implementation of efficient computation.

Economy principles at their core require comparison of the number of steps in a derivation (economy of derivation) or number of symbols in a representation (economy of representation). The basic intuition behind economy principles is that, all else equal, one should minimize the number of operations and symbols necessary for convergence (legitimate output at the interfaces). The basis for comparison, what is known as the reference set (the set of comparable derivations/representations), was a matter of debate in the early minimalist literature: should derivation D_1 be compared to derivation D_2 if they are both convergent and start with the same numeration (lexical items) (Chomsky 1993)? Or should they be compared on the basis of their interpretation (Adger 1994, Reinhart 2006, and especially Fox 1995, 2000)? As Collins (2001: 53) notes in his survey of economy conditions in syntax,

Of all the economy conditions, the Shortest Derivation Requirement is the one with the least intuitive appeal. For example, consider a derivation with 18 steps. By the Shortest Derivation Requirement this derivation will be blocked by any comparable derivation (having the same numeration [*following Chomsky 1993*]) with 17 or fewer steps. This appears to be a case of the grammar counting, in a way that has long been held to be impossible. What grammars seem to be able to do well is to verify whether some simple condition holds of a representation or an operation ...

As Collins (1997, 2001) has shown in detail, examples that were originally thought to make global economy comparisons (i.e. comparisons over entire derivations/representations) can be explained in different ways.[30] Global economy principles gradually made way to *local* economy conditions, conditions that compare steps in a derivation at the point when those steps should be taken, not once the entire derivation has been computed. Local economy was seen as a reduction of the space of the reference sets, in a way that was seen as lessening the computational memory load, hence more efficient from a computational perspective.[31]

As I alluded to earlier, the original economy arguments provided in Chomsky (1993) were heavily criticized in Levine (2002: 327 n. 3), Lappin and Johnson (1999), Lappin et al. (2000a, 2000b, 2001), Pinker and Jackendoff (2005), and Seuren (2004), and were taken to be lethal to the entire program. Though some of the criticisms (especially Lappin and Johnson 1999) correctly pointed out weaknesses in the original formulations of economy principles,

---

[30] See Jacobson (1998) and Singh (2003) for attempts to reanalyze the data that led Fox (1995, 2000) to propose his influential theory of scope economy that does not appeal to explicit economy principles.

[31] In this context, the work of Frampton and Gutmann (1999, 2002) is worth mentioning, as it develops a fully minimalist theory which (as far as syntax is concerned) allows sentences to be constructed without backtracking, without comparison of derivations, and without the device of numerations. Highly derivational theories such as those explored in Epstein et al. (1998) and Epstein and Seely (2002, 2006) also contribute to the effort to reduce computational complexity by reducing the size of the cycle (the space of comparison) down to each merging operation: each pairing of *a* and *b* defines a cycle (or phase), a domain within which economy conditions apply. In the absence of numerous elements within that domain, the scope of comparison is drastically reduced.

'false starts' like principles demanding global comparisons (huge comparison sets) were useful, and almost necessary to get minimalism off the ground (and in fact the problematic aspects of global economy conditions was obvious to minimalist practitioners before the criticism were raised in other theoretical circles (see e.g. Brody (1997: section 1.1; 1998a: section 1; 1998b: section 4), 'on wh[om] much [current] work relies' (Chomsky 2004a: 125 n. 24)).

The next step, which led to less explicit discussion of economy principles in the minimalist literature, consisted in developing ways in which economy 'effects' (effects of efficient computation) fall out (without ancillary machinery computing comparisons across derivations, etc.) once principles are properly constrained.[32] This, of course, takes time. But this is not a weakness, but the very nature of research programs.[33]

3.3.2.5 *Falsifiability* Although I have been at pains to point out the advantageous flexibility and openness of programs and of minimalism in particular, it is not the case that 'anything goes'. Though often vague, the elements of a program's core nevertheless have enough empirical bite to specify options that cannot be entertained within the limits of the program, or situations that would severely threaten the scope of the program and its ultimate success, or cases where the program would implode due to a deep conflict among its basic ingredients. In the remainder of this chapter

---

[32] Central here was the role of the cycle. As is made clear in Freidin (1999), Richards (1999, 2001), Bošković and Lasnik (1999), Lasnik (2006), and the recent development of phase-based derivations (Chomsky 2001, Bošković 2005, Fox and Pesetsky 2005, Epstein and Seely 2006, Heck and Müller 2000, Grohmann 2003, Uriagereka 1999, 2003), this is a domain where one finds plenty of room for innovation, with each specific characterization of the cycle yielding different ways in which efficient computation emerges.

[33] The one specific implementation of computational efficiency that has remained constant is the Last Resort condition, the idea that a syntactic operation may apply only if the derivation would otherwise result in an illegitimate representation at the interfaces. While the various formulations of the cycle have had the effect of drastically reducing the search space or reference set, limiting the domain of application of syntactic operations, the Last Resort condition has helped eliminate superfluous steps in derivations.

I would like to discuss a few cases of this sort in the context of minimalism.

Let me start with an example involving economy principles.

In the realm of syntax it is now a well-established fact that if you try to front an element X of type Y to a position Z, you cannot do this if there is an element W of type Y that is in between X and Z. This is the basic idea behind Rizzi's (1990) Relativized Minimality principle or Chomsky and Lasnik's variant in terms of Shortest Move. If a Nobel prize in linguistics existed, I think Rizzi's insight ought to be rewarded with it. It is a very simple and yet powerful idea. It accounts for why you must front the first auxiliary in an auxiliary sequence when you want to form questions.

(17) a. Has John seen it? Cf. John *has* seen it
      b. *Seen John has it?

It also accounts for why you must take the first object of a ditransitive clause when you passivize it (18)

(18) a. The boy was given the toy. Cf. Somebody gave the boy the toy
      b. *The toy was given the boy

Interestingly, note that it is fine to say *The toy was given to the boy* because this sentence starts off as *Somebody gave the toy to the boy*, where *toy* is the first object in the sequence.

Finally, Rizzi's principle accounts for why a sentence like *Somebody bought something* can be converted to a question like *Who bought what?*, but not into *What did who buy?*

In all these examples, you have the choice between two auxiliaries, two objects, or two *wh*-words, and in each case you front the 'first' one (or the one closer to the target position; recall that by 'first' I really mean 'higher', as syntactic processes rely on hierarchical structure, not linear structure). Once you recognize the workings of Rizzi's idea, you can't fail to see it at work everywhere in syntax. A lot of the work on minimalist syntax has broadened its scope, and thereby shown how economy concerns regulate syntactic processes like fronting.

Needless to say, as with every principle or law in science, counter-examples are not hard to find. When faced with such cases, as Lakatos has correctly pointed out, scientists will try to save the correctness of the principle that makes sense to them by appealing to independent factors that must somehow conspire to obscure the workings of the principle that they believe to be true. It so happens that, in the context of passivization and questions, some languages that are not too different from English display effects that suggest that the economy principle behind Rizzi's insight is not general.

For example, Serbo-Croatian fails to display superiority effects in some contexts.

(19) a. ko   je Šta   kupio
          who is what bought
          'Who bought what?'
      b. *Šta je ko kupio

Similarly, a Bantu language like Kinyarwanda allow either object of a ditransitive verb to passivize.

(20) a. Umuhuûngu a-ra-andik-ir-a   umukoôbwa íbárúwa
          boy   SP-Pres-write-Appl-Asp girl   letter
          'The boy is writing a letter for the girl'
      b. Umukoôbwa a-ra-andik-ir-w-a   íbárúwa n'ûmuhuûngu
          girl   SP-Pres-write-Appl-Pass-Asp letter   by boy
          'The girl is having the letter written for her by the boy'
      c. Íbárúwa i-ra-andik-ir-w-a umukoôbwa n'ûmuhuûngu
          'The letter is written for the girl by the boy'

There are several moves one can make to explain away these counter-examples, and I am not interested in reviewing them here (on super-iority, see e.g. Bošković 1998, 1999, 2002b, Richards 2001, Pesetsky 2000a, Kitahara 1997; on passivization, see e.g. Anagnostopoulou 2003, McGinnis 1998, 2001, Jeong 2006, Lee 2004, and Ura 2000). This is the delight of programs: the space of auxiliary hypotheses is quite vast. Virtually everyone can give it a try. But the space of possibilities, though vast indeed, is not infinite. One thing that a minimalist should resist at all costs is the claim that Rizzi's Relativized Minim-ality principle (in any of its economy incarnations) is parametrized, meaning that some languages may abide by it, while some other languages would be free of its effects.[34] Such a possibility clearly falls out of the set of minimalist grammars. Put differently, if Relativized Minimality is a parameter, the minimalist program is not a program worth pursuing.

Let me now turn to another case where non-minimalist moves may be made. This time, I will look at so-called reconstruction effects. These refer to situations where a displaced element must be interpreted in a position that it occupied prior to fronting. Consider a sentence like (21).

(21)   which picture of himself does everyone like?

Elements like *himself* must in typical cases follow their antecedents. You typically cannot say **Himself likes John* or **Heself likes John*. You must say *John likes himself*. Linguists have a principle enforcing this fact (it's called Principle A of the Binding Theory). The principle appears to be violated in (21). To solve this problem, linguists claim that the fronted *wh*-element, *which picture of himself*, is interpreted in a position lower than the one it is pronounced in. In fact, they claim that *which picture of himself* is interpreted in the position it occupied before fronting, that is, the position it occupies in a declarative sentence like *Everyone likes some picture of himself*, where the anaphor *himself* appears lower in the structure than its antecedent. When this 'lower' interpretation happens, the fronted element is said to be reconstructed.

About thirty years ago linguists determined that in order to handle reconstruction effects and other phenomena it would be a good idea to keep track of the points of origin of fronted elements. Chomsky (1973) proposed that fronted elements leave a trace (represented as *t*) in their original positions. The concept of trace was investigated extensively in the GB literature. But it is not minimalist in spirit.

Recall that Chomsky (1993) imposed an Inclusiveness Condition on syntactic derivations. Inclusiveness requires that the computa-

[34] That Relativized Minimality is a parameter has been suggested in Baker and Collins (2006). I think that both Baker and Collins would admit that this is a very bad move.

tional system only manipulate lexical features (the virtual minimum). Effectively, this forbids adding new kinds of 'objects' during the syntactic computation, including devices such as traces, which do not exist in the lexicon. To retrieve the empirical benefits of traces but without their use, Chomsky (1993) claimed that displacement should be thought of as a copying operation.[35] That is, when fronting is required, an element will create a copy of itself, which will be re-merged in the fronted position. This is a minimal departure from the notion of trace, but it has the advantage of abiding by Inclusiveness, since what is being left behind upon displacement is (a copy of) a lexical item.

Under the displacement-as-copying view, reconstruction arises when the copy in the original position feeds interpretation. For example, the reflexive *himself* in (21) is licensed under the interpretation of the copy of *which picture of himself* in the thematic position, as illustrated in (22). (The angled brackets are just there to indicate that the copy is not being pronounced.)

(22)   Which picture of himself does everyone like <which picture of *himself*>?

The copy-theory-based analysis of reconstruction has been widely adopted.[36] It exploits central minimalist intuitions (virtual conceptual necessity) and provides broad empirical coverage (for additional cases, see Chapter 5). Like the economy condition underlying accounts of Superiority, the link between movement and reconstruction forged by the copy theory of movement is now a central feature of minimalist theory. They both illustrate how general guidelines forming the core of the program (economy and virtual conceptual necessity) can find their way into concrete principles and

---

[35] Notice that copying is not a new operation of the grammar introduced just to keep track of displaced expressions. One could argue (as I have done in Boeckx (2005a)) that copying also underlies the procedure by which the head of a phrase projects (and becomes the label of that phrase).

[36] For some references, see Aoun and Benmamoun (1998), Aoun et al. (2001), Bhatt (2002), Brody (1995), Fox (1999, 2000, 2002), Grohmann (2000), Hornstein (1995), Kim (1998), Lasnik (2003a), Pesetsky (2000a), Rizzi (2001), Romero (1998), Safir (1999), Sauerland (1998), (2004), Sportiche (2001), Witkoś (2002), among many others.

processes of grammar. This not only allows linguists to broaden the empirical scope of the program, it also defines a space of conflict that may threaten the balance of the program as whole. The best illustration of a severe conflict among minimalist principles comes from data discussed by Aoun and Li (2003) and reexamined in Boeckx and Hornstein (forthcoming c). The data comes from Lebanese Arabic. Aoun and Li show that Lebanese Arabic, like English, forms questions by fronting interrogative words.

(23) Miin ʃəft
      Who saw.2sg
      'Who did you see?'

Like English, this fronting process is sensitive to islands:

(24) *Miin btaʕrfo   l-mara   yalli ʃeefit   — bə-l-maTʕam
      Who know.2pl   the-woman   that saw.3sgfem in-the-restaurant
      'Who do you know the woman that saw in the restaurant?'

And like English, the language can obviate island effects by using a resumptive pronoun.

(25) Miin btaʕrfo   l-mara   yalli ʃeefit-o   bə-l-maTʕam
      Who know.2pl   the-woman   that saw.3sgfem-him   in-the-restaurant
      'Who do you know the woman that saw him in the restaurant?'

The traditional view is that the resumptive pronoun in such cases indicate that fronting has not taken place. The resumptive pronoun basically acts as a signal that if there had been no island the interrogative word would have been displaced from there.

Aoun and Li conclusively show that when resumptive pronouns are used in island contexts like (26), there are no reconstruction effects.

(26) *ʔayya taalib   min   tulaab-a$_i$ ʔənbasatto   laʔinno   kəll
      which student among students-her   pleased.2pl because   every
      mʕallme$_i$ ħatnaʔ-ii
      teacher.fs will.3fs.choose-him
      'Which of her$_i$ students were you pleased because every teacher$_i$ would choose (him)?'

This immediately follows if, as discussed above, reconstruction is the result of interpretation of a lower copy left from the displaced expression. In the absence of genuine displacement (resumption), no copy will be left behind, and reconstruction effects cannot arise.

The fascinating twist in Aoun and Li's discussion is that even in those island contexts where no reconstruction effects obtain (suggesting that no movement took place), superiority effects still obtain, as the following examples show.

(27) a. miin   ʔənbasatto   laʔinno   saami   ʕarraf-o   ʕa-miin
who   pleased.2pl   because   Sami   introduced-him   to-whom
'Who were you pleased because Sami introduced (him) to whom?'

b. *miin   ʔenbasatto   laʔinno   saami   ʕarraf   miin   ʕəl-e
who   pleased.2pl   because   Sami   introduced   whom   to-him
'Who were you pleased because Sami introduced who to him?'

At this point we face a big problem: if superiority is a reflex of fronting the closest element, how can superiority effects arise in non-movement contexts? Minimalists are now facing a dilemma: either we give up the idea that superiority is an effect of economy conditions on movement, or else (if we say that movement obtains in island contexts) we have to say that copying does not entail reconstruction, which begs the question of whether reconstruction data can then be taken as evidence for copying and the core minimalist notion of Inclusiveness. We could for instance say that some instances of movement do not leave a copy behind.[37] This strikes me as a non-minimalist possibility, as copying appears to be the most efficient way of keeping track of movement—a task that seems required on grounds of virtual conceptual necessity. In particular, the external processing systems appear to operate on the basis of filler–gap structures (i.e. antecedent–trace relations, or relations among copies). If filler–gap effects are real, it is necessary to have a mechanism to encode them. Copying, coming for free on grounds of Inclusiveness, is the most optimal mechanism linguists have been able to think of.

Boeckx and Hornstein (forthcoming c) suggest that we need not abandon economy principles or the copy-based view on

---

[37] As Lasnik (2003a) and Fox (1999) have suggested. Fox and Lasnik differ on whether something else is left behind. For Lasnik, nothing is left behind. For Fox, a simple trace is left behind. Neither answer is satisfactory from a minimalist point of view.

reconstruction. What is required is the claim that copying is a necessary, but not a sufficient, condition on movement. I will not explore the ramifications of this proposal here. All I wanted to illustrate, on the basis of the Lebanese Arabic data just discussed is that the minimalist guidelines we have discussed have already given rise to concrete principles, and that data can be found that could falsify these. In other words, minimalism appears to be precise enough to give rise to concrete challenges—a very good thing in my opinion.

3.4 Conclusion

Following Gould's (2002) claim that important theoretical enterprises have both history and essence, I have highlighted in this chapter what I take to be the essence, the fundamental claims, the core of the minimalist program: economy, virtual conceptual necessity, and symmetry. I have illustrated each concept on the basis of concrete principles it has given rise to. The concepts are general, and precise definitions cannot yet be given for what counts as, say, efficient computation. But we know that it will be some formulation like 'Favor or Select *x*-est', where *x* may turn out to be 'short', 'close', 'high', etc.

I have also stressed the importance of recognizing that minimalism is a program: in addition to the core, minimalism comes with a space for auxiliary hypotheses, a heuristic, and other features that must be borne in mind when evaluating the claims it makes.

4

The Minimalist Impact

Having clarified the context of emergence and essential logic of the minimalist program in the two preceding chapters, I would now like to expand on the 'bigger' picture and examine what it means to investigate the minimalist character of a natural object like the language faculty.

I will examine this issue by focusing on two phrases that Chomsky has used repeatedly in his most recent writings (using them as titles in Chomsky 2004a, 2005): 'beyond explanatory adequacy' and 'the three factors in language design'. As I will show in this chapter, both phrases can be seen as specific references to a methodological principle, a *Weltbild* in fact, that has defined modern science since the Copernican revolution, and that I will refer to as the Galilean style in science.[1] Once properly understood, the minimalist attempts to go beyond explanatory adequacy and to identify three factors in language design will be seen as forming an integral part of this Galilean mode of thought. What I find particularly appealing here, and what I will stress, is that the questions biolinguists address 'arise for any biological system, and are independent of theoretical persuasion, in linguistics and elsewhere' (Chomsky 2005: 2), and the conclusions are bound to be 'of some significance, not only for the study of language itself' (Chomsky 2004a: 124). This is the passage I had in mind when I decided to call this chapter 'The Minimalist Impact'.

Let me stress right from the start that, although I will very often make reference to theoretical physics in the pages that follow, it is

[1] Chomsky first refers to the Galilean style in (1980: 8–9), well before the advent of an explicit minimalist program.

not (*contra* Levine 2002: 326) 'to exploit the prestige of the natural sciences' (what is sometimes called 'physics-envy'). I do so simply on considerations of methodological naturalism (in Chomsky's (2000b) sense), that is, on the assumption, that language should be studied just like anything else in the universe. I agree with Chomsky that 'it makes sense to think of this level of inquiry as in principle similar to chemistry ... : in principle that is, not in terms of the depth and richness of the "bodies of doctrine" established' (Chomsky 2000c: 26). As I pointed out in the previous chapter, I think that physics ought to play an important inspirational role, since this is the area where theoretical investigation has been most fully developed. Freidin and Vergnaud (2001: 647) make the issue clear when they note that although 'linguistics and physics have the same Galilean character', the two disciplines 'are at very different stages of mathematical maturation. From this perspective, it is useful to distinguish the "Galilean character" of an area of study, i.e., how much of the subject matter can be analyzed mathematically, from what one could call its "Pythagorean character", how much of mathematics is put to use in the Galilean treatment.'

4.1 The Galilean style in science

Physicist Steven Weinberg 1976 characterizes the Galilean style in science as follows:

... we have all been making abstract mathematical models of the universe to which at least the physicists [*read: scientists*—CB] give a higher degree of reality than they accord the ordinary world of sensation.

The Galilean style is informed by a methodological principle, a thema in Holton's (1973) sense, that is made explicit in the following passage from Galileo's work:

[in studying acceleration] ... we have been guided ... by our insight into the character and properties of nature's other works, in which nature generally employs only the least elaborate, the simplest and easiest of means. For I do not believe that anybody could image that swimming or flying could be accomplished in a simpler or easier way than that which fish and bird actually use by natural instinct. (Galilei 1974 [1638]: 153)

Elsewhere, Galileo notes that nature 'always complies with the easiest and simplest rules', and that 'nature ... does not that by many things, which may be done by few' (1962 [1632]: 99).

As historians of science Redondi (1998) and Shea (1998) have emphasized, Galileo was indeed guided by the ontological principle that 'nature is perfect and simple, and creates nothing in vain' (see e.g. Galilei 1962 [1632]: 397).

In this belief Galileo was not alone. Copernicus knew that the motion of the heavenly bodies could be charted according to Ptolemy just as correctly as according to his sun-centered model. In fact, as Burtt (1932: 37–8) discusses in detail, the Copernican view of the universe faced serious empirical objections. In the face of these, Copernicus could only plead that 'his conception threw the facts of astronomy into a simpler and more harmonious mathematical order', praising his system as representable 'paucioribus et multo conventioribus rebus', 'by fewer and much more agreeable things' (Burtt 1932: 38–9). It was simpler in that in place of eighty epicycles in the Ptolemaic system, Copernicus was able to capture the phenomena with only thirty-four (all those which had been required by the assumption that the earth remained at rest now being eliminated). It was more harmonious in that the major part of the planetary phenomena could now fairly well be represented by a series of concentric circles around the sun (the moon being the only irregular intruder). So Copernicus too was guided by the principle that nature is simple. In fact, as Burtt (1932: 39) stresses, both ancient and medieval observers had noted that in many respects nature appeared to be governed by the principle of simplicity: falling bodies moved perpendicularly towards the earth, light traveled in straight lines, projectiles did not vary from the direction in which they were impelled, etc.

These observers had recorded the substance of their observations to this effect in the form of crisp, proverb-like statements such as

'Nature does nothing superfluous or any unnecessary work' (Olympiodorus) or 'Nature is economical' (Leonardo da Vinci).[2]

Kepler placed the principle of simplicity and unity of nature at the center of his system, asserting that 'natura simplicitatem amat' (nature loves simplicity), stating that 'numquam in ipsa quicquam otiosum aut superfluum exstitit' (never in it is there found anything useless or superfluous), 'natura semper quod potest per faciliora, non agit per ambages difficiles' ('because nature is always able (to accomplish something) through rather simple means, it doesn't act through difficult winding paths') (Kepler 1858: i. 112ff.).

Clearly, Galileo was not the first scientist to recognize nature's simplicity and economy. Nor was he the last. Another great architect of modern science, Isaac Newton, following in the immediate footsteps of Galileo, expressed the same view in formulating his first rule of reasoning in philosophy: 'We are to admit no more causes to natural things than such as are both true and sufficient to explain their appearances. To this purpose, the philosophers say, that nature does nothing in vain, and more is in vain when less will serve; for nature is pleased with simplicity, and affects not the pomp of superfluous causes' (Newton 1687: ii. 160ff.) Similarly, Albert Einstein (1954: 274) searched for a theory that would describe the belief that 'nature is the realization of the simplest conceivable mathematical ideas'.

The idea that 'if Nature be most simple and fully consonant to herself she observes the same method in regulating the motions of smaller bodies which she doth in regulating those of the greater' (Newton, 1687: ii. 160) indeed runs through the work of all major modern scientists. Naïve Popperian empiricism pays no attention to such methodological principles like the principle of simplicity, taking them to be idols of the cave that one had better dispense with. But it is quite clear that one cannot begin to understand the course

---

[2] Burtt (1932: 39) provides other similar statements such as 'natura semper agit per vias brevissimas' ('nature always acts through the shortest pathways') and 'natura neque redundat in superfluis, neque deficit in necessariis' (nature does not abound in unnecessary things, nor does it lack in the necessary).

of modern science if one ignores the idea that 'there is unity at the foundation' (Einstein 1938 letter, reported in Holton 1973: 241), not just in the context of (empirical) discovery but also (and crucially, for our purposes) in the context of justification and perseverance in the face of (apparent) counterexamples (see especially Maxwell (2003) on this point).

Minimalism can be seen as a thorough investigation of the principle of simplicity, interpreted realistically, that is, as applying to a real object, the human language faculty. The inquiry amounts to the following task. Once the shape of the human language faculty has been fixed (the task of the Principles and Parameters approach), can we show that (to paraphrase Galileo) language always complies with the easiest and simplest rules, that it employs only the least elaborate, the simplest and easiest of means?

It is important to note that asking this minimalist question is an integral part of the development of the Galilean style in linguistics. Methodologically, it is a necessary step. It 'may still be premature' (Chomsky 2001: 1), or 'not be appropriate at the current level of understanding' (Chomsky 2000a: 93), in the same way in which Einstein's attempt to unify all the forces of physics was premature. But it is a central part of the generative program. Without it, linguistics would be, in the words of Kant, '*eine Wissenschaft, aber nicht Wissenschaft*' (a science, but not Science; that is, a special, isolated scientific inquiry, as opposed to a part of Modern Science).

4.2 *Why*-questions

The reason the principle of simplicity is so important in science is because it provides an answer to the deepest question of all: why is nature the way it is? Indeed, the principle of simplicity provides the most satisfactory answer to the deepest *why*-questions. As physicist Weinberg (2001: 15) notes:

In all branches of science we try to discover generalizations about nature, and having discovered them we always ask why they are true. ... Why is nature that way? When we answer this question the answer is always found partly in contingencies, ... but partly in other generalizations. And so there is a sense of direction in science, that some generalizations are 'explained' by others.

Nature may be the way it is because of some accident that happened at some point in time. Call this the historical answer. Or nature may be the way it is because that is the simplest way it could be. Call this the Galilean answer. The historical answer may be true in many cases, but it is never deep. Things could well have been otherwise. Rewrite history, rewind the sequence of past events, and a different outcome may result in no contradiction. By contrast, the Galilean answer, when true, implies that things could not have been otherwise. And for this reason the Galilean answer is much more satisfactory. Precisely for this reason, the Galilean style of investigation enjoys a certain privilege in scientific investigation. It should be tried first, because if it succeeds, it is satisfactory.

Minimalism is precisely that: an attempt to 'ask not only *what* the properties of language are, but *why* they are that way' (Chomsky 2004a: 105), and to provide an answer that is satisfactory, an answer that makes sense of language.

The way to proceed is to

show that the [richly documented] complexity and variety [in language] are only apparent, and that the ... kinds of rules can be reduced to a simpler form. A 'perfect' [optimal] solution ... would be to eliminate [those rules] entirely in favor of the irreducible operation that takes two objects already formed and attaches one to the other ..., the operation we call Merge [the simplest, smallest conceivable linguistic process]. (Chomsky 2001: 13)

This is identical to Weinberg's (2001: 17–18) statement:

There are arrows of scientific explanation, which thread through the space of all scientific generalizations. Having discovered many of these arrows, we can now look at the pattern that has emerged, and we notice a remarkable thing: ... These arrows seem to converge to a common source! Start anywhere in science, and like an unpleasant child, keep asking 'Why?' You will eventually go down to the level of the very small.

Of course, at some point, one will face the 'infinite regress' question: at which level of the very small do we stop? Here again, Weinberg is illuminating:

John Wheeler has predicted that, when we eventually know the final laws of physics, it will surprise us that they weren't obvious from the beginning. ... That's our quest: to look for a simple set of physical principles, which have about them the greatest possible sense of inevitability. (1987: 63)

Scientists 'are looking for a sense of uniqueness, for a sense that when we understand the final answer, we will see that it could not have been any other way' (Weinberg 2001: 39). They are looking for principles that 'give theories a sense of rigidity' (1993: 147).

Weinberg (1993: 135) cites Einstein as making a similar point: 'The chief attraction of the theory lies in its logical completeness. If a single one of the conclusions drawn from it proves wrong, it must be given up: to modify it without destroying the whole structure seems to be impossible.' Likewise, Richard Feynman (1965b: 26) states:

Now in the further advancement of science, we want more than just a formula. First we have an observation, then we have numbers that we measure, then we have a law which summarizes all the numbers. But the real *glory* of science is that *we can find a way of thinking* such that the law is evident.

Such themes resonate strongly among minimalist practicioners, who seek to follow guidelines that distinguish between 'engineering solutions' and 'genuine explanations' (Chomsky 2000a: 93). In fact, the clearest sense in which we may understand the central minimalist question, 'To what degree is language "perfect"?' is (for me at least) in terms of what Albert Einstein called the 'inner perfection' of a theory, which he defined thus: 'we prize a theory more highly if, from a logical standpoint, it is not the result of an arbitrary choice among theories which, among themselves, are of equal value and analogously constructed' (1949: 23). Theories that 'give us a sense that nothing could be changed' are 'the theories that [scientists] find beautiful' (Weinberg 2001: 39).

4.3 Beauty in science

That there is beauty in science is a feeling shared by all scientists. Copernicus started his epoch-making work, *The Revolutions of the*

Heavenly Spheres (1542), by stating that 'among the many and varied literary and artistic studies upon which the natural talents of man are nourished, I think that those above all should be embraced and pursued with the most loving care which have to do with things that are very beautiful'. As the Nobel prize-winning physicist Chen Ning Yang (1982) notes, the fact that Copernicus chose this sentence indicates how much he appreciated the aesthetic dimension of science. Poincaré (1958 [1904]: 8) made an even stronger statement when he said that 'if nature were not beautiful, it would not be worth studying'. Poincaré's statement captures something deep, and, once dissected, it will help us make sense of the need to go beyond explanatory adequacy. So allow me the opportunity to make the concept of beauty in physics precise.

Yang (1982) and Weinberg (1993), two physicists recognized worldwide for having developed beautiful theories, have addressed this issue in detail, and I will extract ideas and insights from these works that I think are directly relevant to minimalist theorizing.

Both Yang and Weinberg agree that the concept of beauty in physics is 'deeply related to the concept of beauty in mathematics' (Yang 1982: 26). And, as Poincaré once pointed out (cited in Weinberg 1993: 134), 'although it may be very hard to define mathematical beauty, that is just as true of beauty of all kinds'. Yang (1982: 32) suggests three categories of beauty: the beauty of phenomena, the beauty of theoretical description, and the beauty of the structure of the theory. Yang hastens to add that, as in all discussions of this type, these are not sharply different types of beauty: they overlap, and there are beautiful developments that one may find difficult to put into any one category. But I find it interesting that the three kinds of beauty Yang suggests correspond in an obvious way to the three levels of adequacy recognized in linguistics: observational adequacy, descriptive adequacy, and explanatory adequacy. What is more, Yang notes that, as the field of theoretical physics grew, as the mathematization of the field became more important and central, the scientific appreciation of the three different types of beauty changed weights.

For reasons that should be pretty clear by now, the beauty of the structure of the theory—the type of beauty directly associated with the level of explanatory adequacy—will be most relevant for the nature of minimalism in linguistic theory. But before clarifying this type of beauty, it may be useful for me to suggest one linguistic instance of each type of beauty identified by Yang. I think that typological generalizations understood as the clustering of parametric choices, what Baker (1996, 2001) calls macroparameters, fall within the class of beautiful phenomena. It is indeed quite remarkable to see how English and Japanese phrases consistently mirror one another (cf. Chapter 2). Similarly, Cinque (1999) has discovered that the order of adverbs across languages mirrors the order of various inflectional morphemes. For example, the ordering relation between adverbs like *once* and *usually* remains constant across English, Dagaare (West Africa), and Canela-Crahô (Brazil), and is consistently flipped in languages of the Japanese type such as Aleut (North America), Khalkha Mongolian, and Turkish. (My selection of examples here was inspired by Pesetsky's (2000b) handout.)

(1)   a. *English adverbs*
         He was **once usually** willing to help
         *He was **usually once** willing to help
      b. *Dagaare (West Africa) tense particles*
         O da man nmiere ma
         (S)he **PAST HABITUAL** beat-PROG me
         '(S)he was usually beating me'
      c. *Canela-Crahô (Brazil) tense particles*
         pê wa ajco apu to hane
         PAST I **HABITUAL** PROG do thus
         'I always used to do that'
      d. *Aleut (North America) tense suffixes*
         chisi-lga-**qali-qa**-x ...
         distribute-PASS-**INCEPT**-**HABITUAL**-**PAST**-sg ...
         'It was distributed ...'
      e. *Khalkha Mongolian tense suffixes (Asia)*
         bi: [...] moGoi-g cωlωd-**dδg** bai-**sδn**
         I snake-ACC throw-**HABITUAL** be-**PAST**
         'I used to throw it at the snake'

f. *Turkish tense suffixes*
Hasan piyano çal-**ar-di**
Hasan the piano play-**HABITUAL-PAST**
'Hasan used to play the piano'

Based on such correspondences, Cinque proposed a rigid sequence of elements in the sentence, valid for all languages:

(2)   The Cinque Hierarchy

[*frankly* Mood*sentence type*
　[*luckily* Mood*evaluative*
　　[*allegedly* Mood*evidential*
　　　[*probably* Mod*epistemic*
　　　　[*once* T(Past)[*then* T(Future)
　　　　　[*perhaps* Mood*irrealis*
　　　　　　[*necessarily* Mod*necessity*
　　　　　　　[*possibly* Mod*possibility*
　　　　　　　　[*usually* Asp*habitual*
　　　　　　　　　[*finally* Asp*delayed*
　　　　　　　　　　[*tendentially* Asp*predispositional*
　　　　　　　　　　　[*again* Asp*repetitive(I)*
　　　　　　　　　　　　[*often* Asp*frequentative(I)*
　　　　　　　　　　　　　[*willingly* Mod*volition*
　　　　　　　　　　　　　　[*quickly* Asp*celerative(I)*
　　　　　　　　　　　　　　　[*already* T(Anterior)
　　　　　　　　　　　　　　　　[*no longer* Asp*terminative*
　　　　　　　　　　　　　　　　　[*still* Asp*continuative*
　　　　　　　　　　　　　　　　　　[*always* Asp*continuous*
　　　　　　　　　　　　　　　　　　　[*just* Asp*retrospective*
　　　　　　　　　　　　　　　　　　　　[*soon* Asp*proximative*
　　　　　　　　　　　　　　　　　　　　　[*briefly* Asp*durative*
　　　　　　　　　　　　　　　　　　　　　　[*almost* Asp*prospective*
　　　　　　　　　　　　　　　　　　　　　　　[*suddenly* Asp*inceptive*
　　　　　　　　　　　　　　　　　　　　　　　　[*obligatorily* Mod*obligation*
　　　　　　　　　　　　　　　　　　　　　　　　　[*in vain* Asp*frustrative*
　　　　　　　　　　　　　　　　　　　　　　　　　　[*completely* Asp*SgCompletive(I)*
　　　　　　　　　　　　　　　　　　　　　　　　　　　[*tutto* Asp*PlCompletive*
　　　　　　　　　　　　　　　　　　　　　　　　　　　　[*well* Voice
　　　　　　　　　　　　　　　　　　　　　　　　　　　　　[*early*Asp*celerative(II)*
　　　　　　　　　　　　　　　　　　　　　　　　　　　　　　[*again* Asp*repetitive(II)*
　　　　　　　　　　　　　　　　　　　　　　　　　　　　　　　[*often* Asp*frequentative(II)*
　　　　　　　　　　　　　　　　　　　　　　　　　　　　　　　　Verb

I find the classic X-bar theory introduced in Chapter 2 a beautiful description, an elegant way to capture the combinatorial properties of all phrases:[3]

(3)

By its very nature, the third type of beauty, beauty of the structure of the theory, applies to entire theories. Work within minimalism seeks to develop beautiful theories. As I have stressed in previous chapters, before the advent of the P&P model, a premium was placed on developing explanatory theories. The aesthetic considerations that lie beyond the level of explanatory adequacy were secondary. At this point in time we have glimpses of beautiful theories, based on specific minimalist proposals. I will describe some of these proposals in Chapter 5. For now I will follow Weinberg (1993) and list a couple of ingredients of beautiful theories. In doing so, I hope that these ingredients will lead to a better understanding of minimalist research, and I also hope that these ingredients will figure more prominently in linguistic analyses.

Weinberg (1993: 134) starts off by noting that 'by beauty of a physical theory, I certainly do not mean merely the mechanical beauty of its symbols on the printed page'. He also wishes

to distinguish the sort of beauty I am talking about from the quality that mathematicians and physicists sometimes call elegance. An elegant proof or calculation is one that achieves a powerful result with a minimum of irrelevant

---

[3] For linguists: I also find the subjacency account of the range of possible long-distance dependencies a neat characterization, with different languages falling into place as a result of a simple set of parameters (see Rizzi 1978, Lasnik and Uriagereka 1988: 110). (Subjacency expresses the idea that languages identify some nodes in syntactic representations as major hurdles for movement. Although languages vary as to which elements count as hurdles, no language allows movement to cross two such hurdles at a time. When two hurdles are crossed at a time, an island results.)

complication it is not important for the beauty of a theory that its equations should have elegant solutions.[4]

Weinberg adds: 'simplicity is part of what I mean by beauty, but it is a simplicity of ideas, not simplicity of the mechanical sort that can be measured by counting equations or symbols' (cf. Chomsky's (1951) notion of simplicity discussed in Chapter 3). Weinberg goes on to note: 'there is another quality besides simplicity that can make a physical theory beautiful—it is the sense of inevitability that the theory may give us, … the sense that nothing … could be changed.'

Weinberg indicates how Einstein's theory of general relativity meets these criteria of beautiful theories. He also makes the interesting point (p. 136) that '[t]here is one common feature that gives [theories] most of their sense of inevitability and simplicity: they obey *principles of symmetry*' (emphasis original). One of the most important developments in theoretical physics is the recognition that the symmetries that are really important in nature are not the symmetries of things, but the symmetries of laws. As physicist Abdus Salam once stated (quoted in Weinberg 1993: 149), 'it is not particles or forces with which nature is sparing, but principles'. (Heisenberg expressed a similar point when he said in 1973 (cited in Yang 1982: 39), 'we … have to abandon the philosophy of Democritus and the concept of elementary particles. We should accept instead the concept of fundamental symmetries.')

The role of symmetry in bringing about the inevitable, rigid, and beautiful character of a theory is easy to grasp. From an explanatory point of view, asymmetries are always problematic, for they always

---

[4] I find Weinberg's distinction between beauty and elegance reminiscent of the subtle distinction that Chomsky (2000a) and other minimalist practitioners such as Martin and Uriagereka (2000) have made between 'methodological minimalism', a methodologically driven effort to improve scientific theories, and what has been called 'substantive/ontological minimalism', or 'the strong minimalist thesis', which claims that the object of our inquiry itself (the human language faculty) has a certain optimal character. As Chomsky (2004b: 154ff.) himself admits, the distinction is a very subtle one, and I will not attempt to elucidate it any more than Chomsky himself has done in his writings, other than by relating it to 'beauty' vs. 'elegance'.

beg further questions. Why did the asymmetry go this way and not that way? What would the system look like if the directionality of the asymmetry were switched? Asymmetries leave enough room for things to turn out differently. Symmetries avoid such questions altogether. Symmetries provide a satisfactory answer to *why*-questions. We can now understand Poincaré's remark that 'if nature were not beautiful, it would not be worth studying'. If our theories, our best attempts to describe nature, lacked symmetry, rigidity, and inevitability, we would never be able to understand nature in a satisfactory way; hence, nature would not be worth theorizing about.

Although Weinberg recognizes that the beauty of a theory is 'a matter of taste and experience, and cannot be reduced to formula' (1993: 148), he stresses that 'we demand a simplicity and rigidity in our principles before we are willing to take them seriously. Thus not only is our aesthetic judgment a means to an end of finding scientific explanations and judging their validity, *it is part of what we mean by an explanation*' (p. 149; emphasis original). It is for this reason that symmetry principles play such an important role in modern theoretical physics (see Ledermann and Hill 2004 for an overview of the central applications of symmetry in fundamental physics; see also Feynman 1965a, Greene 1999, and Randall 2005), and that scientists which adopt a Galilean style demand that a theory be beautiful.

Einstein also admitted that an 'exact formulation' of the 'firm belief' in some underlying unity 'meets with great difficulty'. But that belief has nonetheless 'played an important role in the selection and evaluation of theories since time immemorial' (Einstein 1949: 21–3). This remark is worth bearing in mind when one read that 'the [Minimalist Program] does not ... enjoy the same clarity of specification as its predecessors' (Lappin et al. 2000a: 888). Lappin et al. find it unacceptable that the central notion of perfection itself 'is never given independent formal or empirical substance' (p. 880). But if a precise formulation of 'inner perfection' in physics is hard to attain, why should we expect a clear(er) exposition of it in linguistics? This is another domain in which requirements are imposed on linguistic theory that no one imposes on more advanced sciences with richer bodies of doctrines; in short, another instance of methodological dualism that isolates linguistics in the larger scientific landscape, as Chomsky has repeatedly pointed out over the years (see Chomsky (2000b, 2002); for recent statements; see already Chomsky (1980: 22–3)).

Let me close this general overview of the Galilean style in science by saying that the goal behind the attempt to go beyond explanatory adequacy is, in the words of Einstein, 'not only to know how nature is and how her transactions are carried through, but also to reach as far as possible the Utopian and seemingly arrogant aim of knowing why nature is thus and not otherwise' (cited in Weinberg 2001: 127).

I suspect that this 'seemingly arrogant' aim of the Minimalist Program is what many have found irksome. But recall Feynman's (1965b: 26) quote mentioned above: 'in the further advancement of science, we want more than just a formula. First we have an observation, then we have numbers that we measure, then we have a law which summarizes all the numbers. But the real *glory* of science is that *we can find a way of thinking* such that the law is evident.' This statement makes clear that once observational (observation), descriptive (numbers), and explanatory ('law') levels of adequacy are reached, the desire to go 'beyond explanatory adequacy' naturally emerges, and makes sense in the context of an approach that takes language to be a natural object. The approach responds to a deep-seated urge characteristic of the Galilean mode of thought.

4.4 The Galilean style and biology

There is another integral part of the Galilean style which I would now like to turn to.

As Chomsky notes, implementing the Galilean style entails a 'readiness to tolerate unexplained phenomena or even as yet unexplained counterevidence to theoretical constructions that have achieved a certain degree of explanatory depth in some limited domain, much as Galileo did not abandon his enterprise because he was unable to give a coherent explanation for the fact that objects do not fly off the earth's surface' (Chomsky 1980: 9–10). As the physicist Chen Ning Yang (1982: 28) observes, 'Galileo ... taught the world of science the lesson that you must make a selection, and if you judiciously select the things you observe, you will find that the purified, idealized experiments of nature result in physical laws which can be described in precise mathematical terms.' Sometimes, the mathematical results are too beautiful to be untrue, so that it seems justifiable to stick to the theory, while setting aside problematic or even conflicting data. As Dirac (1963) expressed it, 'it is more important to have beauty in one's equations than to have them fit experiment', emphasizing that 'a theory that has some mathematical beauty is more likely to be correct than an ugly one that gives a detailed fit to some experiments'.

Idealization, then, is a very misleading term. Far from having a negative character, it brings us closer to the truth. It is intrinsic to the Galilean style. As the Nobel prize-winner Gerard 't Hooft (1997: 4) notes, the model that a scientist constructs, full of artificially isolated elements, 'is a simplification, to be used as a toy to learn to appreciate certain aspects of the world'—those aspects that define the Galilean *Weltbild*.

But, as has often been noted, the tendency to idealize is at odds with the general beliefs held by mainstream biologists until very recently, and by the majority of them to this day. As Fox-Keller (2002) clearly states, biologists are not sympathetic to idealization, seeing it as a 'weakness', a lack of 'satisfying explanation' (p. 74), always requiring 'more measurement and less theory' (p. 87).

Since minimalism has a particularly strong commitment to the Galilean vision of natural phenomena and theory construction, and since it is an integral part of the generative enterprise, which studies the biology of mind, it is therefore crucial to examine the implications of the Galilean style for biological sciences. As we will discuss, minimalism taken seriously poses a challenge to mainstream biology, a challenge that led to claims that the pursuit of the minimalist program only served to 'dissociate linguistics from biology' (Jackendoff 2002: 94). Even the caricature of the minimalist program that reduces it to Occam's razor clashes with a representative statement like that of Francis Crick (1998: 138): 'while Occam's razor is a useful tool in physics, it can be a very dangerous implement in biology.'

It is this challenge that led Chomsky (2005) to emphasize the role of 'three factors' in language design, a theme that I would like to discuss in the remainder of this chapter. I will show that in fact, if successful, minimalism, far from dissociating linguistics from biology, will enrich our understanding of the biology of mind.

4.4.1 *Linguistics as biology*[5]

Let me begin my discussion of the relation between minimalism and biology by stressing that, as Chomsky has repeated at various stages, linguistics, studied from a generative perspective, 'is really theoretical biology' (Sklar 1968: 217). The primary question of the branch of biology known as Theoretical Morphology, quoted immediately below, indeed parallels the one within Generative Grammar outlined in detail in Chomsky (1965: ch. 1).

> The goal is to explore the possible range of morphologic variability that nature could produce by constructing *n*-dimensional geometric hyperspaces (termed 'theoretical morphospaces'), which can be produced by systematically varying the parameter values of a geometric model of form. ... Once constructed, the range of existent variability in form may be examined in this hypothetical morphospace, both to quantify the range of existent form and to reveal nonexistent organic form. That is, to reveal morphologies that theoretically could exist ... but that never have been produced in the process of organic evolution on the planet Earth. *The ultimate goal of this area of research is to understand why existent form actually exists and why nonexistent form does not.* (McGhee 1998: 2; emphasis mine)

An answer to the linguistic equivalent of the central problem of Theoretical Morphology was part of the abstract requirements in (4), stated by Chomsky (1965: 31), to characterize explanatory adequacy (see chapter 2).

---

[5] This section is based on material found in Boeckx and Piattelli-Palmarini (2005).

(4)   ... we must require of such a linguistic theory that it provide for
    (a) an enumeration of the class $s_1, s_2 ...$ of possible sentences
    (b) an enumeration of the class $SD_1, SD_2 ...$ of possible structural
        descriptions
    (c) an enumeration of the class $G_1, G_2, ...$ of possible generative grammars

As I reviewed in Chapter 2, the outline of a solution to the right characterization of the class of grammars the child chooses from and how that choice is made appeared on the horizon only with the introduction of the so-called Principles and Parameters model (Chomsky 1981).

The P&P approach led to an explosion of comparative grammatical research that exploited this combination of fixed principles and varying parametric values. In spite of hard problems, theoretical revisions, and lingering perplexities about many details, this whole novel approach showed that languages, for all their apparent surface diversity, could indeed be seen as patterns with a common fixed core. For the first time linguists had the tools to provide a general answer to why human languages are fundamentally the same, and yet so different. With the aid of parameters, languages whose grammars appear radically different are in fact structurally almost identical, differing by one, or a few, simply stated rules. At the same time, the P&P approach enabled the development of a comprehensive explanatory theory of language acquisition and language change (on language acquisition, see Roeper and Williams 1987, Hyams 1986, and for a recent review, Guasti 2002; on language change, see Lightfoot 1999). In particular, it helped linguists formulate a selective theory (as opposed to an instructive one) of language growth (in the well-consolidated sense given to these notions in biology; see Piattelli-Palmarini 1986, 1989).[6] This is a remarkable achievement. As Jacob (1982: 15–18) discusses, selectionism has gradually replaced instructionism in several areas of science (evolution, heredity, immunology). For example, Niels Jerne's work (1967, 1985) introduced a selective theory (in his terms, a 'generative grammar') of antibody formation, whereby antigens select antibodies that already exist in an

---

[6] See also Chomsky (1980: 136–7), where a parallel is made with Peircean abduction.

individual's immune system. Tonegawa's work also unraveled the details of the genetic recombinations that give rise to the awe-inspiring immune repertoire generated anew in each individual (see Tonegawa 1993).

According to Jacob, 'there remains [only] one domain in which the instruction versus selection argument has not been settled yet: the nervous system [and mental life]'. Jacob concludes his discussion by noting that 'it will probably take time before the instructionist versus selective nature of the learning process can be resolved' (1982: 18). In linguistics at least, the success of the P&P approach suggests rather strongly that selectionism will prevail in the area of learning, as it did in other areas of biology. The gradual abandonment of the traditional associative models of instructive, general-purpose learning in animal psychology (Gallistel 1990, 2001, 2005), with a radical reinterpretation of the data on classical conditioning, and a strong plea for the switch to neurally specialized learning modules, subject to selection, and parametrization, gives me confidence that selectionism will soon be the only game in town.

In addition to this important step forward in the resolution of the nature/nurture debate, the detailed theory of language acquisition elaborated in the last twenty years has been put to remarkable use in the context of language deficits such as Specific Language Impairment, whose genetic basis is now understood (see Marcus 2004 and references therein). This led Wexler (2004) to claim that the P&P model may well provide the basis to fulfill 'Lenneberg's dream' of unifying mind and brain by finding the precise 'biological foundations of language' (Lenneberg 1967).

Significantly, the broad outlines of the P&P view found rather direct parallels in biology. As Chomsky (1980: 67) had already noted, the P&P approach was 'rather similar' to the problem of biological speciation, as discussed by molecular biologist François Jacob (1976).[7] Focusing on the remarkable constancy of biochemical building blocks

---

[7] Noam Chomsky (personal communication, September 2005) tells me that Jacob and Monod's findings were a great source of inspiration when he elaborated the P&P approach in the late 1970s.

throughout the living world, and on their combinatorial powers, Jacob had written:

It was not biochemical innovation that caused diversification of organisms ... What accounts for the difference between a butterfly and a lion, a chicken and a fly, or a worm and a whale is not their chemical components, but varying distributions of these components ... specialization and diversification called only for regulatory circuits, which either unleash or restrain the various biochemical activities of the organism, that the genetic program is implemented. [In related organisms, mammals for example], the diversification and specialization ... are the result of mutations which altered the organism's regulatory circuits more than its chemical structures. The minor modification of redistributing the structures in time and space is enough to profoundly change the shape, performance, and behavior of the final product. (Quoted in Chomsky 1980: 67)

On his way toward developing the P&P framework in linguistics, and stressing a close parallel with biology, Chomsky observed (p. 67):

In a system that is sufficiently intricate in structure, small changes at particular points can lead to substantial differences in outcome. In the case of growth of organs, mental organs in our case, small changes in parameters left open in the general schematism can lead to what appear to be very different systems.

The explanatory model based on a fixed and rather limited repertoire of constituent blocks, susceptible of being multiply recombined and integrated into larger functional units, under precise constraints, has been extended from the biochemical constituents all the way up to the assembly of whole genomes. In the last few years, in fact, the discovery of regulatory 'master' genes, and the remarkable conservation of their sequences and modes of operation across the living world, give new substance to, and specify remarkable details for, the very idea that minute parametric variations in the developmental plan of the organism lead to dramatic differences in the terminal phenotypes (for an earlier entry-level summary, see McGinnis and Kuziora 1994).[8]

---

[8] Even more recently, the epigenetic modulation of traits encoded in identical genomes opens up a further dimension of biological variability whose bounds and consequences are still being debated as I write (for an early insight, see Changeux

Such parallelisms between biology and cognitive science, and between biology and linguistics in particular, reinforced the position of linguistics as a branch of biology, a position characterized as making 'eminent sense' already several years ago by Luria (1973: 141) (see also Monod 1974: 129, Jacob 1976: 322, and Jerne 1985: 1059).

In light of the success of the P&P model,[9] Chomsky returned to an early concern of his, stated in Chomsky (1965) but which had so far resisted genuine breakthroughs: why is language the way it is? He had already noted (1965: 6):

There is surely no reason today for taking seriously a position that attributes a complex human achievement [language in this case] entirely to months (or at most years) of experience, rather than to millions of years of evolution or to principles of neural organization that may be even more deeply grounded in physical law.

The appeal to physical (or, equivalently, to formally necessary and universal) explanations, over and beyond the biologically contingent ones has been amplified in recent years. Chomsky (2005: 6) clearly delineates three factors that enter into the growth of language in the individual: (1) genetic endowment, (2) experience, and (3) principles not specific to the faculty of language. These match point by point the defining elements of the program of the biological sciences, elements

1980; for a recent entry-level summary, see Gibbs 2003; for the very idea of a 'histone code', see Grewal and Moazed 2003, Jaenisch and Bird 2003). I strongly suspect that such findings will have to be taken into consideration as linguists seek to refine the nature of parameters from a minimalist perspective. Unfortunately, I will not be able to sketch here the outlines of what a refined, minimalist view on parameters may look like. But I hope to turn my attention to this important issue in the near future.

[9] There is a sense in which a parametric model of language acquisition is, I think, 'logically' necessary, under the constraints of the poverty of stimulus, a selective (not instructive) acquisition process, the morpholexical variability of languages, and the computational-representational theory of mind that is standardly assumed in cognitive science (see Pinker 1997). This 'logical' necessity is suggested by the insurmountable difficulties faced by the pre-parametric (transformational) theories of language learn-ability and the considerable progress suddenly made possible by parametric ap-proaches. This logical necessity holds, I think, in spite of lingering uncertainties, some of which are considerable, as to a final exact characterization of all the param-eters. Put differently, whatever the right view on parameters turns out to be, some notion of parameter is required.

which Lewontin (2000) calls 'the triple helix': genes, environment, and organism. Lewontin surveys the large and growing body of evidence that demonstrates that the development of any individual organism is the consequence of a unique web of interactions among the genes it carries; the complex, multi-determined molecular inter-actions within and across individual cells; and the nature and sequence of the physical, biological, and social environments through which it passes during development. Disentangling all these factors to examine their respective contributions is no easy matter, and, as Lewontin notes in conclusion, clearly requires new directions in the study of biology. As D'Arcy Thompson (1917: 5) wrote:

The use of the teleological principle is but one way, not the whole or the only way, by which we may seek to learn how things came to be, and to take their places in the harmonious complexity of the world. To seek not for ends, but for 'antecedents' is the way of the physicist, who finds 'causes' in what he has learned to recognize as fundamental properties, or inseparable concomitants, or unchanging laws, of matter and of energy. In Aristotle's parable, the house is there that men may live in it; but it is also there because the builders have laid one stone upon another: and it is as a *mechanism*, or a mechanical construc-tion, that the physicist looks upon the world. Like warp and woof, mechanism and teleology are interwoven together, and we must not cleave to the one and despise the other.

Lewontin's admonitions concerning the triple helix converge with Gould's (2002) 'plea for pluralism', the need to recognize the three axes of causal influences underlying the genesis of natural objects: historical, functional, and formal. Generative grammar has consist-ently focused almost exclusively on the formal axis. And just like the emergence of generative grammar and its immediate success helped shape the landscape in cognitive science, and turn the attention back on to problems of central importance to any serious inquiry into the structure and function of the mind, minimalism, if not unduly premature, could signal a return to central formalist concerns shared with what Kauffman (1993) calls the Rationalist Morphologists in biology: internalists like Goethe, Geoffrey Saint-Hilaire, Severtzov, Remane, Riedl, Owen, Golton, Bateson, and Goldschmidt. This is in fact what I will be arguing in the remainder of this chapter.

4.4.2 *Two scientific cultures*

Let me go back to Crick's statement, quoted earlier, that 'while Occam's razor is a useful tool in physics, it can be a very dangerous implement in biology'.

The divide between theoretical physics and biology illustrates what Dyson (1982: 49) calls 'two styles of science', the 'unifiers' and the 'diversifiers'.[10] The two groups have 'fundamentally different concepts of the nature and purpose of science' (p. 48), and, I would add, different concepts of nature itself. According to Dyson (p. 51),

unifiers look inward ... diversifiers ... outward. Unifiers are people whose driving passion is to find general principles which will explain everything. They are happy if they can leave the universe looking a little simpler than they found it. Diversifiers are people whose passion is to explore details. They are in love with the heterogeneity of nature. ... [[11]] They are happy if they leave the universe a little more complicated than they found it.

Dyson notes (1982: 51) that especially in physics the very great scientists are unifiers. In fact, it is almost taken for granted that the

---

[10] Dyson's distinction has a long historical pedigree. Adapting a similar distinction made by the French philosopher and scientist Blaise Pascal, the physicist and historian of science Pierre Duhem distinguished between two kinds of minds—the strong and narrow mind and the weak and ample mind. The ample mind relishes in a multitude of details and facts, but it is too weak to grasp abstract principles. The strong mind, conversely, understands abstract principles with ease, but it is so narrow that details tend to overload and confuse it.

Similarly, in his *Critique of Pure Reason* (1925 [1781]: 403), Kant distinguished two cognitive styles when he discussed the 'very different thinking styles of scientists, some of whom (who are supremely speculative) are adverse to dissimilarity and always aim at the unity of a category, others of whom (supremely empirical minds) incessantly seek to split nature into so much diversity that one might almost have to abandon the hope that one would be able to evaluate natural phenomena according to general principles'.

[11] Contrast Dyson's statement to Weinberg's (1993: 58) quip that 'if you have seen one electron, you have seen them all'. Gould (2002: 1334) puts it in a more poetic fashion: 'Note how Darwin contrasts the dull repetitiveness of planetary cycling (despite the elegance and simplicity of its quantitative expression) with the gutsy glory of rich diversity on life's ever rising and expanding tree.' Or elsewhere (Gould 2003: 150), 'no one celebrates diversity more than evolutionary biologists like myself; we love every one of those million beetle species, every variation in every scale on a butterfly's wing, every nuance in the coloration of each feather of a peacock.'

road to progress in physics is a wider and wider unification, bringing more and more phenomena within the scope of a few fundamental principles. Although some—most forcefully Philip Anderson (1972) in his seminal paper 'More is Different'[12]—have proclaimed the end of reductionism in physics, Anderson himself clearly states (and 'fully accepts') that 'we must all start with reductionism' (p. 394).

In biology, Dyson points out, the roles are reversed. Few biologists are unifiers. Although Darwin succeeded in encompassing the entire organic world within his theory of evolution,

the organic world remains fundamentally and irremediably diverse. The essence of life is diversity, and the essential achievement of Darwin's theory was to give intellectual coherence to that diversity. The working lives of ninety-nine out of a hundred biologists are spent in exploring the details of life's diversity, disentangling the complex behavior patterns of particular species or the marvelously intricate architecture of particular biochemical pathways. (p. 53)

Dyson concludes by saying that 'biology is the natural domain of the diversifiers, and physics the natural domain of the unifiers' (p. 53).

Ernst Mayr has amplified this point in his recent (2004) book, whose title, *What Makes Biology Unique?*, is meant to convey the idea that biology is a science very distinct from the natural sciences like physics and chemistry. Mayr questions the assumption that biology (more precisely, evolutionary biology) is a science exactly like any of the physical sciences. Like Dyson, he argues for the need to distinguish between two kinds of science, cutting across traditional disciplines like biology, for instance. Mayr (see e.g. pp. 13, 24) leans toward attaching functional/'mechanistic' biology (molecular biology) to the natural sciences, and evolutionary biology to the

---

[12] Anderson's message is clearly expressed in a reprise by Laughlin and Pines (2000: 30), where the 'reductionist ideal' is said to have 'reached its limits as a guiding principle'. According to Laughlin and Pines, 'the central task of theoretical physics in our time is no longer to write down the ultimate equations but rather to catalogue and understand emergent behavior in its many guises', research 'firmly based in experiment, with its hope for providing a jumping-off for new discoveries, new concepts, and new wisdom' (p. 30) In the words of Schweber, 'an ever larger fraction of the efforts in the field [are] being devoted to the study of novelty rather than to the elucidation of fundamental laws and interactions' (1993: 34).

historical sciences (as Gould (2002: 1055) notes, 'most evolutionists are historians at heart'), each with its own methodology and principles. In particular, Mayr takes issue with 'reductionist' statements like the following quote from Weinberg (2001: 17–18), discussed above in the context of the Galilean style:

There are arrows of scientific explanation, which thread through the space of all scientific generalizations. Having discovered many of these arrows, we can now look at the pattern that has emerged, and we notice a remarkable thing: ... These arrows seem to converge to a common source! Start anywhere in science, and like an unpleasant child, keep asking 'Why?' You will eventually go down to the level of the very small.

Mayr writes (p. 69) that 'to have isolated all parts, even the smallest ones, is not enough for a complete explanation of most systems' and notes (p. 28) that 'laws certainly play a rather small role in theory construction in biology', 'because evolutionary regularities do not deal with the basics of matter as do the laws of physics. They are invariably restricted in space and time, and they usually have numerous exceptions' (p. 93).[13]

Very few would disagree with Mayr's statement about the usefulness of laws in biology. As C. H. Waddington famously said, 'the whole real guts of evolution—which is, how do you come to have horses and tigers, and things—is outside the mathematical theory.'

Gould (1995: 36) makes a similar point:

Apply all the conventional 'laws of nature' type of explanations you wish; add to this panoply all that we will learn when we grasp the laws and principles of higher levels, greater magnitudes and longer times, and we will still be missing a fundamental piece of 'what is life?' The events of our complex natural world may be divided into two broad realms—repeatable and predictable incidents of sufficient generality to be explained as consequences of natural law, and uniquely contingent events that occur, in a world of full chaos, and genuine ontological randomness as well, because complex historical narratives happened to unfurl along the pathway actually followed, rather than along any of the myriad equally plausible alternatives. ... Contingency's domain embraces questions of the common form: 'why this, and not any one of a thousand something else?'

---

[13] On the interesting issue of lawfulness vs. regularity, or Galileo vs. Aristotle, see Lewin (1935).

In a similar vein, Gould notes (2002: 85):

The contingent and phyletically bound histories of particular complex lineages ... constitute the 'bread and butter' of macroevolution ... validation in natural history rarely follows the criterion of 'never in principle for this would violate nature's laws,' as favored in some constructions of the so-called exact sciences, but rather the standard of 'conceivable in principle, but not occurring often enough to matter.' (Gould 2002: 1028)

Lewontin (2000: 93) reinforces Gould's and Mayr's points:

The problem for biology is that the model of physics, held up as the paradigm of science, is not applicable because the analogues of mass, velocity, and distance do not exist for organisms. Organisms are of intermediate size and take odd shapes. As a result, it is not the first book of Newton's *Principia*, which deals with idealized systems in vacuums, but the second, which discusses friction, buoyancy, and the movement of real objects in real media, that is most relevant to them.

Weinberg (2001: 15), the author of the 'reductionist' quote above, says nothing different when he writes: 'Why is nature that way? When we answer this question the answer is always found partly in contingencies', stressing that 'the separation of law and history is a delicate business' (1993: 38).

Chomsky (2004a: 105) also acknowledges that the answer to why our generalizations about the nature of language are the way they are will lie in part in contingent facts:

Assuming that these questions can now be seriously placed on the research agenda, we can proceed further to disaggregate [the properties of language] into elements that have a principled explanation, and others that remain unexplained at this level of analysis, and must be attributed to something independent: perhaps path-dependent evolutionary processes ...

Samuel Johnson, in the fourteenth *Rambler* (5 May 1750), expressed a similar view: 'The mathematicians are well acquainted with the difference between pure science, which has to do only with ideas, and the application of its laws to the use of life, in which they are constrained to submit to the imperfections of matter and the influence of accident.' As Herschel (1831: 221) notes, 'natural history ... is either the beginning or the end of physical science.'

Both Johnson's and Herschel's quotes are printed on the epitaph of D'Arcy Thompson's magnum opus *On Growth and Form* (1917), together with a telling quote by Karl Pearson, where he expresses his belief that 'the day must come when the biologist will—without being a mathematician—not hesitate to use mathematical analysis when he requires it.'

Of course, evolutionary biology as we now know it incorporates a substantial amount of insightful mathematical work, the result of the unification of Mendelian genetics and Darwinian evolution under the guidance of Ronald Fisher, Sewall Wright, and J. B. S. Haldane, the fathers of evolutionary dynamics (see Nowak 2004). But the ambition that Thompson wished to express in *Growth and Form* was altogether different. The issue was not how to model the workings of natural selection in precise mathematical terms, but rather to stress that biologists of his day had overemphasized the role of evolution, and underemphasized the roles of physical and mathematical laws in shaping the form and structure of living organisms, the 'third factor' highlighted in Chomsky (2005).

4.4.3 *Back to laws of form*

Thompson's sketch of 'Laws of Forms', his graphic, formally simple, topological transformations to which differences in the forms of related animals could be attributed, are still well known (and have figured more prominently in the biological literature in recent years). But although such early work was very promising, it is now quite clear that the immense progress in biology we have witnessed since the mid-1950s *could* not have come from these general mathematical analyses. The revolution in genetics and in biology was marked by the advent of the what Piattelli-Palmarini (1981) aptly called 'the age of specificity'. Biophysics and biomathematics became micro-structural and, powerfully boosted by the quantum revolution in physics, turned their attention to the various kinds of chemical bond in biological macro-molecules, to the X-ray diffraction of crystals of nucleic acids and proteins, the generation and conduction of the nerve impulse, the modeling of motor control and motor planning, and later on, to the logical modeling of neuronal networks. The lesson here, taken from Piattelli-Palmarini (2005), that the legitimate desire to capture mathematical, formal, and physical invariants in biology could not be satisfied by those equations and by Thompson's topological shears.

Recently, however, Thompsonian themes have made an extraordinary comeback, suggesting that Thompson's program was right on target, though premature.

A key aspect of this comeback was the discovery of the omnipresence in evolutionary quite distant organisms of certain regulatory genes such as the *Homeobox* genes whose activity can produce a wide array of different forms on the basis of simple parameter switches. Take the case of the eye. For several decades, the eye has been the evolutionary biologists' stock example of analogical development, a device so exquisitely tuned to function that nature supposedly has 're-invented' it several times, perhaps five times, perhaps fifty.

Recently, biologists have demonstrated that the PAX6 genetic system is substantially the same from the fruit fly all the way up to humans, but that it gives rise to predictably different kinds of eyes, depending on the signals it receives from the tissues that surround it. *Pace* François Jacob, the eye was not independently invented five times by evolution. Rather, the same set of developmental genes can give rise to five different kinds of eye, under five different kinds of signal. So, nature can be said to have 'invented' the eye once. In the words of Gehring (1998: 53),[14]

We have accumulated more and more evidence that the same homeobox genes are used in both vertebrates and invertebrates to specify the body plan and the mechanisms of the genetic control of development are much more universal than anticipated.

The important phrase here is 'much more universal than anticipated'. Contrary to the still prevailing wisdom (the 'anticipation'), well captured in François Jacob's oft-quoted notion of *bricolage* (tinkering), it may well *not* be the case that *all* the sub-optimal

---

[14] For fuller exposition, see Carroll (2005).

solutions have been tried out in the course of evolution, to be then discarded by selection. As Piattelli-Palmarini (2005) notes, 'when optimal invariants are found across many orders of magnitude and across evolutionarily wildly scattered species it is more likely that they are the result of a regimentation by physicochemical factors than of the 11th-hour filtering of innumerable independent blind trials.' Alan Turing—who, following D'Arcy Thompson, urged biologists to be like physicists, not like historians (see Leiber 2002)—captured the spirit of the enterprise well when he said: 'the primary task of the biologist is to discover the set of forms that are likely to appear [for] only then is it worth asking which one of them will be selected' (Saunders 1992: xii).

This is not to deny that the effects of Jacobian evolutionary tinkering are everywhere to be found in biology; but one should not over-extend the power of tinkering. Put another way, the point is not to deny or belittle any bit of insight that the age of specificity has brought us. The point is to embed such insights into a more comprehensive theory that embraces both the diversity and the unity of the living world.

In this particular respect, the generative enterprise has been remarkably consistent since its inception (Jenkins (2000) traces this consistency better than I could, with extensive quotes from Chomsky's works). The exploration of 'principles of structural architecture and developmental constraints' has particular significance in determining the nature of attainable languages, which is what generative grammar is all about. Recall the parallelism I drew above between the goal of generative grammar as stated in Chomsky (1965) and McGhee's (1998) characterization of the goal of Theoretical Morphology. As Gould (2002: 347) clearly states,

...simple descent does not solve all problems of 'clumping' in phenotypic space; we still want to know why certain forms 'attract' such big clumps of diversity, and why such large empty spaces exist in conceivable, and not obviously malfunctional, regions of potential morphospace. The functionalist and adaptationist perspective ... ties this clumping to available environments, and to shaping by natural selection. Structuralists and formalists wonder if some clumping might not record broader principles, at least partly separate from a simple history of descent with adaptation—principles of genetics, of development, or of physical laws transcending biological organization.

In the context of theoretical morphology, then, these 'broader principles', also known as structural constraints, are critical and primary (which is not to say that contingencies are irrelevant, as even the most structuralist-minded biologists like D'Arcy Thompson readily conceded; see e.g. 1942: 1023).

4.4.4 *The evolution of the language faculty*

Minimalist investigations are fundamental not only to understanding of the nature and functioning of mental organs and their subsystems, but also to investigation of their growth and evolution. In the latter case, however, the divide between 'structural morphologists and teleologists' (Amundson 1998: 154),[15] or between the 'Argument from Pattern' and the 'Argument from Design', is most keenly felt. Not surprisingly, then, it is in the context of the evolution of the language faculty that minimalism has come under heavy attack.

4.4.4.1 *General remarks*   The past decade has witnessed an increase in publications touching on the 'evolution' of language (see Christiansen and Kirby 2003 for a comprehensive overview). This is hardly surprising in light of the success of the P&P model. Once the basic architecture of language is clear, one of the *why*-questions that immediately arise will touch on evolution (to the best of my knowledge, Berwick 1998 was the first to make this point explicit). When addressing the question of evolution of language, most researchers assume that language is the product of adaptive pressures, following standard Argument from Design considerations, well expressed in Pinker and Bloom's (1990) oft-quoted article. (For some dissenting voices, see Piattelli-Palmarini (1989), Uriagereka (1998), Longa (2001), Lorenzo and Longa (2003a, 2003b). For remarks of the same ilk under a broader cognitive

---

[15] Amundson (1998) argues that the divide between teleologists and morphologists was far more significant in the context of Darwin's writings than the more popular 'common descent vs. divine engineering'.

context, see Fodor (2000), Leiber (2002).) Pinker and Bloom (1990: 707) state that 'all languages are complex biological systems. ... It would be natural, then, to expect everyone to agree that language is the product of Darwinian natural selection. The only successful account of the origin of complex biological structure is the theory of natural selection.' Claiming otherwise would be like 'the proverbial hurricane that blows through a junkyard and assembles a Boeing 747' (Pinker 1994: 361) (similar remarks can be found in Pinker 1997, 2005).

Under the 'law of the higgledy-piggledy' (F. Darwin 1887: 2, 37; Herschel 1861: 12; Mayr 2004: 111), which characterizes the workings of natural selection, language is thus expected to consist of a hodge-podge of loosely interacting computational tricks.

Jackendoff (1997: 20) expresses this well when he writes that 'it is characteristic of evolution to invent or discover "gadgets" ... The result is not "perfection".' Jackendoff goes on to say that he would 'expect the design of language to involve a lot of Good Tricks ... that make language more or less good enough. ... But nonredundant perfection? I doubt it.' He also adds:

This is not to say that we shouldn't aim for rigor and elegance in linguistic analysis. Admitting that language isn't 'perfect' is not license to give up attempts at explanation. In particular, we still have to satisfy the demands of learnability [*explanatory adequacy in Chomsky's 1965 sense*]. It is just that we may have to reorient our sense of what 'feels like a right answer' away from Chomsky's sense of 'perfection' toward something more psychologically and biologically realistic. It may then turn out that what looked like 'imperfections' in language ... are not reason to look for more 'perfect' abstract analyses, as Chomsky and his colleagues often have done; rather, they are just about what one should expect. (p. 20)

Jackendoff is quite correct on one historical point. Perfection is not what we expect from biological systems, at least when it comes to their use, and to the extent that they have arisen through the pressures of natural selection. But, as Noam Chomsky points out (personal communication, December 2004), Jacob is not pronouncing a dogma when resorting to his notion of tinkering quoted above. He is merely noting that to the extent that something evolves through a long and intricate process of natural selection, with path-dependent effects on later steps, accidents, etc., then we expect tinkering. But we certainly don't expect tinkering for cell division into spheres, or for what Gould and Lewontin (1979) have called 'spandrels', for example. In such cases, Jacob's reasoning just doesn't apply. As Jacob himself noted (1982: 20), following a remark by George C. Williams, 'adaptation is a special and onerous concept that should be used only when and where necessary.' Unless there is some reason to dismiss the hypothesis that language may have been the (inevitable) result of some structural constraints, a forced side-effect of some independent change, Jackendoff's remarks merely point to tangential issues.[16]

To reiterate my point: although the appropriateness of the tin-kering metaphor is being re-evaluated in biology, the prevailing trend for quite some time—and one clearly expressed by Jackendoff and evolutionary psychologists—has been in favor of explanations based on tinkering, rather than optimization and economy. Jacob's tinkering is an undeniable and pervasive fact, but an excessive insistence on it alone may have obscured deeper organizing prin-ciples. Jacob's tinkering metaphor is complemented by his classic work (with Monod) on gene regulation, whereby, for the first time, the digital ('switch-like', in their own terminology, 'modular,' in more recent terminology) and universal nature of the activation and repression of single genes was introduced into the 'logic' of biological thinking.[17] These inner, more abstract constraints on

[16] Jackendoff's appeal to learnability strikes me as a serious misunderstanding of the P&P approach. As noted in Chapter 2, the primary contribution of P&P, in the present connection, was to divorce questions of learning entirely from the question of the 'format for grammar', and thus to make it possible for the first time to address seriously what had always been understood to be the basic problems of biology of language: what is specific to the language faculty and what follows from laws of physical organization?

[17] As a matter of fact, I think that Jacob's use of the notion of tinkering was more a way for him to emphasize the fact that nature makes use of available elements as opposed to inventing new ones (see Jacob 1982: 34ff.), rather than a way to stress the 'higgedly-piggedly' character of evolution. The latter aspect was an almost inevitable consequence of the connotation the word 'tinkering' has in the language, but not obviously what Jacob intended.

biological evolution will surely not deny the role of natural selection, though a radical reappraisal of its power and patterns of action may be expected.

The point of the minimalist program is to invite us to look for such deeper organizing principles, that is, to consider another factor in the role of language design and the emergence of language. And although the program as a whole may still be premature, there is little doubt that it makes eminent sense from a biological point of view, especially in the context of evolution. It is indeed hard to imagine how the human language faculty could have emerged in all its glorious complexity in such a short time on the evolutionary scale (*c.* 50,000 years ago according to most estimates concerning the origins of language). Minimalism can begin to make sense of that if all the apparent complexity is the result of very simple computational mechanisms.

The discoveries of the past fifty years or so have partially vindicated Thom's (1975) statement (quoted in Le Guyader 2004: 244): '[he] would not be surprised if in the future more justice was rendered to the considerations of Geoffrey Saint-Hilaire' (a major unifier and internalist in biology). Indeed, Gould wrote a 1985 article entitled 'Geoffrey and the Homeobox' in which he presented in parallel fashion the thought of Geoffrey Saint-Hilaire and the principal findings of molecular genetics concerning the homeotic genes that determine the anterior–posterior organization of the embryo.

Evidence from genetics, embryology, and developmental biology has indeed converged to offer a more epigenetic and dynamic view of how organisms develop, so much so that we can begin to talk of 'non-genomic nativism' (Cherniak forthcoming, Baker 2005). In some cases, to capture the idea that contrary to the nature/nurture dichotomy, there is a third factor, a set of principles, which, following Gould (2002), I will refer to as 'constraints' that reinforce Harrison's (1937: 370) statement, which has lost none of its relevance to current biology:

The prestige of success enjoyed by the gene theory might become a hindrance to the understanding of development by directing our attention solely to the genome. ... Already we have theories that refer the processes of development to genic action and regard the whole performance as no more than the realization of the potencies of the genes. Such theories are altogether too one-sided.

In this respect, Gould (2002: 21) calls for a renewed appreciation of 'the enormous importance of structural, historical, and developmental constraints in channeling the pathways of evolution, often in highly positive ways', adding that 'the pure functionalism of a strictly Darwinian (and externalist) approach to adaptation no longer suffices to explain the channeling of phyletic directions, and the clumping and inhomogenous population of organic morphospace'.

All major evolutionary theories before Darwin, and nearly all important versions that followed his work, followed a tradition arching back to Plato in presenting a fundamentally 'internalist' account, based upon intrinsic and predictable patterns set by the nature of living systems for development through time, as the term 'evolution' (*evolutio*, unfolding) reveals. As one of the foremost exponents of such internalist accounts, and the person who coined the term 'morphology', Goethe writes (second essay on plant metamorphosis, written in 1790, in Mueller and Engard, 1952: 80):

In my opinion, the chief concept underlying all observation of life—one from which we must not deviate—is that a creature is self-sufficient, that its parts are inevitably interrelated, and that nothing mechanical, as it were, is built up or produced from without, although it is true that the parts affect their environment and are in turn affected by it.

As a common thread, internalist accounts deny exclusivity to natural selection as the agent of creativity, viewing 'adaptation as secondary tinkering rather than primary structuring' (Gould 2002: 290). Internalists claim a high relative frequency of control by internal factors, emphasizing notions like 'unity of type' and 'correlation of growth'.

At the heart of internalist frustrations is the linkage between natural selection and contingency. In the words of Kauffman (1993: 26):

We have come to think of selection as essentially the only source of order in the biological world ... It follows that, in our current view, organisms are largely

ad hoc solutions to design problems cobbled together by selection. It follows that most properties which are widespread in organisms are widespread by virtue of common descent from a tinkered-together ancestor, with selective maintenance of useful tinkerings. It follows that we see organisms as over-whelmingly contingent historical accidents, abetted by design.
My own aim is not so much to challenge as to broaden the neo-Darwinian tradition. For, despite its resilience, that tradition has surely grown without attempting to integrate the ways in which simple and complex systems may spontaneously exhibit order.

Despite the fact that various biologists have complained that phrases like 'adaptation to the edge of chaos' and 'order for free', repeatedly used by Kauffman, Goodwin, and others, lack clear scientific defini-tion and operational utility, Gould (2002: 1213) argues that Kauffman et al. are groping towards something important, a necessary enrich-ment or broadening of biology, with important implications. Gould adds: 'if we have been unable, thus far, to achieve a rigorous formu-lation, we should at least recognize that science itself has been so tuned to other, largely reductionist, modes of thought, that the basic conceptual tools have never been developed.'

   Other authors, such as Cherniak et al. (2004), have recently reported that the principles of surface distribution in the spatial layout of the cerebral cortex minimize total connection costs to an extent previously unsuspected, revealing a remarkable level of 'neuro-optimality' down to best-in-a-billion, and beating even the best results obtained in artificial micro-circuit design optimization. These natural optimization models have predictive power in the reconstruction of the structure of sensory areas in the cat and the macaque cerebral cortices.

   Consider another example. The heart-rate of an elephant is slower than that of a mouse, while its pregnancy time is longer; there are various observations of this sort, across species, about which biolo-gists know their mathematical rate: an idealized proportion of direct or inverse fourth powers involving the creature's mass, depending on the specific system but otherwise constant across species. Why the mathematical expression should be a power *of four* is particu-larly puzzling, as entities existing in the usual three dimensions of space scale by powers of three, one per dimension. West et al. (1997) provide an explanation for the fourth power starting from some abstract assumptions of the sort linguists constantly make: (i) that all eukaryotic organisms have (standard) cells of roughly the same size; (ii) that physiological functions, such as those involved in blood or oxygen distribution or the growth of tissue, are optimal in some definable sense; and (iii) that given these two initial assumptions, and a central core (a heart, lung, growth apex, etc.), the best sort of geometry to describe the system would be fractal— structures whose most important property is recursion under conditions of self-similarity. Standard recursion is familiar to linguists, but self-similar recursion is a sub-case with a curious property: it must present a kind of structural optimality that can be easily and intuitively grasped by merely observing a Fibonacci structure in nature (flower corollas, sea-shells, skin patterns in cordates, etc.). As it turns out, networks of this sort require a fourth dimension to describe them, which accords with the initial description of scaling conditions.

All in all, as Thompson and Turing had insightfully anticipated, powerful unifying mechanisms and deeper optimization criteria are at play in biology (see Uriagereka 1998 for additional examples and fuller exposition). Jacques Monod always made it very clear (Massimo Piattelli-Palmarini, personal communication, November 2003) that the role of chance in determining the manifold structures of living beings could be properly understood only within the boundaries of physico-chemical (and today we may add computational and algorithmic) necessity (see Monod 1972). It was the 'necessity' half of his unified conception of life as 'chance and necessity'. It is that 'necessity' that the minimalist program sets out to explore in detail. In harmony with this more general picture, minimalism is concerned with developing a view of the language faculty that will help identify (in the words of Thomas Huxley) the 'predetermined lines of modification', 'the limitations of phenotypic variability', 'caused by the structure, character, composition or dynamics of the developmental system' (Maynard-Smith et al. 1985). Even if such internalist accounts as Kauffman's have only partial validity, that validity needs to be recognized, and such accounts must be integrated within the biological sciences.

4.4.4.2 *A concrete research program* Although still in its preliminary stages, minimalism has allowed the formulation of a concrete hypothesis concerning the emergence of the language faculty that is very much in the spirit of the internalist accounts just discussed. The hypothesis was first formulated in Hauser et al. (2002), and was expressed in more detail in Fitch et al. (2004), in a reply to Jackendoff and Pinker's (2005) criticism of Hauser et al. (2002). Let me stress right away that my reason for presenting Hauser et al.'s analysis is not because I think it is correct in every detail. It is certainly in need of refinements; but it offers a concrete example of what kind of analysis minimalism makes possible. As Fitch, Hauser, and Chomsky note, although their hypothesis is logically independent from the minimalist program, the latter renders the former far more plausible.

According to Hauser et al., what distinguishes humans from other species is the computational system that constitutes Narrow Syntax, or the narrow language faculty, specifically its recursive quality (the ability to effect infinite embedding) and the way this quality maps the syntactic objects it constructs onto the conceptual-intentional and sensorimotor systems. They claim that there is evidence that other species possess sensorimotor and conceptual-intentional systems similar to our own. These constitute the broad language faculty. Hauser et al. propose that their hypothesis may have important evolutionary consequences. The hypothesis that only narrow language faculty is unique to humans

raises the possibility that structural details of [the narrow language faculty] may result from such preexisting constraints, rather than from direct shaping by natural selection targeted specifically at communication. Insofar as this proves to be true, such structural details are not, strictly speaking, adaptations at all. (Hauser et al. 2002: 1574)

The idea that the language faculty was not shaped by adaptive demands is a recurring theme in Chomsky's writings (see Jenkins 2000: ch. 5 for extensive review and references). In the GB era, in fact, generative grammar invited this conjecture by focusing on the specificities of the language organ, making it very unlikely that central linguistic concepts such as c-command, government, empty categories, and cyclicity, just to name a few, may have found analogs or precursors in motor control, vision, or action. It was inconceivable that adaptive pressures, generically rewarding better communication and planning, might have given rise to such peculiar linguistic structures and computations. (See Piattelli-Palmarini (1989) for a clear formulation of this position.)

In practice, however, the GB architecture, with its richly modular structure, made it hard to formulate a precise non-adaptive alternative. Roughly speaking, the GB era offered a picture of the language faculty that was too complex for structural constraints to account realistically for its emergence. Views like Thompson's and Turing's gain in plausibility when applied to simple systems. As Thompson (1917: 251–2) himself noted (the opening quote is a conventional defense of phylogenetic reasoning by E. Ray Lankaster):

'The fact that we are able to classify organisms at all in accordance with the structural characteristics which they present, is due to the fact of their being related by descent.' But this great generalization is apt, in my opinion, to carry us too far. It may be safe and sure and helpful and illuminating when we apply it to such complex entities,—such thousandfold resultants of the combination and permutation of many variable characters,—as a horse, a lion, or an eagle; but (to my mind) it has a very different look, and a far less firm foundation, when we attempt to extend it to minute organisms whose specific characters are few and simple, whose simplicity becomes much more manifest when we regard it from the point of view of physical and mathematical description and analysis, and whose form is referable, or (to say the least of it) is very largely referable, to the direct and immediate action of a particular physical force.

Minimalism invites us to view the language faculty as a 'minute organism [the "language organ"] whose specific characters are few and simple'. As Thompson notes, this 'simplicity becomes much more manifest when we regard it from the point of view of physical and mathematical description and analysis', that is to say, when one adopts a Galilean attitude to the study of language.

Put differently, the emphasis on 'virtual conceptual necessity' within minimalism reduces considerably the evolutionary load that previously fell upon adaptations and tinkering. This is a welcome consequence, because according to everyone's best guesses, the human language faculty emerged very, very recently in the species, which makes it hard seriously to entertain an adapatationist story (especially if the language faculty is as complex as Pinker and Jackendoff 2005, Jackendoff and Pinker 2005, and so many others claim). There is just not enough time for such a complex object to be built step by step.

4.4.5 *Language and cognition*

In its search for elementary operations, symmetric representations, and efficient derivations, minimalism is beginning to reach a level of 'conceptual granularity' that allows one to formulate precise, testable hypotheses in the context of language evolution. This same conceptual granularity may also help reduce the gap between studies of competence and studies of performance, or between linguistics and cognitive neuroscience (see Poeppel and Embick 2005, Poeppel 2005, and Phillips 2004 for remarks to that effect). Minimalism may also help us identify the right building blocks to illuminate the relationship between language and thought, along the programmatic lines suggested by Spelke (2003), Carey (forthcoming), and Hauser and Carey (1998). Indeed, the minimalist program has an extraordinarily programmatic character, for one way of answering the minimalist question, 'How many aspects of the language faculty can be given a principled explanation?' is 'to find out the extent to which principles of language ... are unique to this cognitive system or whether similar "formal arrangements" are found in other cognitive domains in humans or other organisms' (Chomsky 2005: 1–2; see Hauser et al. 2002 and Fitch et al. 2004 for a clear outline of this interdisciplinary research program).

The effort to sharpen and to investigate these questions defines a major aspect of research in minimalism. In particular, minimalism attempts to elucidate (i) principles of data analysis that might be used in language acquisition and other domains (see especially Yang 2002) and (ii) 'principles of structural architecture and developmental constraints that enter into canalization, organic form, and action over a wide range', including principles of efficient computation and symmetry.

This research program inevitably reopens the question of specificity and biological isolation of the language faculty.[18] There is little doubt that nature makes available some structure, a mental organ, dedicated to language. Without such structure, one could not account for why all human beings barring pathology display an irrepressible 'instinctive tendency' for language, as Darwin (1981 [1871]) called it.

Much work in generative grammar until now has been devoted to figuring out the internal structure of this biologically determined capacity. Language has been studied by generativists in a very modular, autonomous fashion, in part because (as I pointed out above, citing Jacob) micro-modularization is often the key to success in science. But autonomy has also been assumed and emphasized as a reaction to the Piagetian view that language learning is an expression of intelligence, a specific expression of a general mental skill. For reasons that have been well documented (see Piattelli-Palmarini 1980), the Piagetian view does not carry much explanatory weight, much as the behaviorist insistence on general learning mechanisms with little or, worse, no dedicated structure does not even begin to characterize linguistic properties adequately (see Chomsky 1959).

The specificity and distinctness of language, its isolability in the mental world, has been extremely well documented in the past twenty years, based on dissociation cases like language savants (Smith and Tsimpli 1995), aphasics, language deprivation (Curtiss 1977), genetic deficits (Van der Lely 2004, 2005, Marcus 2004, Fisher 2005, Bellugi and St George 2001), and so on. The list is growing as I write, and I suspect that it will continue to grow as we learn more

---

[18] Fitch et al. (2004) make this clear in the context of the now standard assumption that 'Speech is Special'.

about the genetic and neural substrates of the language faculty. Until the advent of the minimalist program, the specificity of language appeared to many so inescapable that they considered it futile to consider how much of the internal structure of the language faculty is unique to language, and how much is shared with, recruited from, and/or determined by other mental faculties, at the ontogenetic and/or phylogenetic levels. As Rizzi (2004: 340) points out, this question is much harder than just figuring out the content of the language faculty, as it necessarily involves comparisons between the language faculty and other non-linguistic mental faculties in humans and other species, which (to make the comparison meaningful) should be modeled and expressed in a somewhat commensurable format.

Part of the minimalist impact, already noticeable at the present stage of research (see e.g. Hauser 2006, Poeppel 2005), is to force this interdisciplinary dialog, and to some extent make it possible and concrete. By recasting much of GB's concepts and analytic devices into a more general mold emphasizing symmetry and computational efficiency, it becomes possible to find analogs and homologs of some linguistic processes in other domains of the human mind or in other species. This naturally leads to the hypothesis, expressed in Rizzi (2004: 340), 'that much of the specificity of the language faculty is linked not so much to the use of special computational devices, but rather its place in the "topography" of the mind, to the overall function it must perform (relating sound and meaning), [and] to the contiguity with the other systems it must interact with at the interfaces'. As Tony Kroch pointed out to me (personal communication, January 2005), it is the mental organization that makes language special, not the physical organs themselves. Descartes may very well have agreed to this, since he pointed out in his *Discourse on Method* that the absence of linguistic ability in animals is 'not [due to the fact that] they lack the necessary organs'.

By its very nature, minimalism forces researchers to look for uniformity across cognitive systems, and in fact even more broadly across complex systems, at a level that is much more abstract and refined than the Piagetian perspective. The fact that it opens new research possibilities is a sign of fecundity that characterizes progressive programs.

4.5 Conclusion

Dyson (1982: 54) observes that 'every science needs for its healthy growth a creative balance between unifiers and diversifiers'. When when one studies a biological system, it is not the unity that strikes us, but rather the extraordinary diversity, the source of biodiversity. This is certainly the case in language. The first thing that strikes us is the diversity of languages, the range of variation. But as the generative program has shown in its short but rich history, this range of variation is to be understood against the background of a universal language faculty. The minimalist program calls attention to the underlying simplicity of this Universal Grammar, and in so doing emphasizes the Unity of Type that must be part of the explanation of the emergence and growth of this aspect of the natural world. Because this unity is especially hidden in the daily diversity of languages, it is critical to adopt a Galilean perspective at the core of minimalism so as not to lose sight of the (positive) constraints that in part, perhaps in large part, helped shape our language faculty.

Not surprisingly, the few biologists like Thompson and Turing who have devoted their energy to carry out a Galilean program for biology have figured prominently in generative approaches to language (they are mentioned in Chomsky's writings as early as 1982: 50, but Lenneberg 1967 already alludes to them). Thompson (1942: 643) was quite clear that attention should be drawn to 'simple, or simplified, cases of phenomena which in their actual and concrete manifestations are usually too complex for mathematical analysis'—a good example of the idealizing method typical of Galilean science. Thompson was at pains to emphasize the need of 'a principle of negligibility' (p. 1029), to 'learn from the mathematician to eliminate and discard; to keep the type in mind and leave the single case, with all its accidents, alone' (p. 1032) Without this method, 'there would have been no Kepler, no Newton, and no astronomy' (p. 1029).

I have tried to show here that adherence to the Galilean style, as described in this chapter, promises to yield important hypotheses not just in the strictly linguistic realm of grammatical analyses but also in the realm of biology at large.

5

The Minimalist Highlights

Minimalism is animated by the belief that the old adage 'Least is best' is not only methodologically desirable but also true of the design of the language faculty. Ultimately, the success of the minimalist program ought to be measured by the range and depth of analyses it has helped generate. As they say, the proof of the pudding is in the eating. In the words of Epstein and Hornstein (1999: ix), 'the proof of a program ultimately rests in how good the detailed products that result from taking its strictures seriously look.'

5.1 *Caveat lector*

The aim of this chapter is to illustrate how minimalist concerns and guidelines of the type discussed in the previous chapters can be made concrete in specific proposals. This is quite a difficult chapter to write for a book like this one, which tries to reach an audience that is not limited to minimalists who may want to have a bird's-eye view of the enterprise, or GB practitioners who may wonder what happened to this or that key aspect of their framework. To measure success one needs some benchmark, and GB is perfect for that. Since I do not assume that everyone will have all the GB tools in hand to measure how far minimalism can go in capturing the same aspects of language in a more natural and interesting fashion, I will try briefly to sketch the GB elements providing the basis for comparison before summarizing minimalist findings. In some cases, inevitably, subtleties will be lost. I apologize in advance to the experts. As for the non-experts, I will have reached my goal if at the end of the chapter they have gained enough of a flavor of the argument and decide that they want to learn more and pick up more detailed texts that address the technical issues I touch on here such as Hornstein et al. (2006) or Lasnik et al. (2005). They may even want to move to the primary literature. For an excellent collection of essential readings, see Bošković and Lasnik (2006).

Let me also point out right from the start that there is no single locus classicus for the Minimalist Program. The results and analyses I will highlight here do not come from the works of a single author. Nor are they necessarily compatible with one another at this stage. This chapter is meant to provide great minimalist snapshots, not panoramas. Remember that this is a program, not a theory. All I want to suggest here is that, taken collectively, the hypotheses discussed below demonstrate that minimalist efforts have already borne some fruits. Given the claims at stake, not just for linguistics but for biology at large (cf. Chapter 4), it is quite remarkable that one can already see glimpses of concrete minimalist results in only fifteen years of research. In the same breath, I would also like to mention that the present chapter is not meant to be a comprehensive survey of minimalist analyses. The analyses discussed below have been selected because they illustrate the specific guidelines I have emphasized in the previous chapters in a way that I will try to make clear at each point. It should be clear, however, that like all selections, the present one pays serious attention to only a limited number of paths among the large number of available possibilities. I apologize in advance to each and every researcher within minimalism who feels his or her work should have been mentioned and/or given a more prominent place in my sketch. What follows inevitably suffers from what has come onto my desk in the past few years, and from my own perception of what constitutes progress and genuine understanding. The reader should never forget that what follows is minimalism through my own eyes; and of course what is seen up close, such as my own work or the work of close colleagues, will appear magnified.

5.2 Evaluating the objections to the program

In my view, minimalism has already shown signs of success in a variety of domains. But, clearly, mine is a controversial view. Indeed, several authors have recently suggested that 'the empirical results of the minimalist program that Chomsky can point to in [2002] do not come close to approaching his level of rhetoric about the program's degree of success' (Newmeyer 2003: 596). Newmeyer goes as far as to suggest that the minimalist program does not 'bring phenomena under its explanatory scope that were outside the scope of [the P&P system]' (p. 589). Furthermore, he claims that 'minimalism in its purest form (the form advocated by Chomsky in [2002] and the only form in which language might conceivably be regarded as "optimal") represented a big step backwards from [P&P] in its ability to derive constructional complexity' (p. 589).[1]

Because it is my overall goal in this book to show that the minimalist program has great merits, I want to show that the criticism is in fact unwarranted, and that the pursuit of the minimalist program in syntactic theory is not only legitimate (resting as it does on solid foundations, of the sort reviewed in the previous chapters) but also rewarding. In addition, examining the logic of some of the critiques leveled at the minimalist program will allow me to clarify and emphasize some of the central features of the latter.

Let us start by considering Newmeyer's (2003) logic further.[2] He states:

[1] Newmeyer's criticism is by no means isolated. For instance, Levine (2002: 325) claims that minimalism is an 'empirically groundless speculation' (Levine 2002: 325), and that therefore adherence to the program amounts to an 'irrational commitment' (Levine 2002: 329). (For additional comments of that ilk, see Lappin et al. 2000a, 2000b 2001, Jackendoff 1997, 2002, Jackendoff and Pinker 2005, Postal 2003a, 2003b, and Seuren 2004.)

[2] My reason for choosing Newmeyer's 2003 critique is twofold. First, Newmeyer's review highlights specific themes that I wish to defend in detail in the present work. Second, other critiques such as those by Lappin, et al. and Jackendoff and Pinker have already been addressed in detail in works that are easily accessible: see *Natural Language and Linguistic Theory*; 18 (2000) and 19 (2001), see also Freidin and Vergnaud (2001) and Fitch et al. (2004). For remarks on Postal (2003b), see Boeckx (2006c); on Seuren (2004), see Grohmann (2005) and ten Hacken (2006).

As many distinct UG principles are being proposed today as were proposed twenty years ago. I would go as far as to claim that no paper has ever been published within the general rubric of the minimalist program that does not propose some new UG principle or make some new stipulation ... about grammatical operations that does not follow from the bare structure of the M[inimalist] P[rogram]. (p. 588)

Newmeyer's remarks betray a misunderstanding of what it means for something to be a program (a theory in the making). Suppose it were true that, as he claims, no paper has ever been published within the general rubric of the minimalist program that does not stipulate a new principle. What would that tell us about the minimalist thesis? Very little indeed. The ambition of Minimalist Syntax is not to avoid all stipulations at all costs. Axioms (i.e. stipulations) will always be needed, and new ones at that, since the conditions under which the axioms are needed will vary as empirical investigations proceed (a sign of progress). Recall Chomsky's comments that '[g]ood design conditions are in part a matter of empirical discovery' (2001: 1). This, of course, affects the nature of the concrete proposals being made under the rubric of minimalism. Furthermore, it is perfectly natural for new axioms and principles to be proposed, for the aim of the minimalist program is to determine under which conditions narrow systems meet interface demands in an optimal fashion. Proposing new axioms helps determine which is more comprehensive, economical, enhances symmetry, etc.

In addition, as Massimo Piattelli-Palmarini pointed out to me (personal communication, November 2003), language may be a perfect system, but linguists clearly aren't perfect. The same is true in all scientific domains. The minimalist program is nothing more than an application of the Galilean outlook on nature, which, as physicists know all too well, is often hard to live up to. As Weinberg (1993: 45–6) points out in a similar context, 'I am concerned here not so much with what scientists *do*, because this inevitably reflects both human limitations and human interests, as I am with the logical order built into nature itself.' This is why I think it is particularly helpful to consider below analyses that come from various authors, and not to fall into the trap of characterizing the minimalist program as 'Chomsky's (or anybody else's) minimalism' (*contra* Seuren (2004) and so many others).³

Having made this clear, let us return to Newmeyer's review. When it comes to empirical results, Newmeyer claims that language would not be less optimal in the absence, in particular, of specific proposals like Relativized Minimality, copies, and last resort:

Belletti and Rizzi [*in their 2002 introduction to Chomsky (2002), specifically pp. 41–4*] point to the copy theory of traces and the explanation that it provides for reconstruction effects (that is, the behavior of a moved phrase as if it were in the position of its trace) as an example of 'optimal design.' The copy theory may or may not be empirically motivated, but it is hard to see why it is more 'optimal' in some a priori sense than a theory that says when an element moves, it moves, tout court. Earlier in the introduction [*to Chomsky 2002*], Belletti and Rizzi endorse economy principles such as movement-as-last-resort, the idea that derivations take place in 'phases' corresponding to V[erb]P[hrase] and C[omplementizer]P[hrase], and the principle of relativized minimality. These principles might be right or they might be wrong, but language would be no more or less 'perfect' if movement were utterly forbidden, if D[eterminer]P[hrase] and A[djectival]P[hrase] were also phases, and if minimality were not relativized. (p. 586)

Here I have to disagree with Newmeyer. As I discussed in Chapter 3, Rizzi's (1990) understanding of locality was the principle within P&P that received an almost immediate minimalist formulation in terms of economy. If minimality were not relativized to types of fronting, no fronting would be allowed to take place in natural

---

³ It is indeed remarkable how limited in scope the critiques aimed at the minimalist program are. Virtually all of them focus almost exclusively on Chomsky's work. To take two examples, Seuren's (2004) book cites no technical work within minimalism other than Chomsky. Pinker and Jackendoff (2005: 222) acknowledge, 'to be fair', that 'recent work on minimalism has tried to fill in the gaps and address the problems of Chomsky's original formulations' but do not cite any such work (nor any work that have explored alternative minimalist hypotheses, such as Brody (1995, 2003), Zwart (2004), Koster (2003), Epstein et al. (1998), Hornstein (2001), Grohmann (2003), Williams (2003), Sportiche (1998), Kayne (2005), Moro (2000), and Boeckx (2003a, 2005a), all of which adopt tenets that have been explicitly rejected in Chomsky's own work). Given the limited set of analyses they consider, it is no surprise that Pinker and Jackendoff can conclude that the critiques of the minimalist program 'are remarkably similar in substance' (2005: 222).

language, since any type of element would block any type of fronting. Since fronting appears to be a true property of language, the best way to implement it, while capturing all the observed restrictions on it, appears to be to relativize minimality. Similarly, copies provide the least stipulative way of handling reconstruction effects, which are part of the 'data structure' in syntax. Other approaches to reconstruction in terms of lowering, indexing, multiple levels, etc. have been shown to be either empirically severely inadequate or (worse) more complex, and at variance with well-motivated principles, such as Inclusiveness (which bars introduction of non-lexical properties in syntax). Copying introduces a kind of conservation principle that makes perfect sense in optimal systems (see Uriagereka 1998 and Lasnik et al. 2005: 53–5, 120–1; see also below). If one has to keep track of where fronting took place from, as language appears to do, copying is the best way to do so.

With respect to last resort and other economy principles, Newmeyer notes: 'Chomsky barely alludes to economy principles in [Chomsky 2002], despite the fact that they were the centerpiece of his minimalist theorizing in the 1990s' (2003: 586, n. 5).

Although I have already touched on the issue of economy in Chapter 3, the points I made there bear emphasis. So, let me repeat the essence of these points. First, last-resort conditions are now subsumed under mechanisms presupposing them. Take, for instance, the notion that Case assignment in a nominal deactivates its derivational accessibility (Lasnik 1999, Chomsky 2004a). Once its case is checked, an NP ceases to be visible for further computation. This is similar to saying that an NP can only move to a case position if it has not yet been assigned a case feature. The 'last resort' strategy has not disappeared—it has just been deeply integrated into the system, in alternative principles. Second, the issue of economy conditions gets naturally reduced the moment syntactic derivations are divided up into cyclic domains that reduce access to elements in the syntactic representations. As soon as cyclic considerations are introduced into the system, comparison sets immediately shrink. In the limit, if radical cycles turn out to force almost immediate transfer to the PF and LF components, as in the level-free model discussed in Chapter 3, derivational comparison will simply have no room actually to arise (see especially Frampton and Gutmann (1999, 2002)). Although it is fair to say that global economy conditions of the type explored in Chomsky (1993) and other early minimalist writings turned out to be a 'false start', it was a useful false start, and forced linguists to think of better principles with the same effects (see e.g. Collins 1997, Brody 2003).[4] Levine (2002: 328) notes that in other sciences "optimization" effects ... are by-products of specific properties', but fails to note that this is precisely what recent research within minimalism has highlighted.

Finally, Newmeyer in the passage just quoted also cast doubt on phase-based computations (see Chomsky 2000a and much subsequent work) as another instance of optimal design. Phase is just a different implementation of the notion of cycle. And I grant that the identity of the relevant 'phases' (cycles) retains a certain stipulative character at this point.[5] But again I should point out that phases are but one specific proposal to capture various locality phenomena that pervade narrow syntax. Not all practitioners of the minimalist program have adopted the model of derivation by phase advocated by Chomsky (2000a, 2001, 2004a). In addition, those researchers who adopt phase-based computations are aware of this current arbitrary character of phases, and have tried to remedy this by extending the notion of phase to all phrases (see e.g. Epstein 2004, Epstein and Seely 2002, 2006, Bošković 2005, Fox and Pesetsky 2005). Such a development, much like the gradual abandonment of explicit economy principles in favor of principles that result in economy effects, is a significant achievement of the minimalist program, a result that should reinforce the intuition behind the minimalist thesis, and not one to be taken as a lack of continuity in minimalist theorizing.

[4] A development that is not recorded in the critiques of Lappin et al. (2000a, 2000b, 2001), Jackendoff and Pinker (2005), and Seuren (2004), among others, who remain focused on long-abandoned global economy considerations.

[5] Boeckx and Grohmann (forthcoming) acknowledge this problem, and point out that phases are not unlike 'bounding nodes' or 'barriers' in earlier models of grammar such as Chomsky (1973) and (1986b).

The points made in Newmeyer's review are characteristic of all the critiques leveled at minimalism. They all appear to boil down to (i) a consistent misunderstanding of the success of the P&P model, which renders the attempt to move beyond explanatory adequacy legitimate, as discussed in Chapter 2, and (ii) a consistent misunderstanding of the fact that minimalism is a program.

5.3 Specific minimalist analyses

Having pointed out common mistakes in the evaluation of minimalist hypotheses, let me now turn to some significant, albeit healthily controversial, results coming from the minimalist literature. Whenever possible I will focus on some specific proposals that revolve around the three core ingredients of the program presented in Chapter 3: virtual conceptual necessity, computational efficiency/ economy, and symmetry.

5.3.1 *Control*

I will start with an illustration of the advantages of eliminating syntax-internal levels of representation, specifically Deep Structure, as dictated by virtual conceptual necessity considerations. The first empirical domain I will discuss is control, a construction introduced in Chapter 3 to refer to situations where a noun phrase participates in the events expressed by different verbs. (For example, in *John tried to kiss Mary, John* participates in the *try*-event and *kiss*-event.)

Control has played an important role in theoretical debates within the Minimalist Program (see e.g. Hornstein 1999, 2001, 2003, Boeckx and Hornstein 2003b, 2004, forthcoming a, Culicover and Jackendoff 2001, 2005, Landau 2000, 2003, Manzini and Roussou 2000). This is because control implicates notions such as module, theta-role, the Last Resort nature of syntactic operations, movement, binding, Case, etc., all relevant when it comes to finding out what the shape of the language faculty is.

5.3.1.1 *The basic idea*   Traditionally (ever since Rosenbaum (1967)), control has been dealt with as a non-movement relation involving a controller (overt referential noun phrase) and a controllee, an unpronounced element, either identical to the controller or a dedicated empty category called PRO. The main task of syntacticians working on control is to figure out the best way to characterize the distribution and interpretation of the controllee in relation to the controller. Various solutions have been proposed (in terms of government, null case assignment, etc.) in the GB era. I will not attempt to review them here. Instead, I will try to show how minimalism offers a radically different conception of control.

The standard view of control brings with it a whole additional module of the grammar (the Control module whose function it is to determine the controllers of PRO and the interpretation carried by a particular control structure), a theory-internal formative—PRO— with its own idiosyncratic distributional requirements (it occurs in the subject positions of non-finite clauses and this prompts other- wise conceptually and empirically problematic technology, for example Null Case (a special feature making sure PRO is phonetically null; see Chomsky and Lasnik 1993), to track this fact), and a set of grammatical processes (construal rules) *added to the movement processes already assumed to be available*, whose function it is to establish dependencies quite similar to those already afforded by movement.

As explored in Hornstein (1999, 2001), minimalism offers the possibility of a movement theory of control (MTC), which holds that control[6] is a subspecies of movement. In standard cases, then, control approximates familiar instances of raising. Specifically, just as raising takes an element from the (embedded) lexical domain and moves it to the subject position of the finite clause (1), control takes

---

[6] More precisely (for experts), obligatory control (the type of control that requires the controller to be present in the sentence). I ignore the obligatory control/non- obligatory control distinction. For some discussion, see Hornstein (1999, 2001, 2003), Boeckx and Hornstein (2004), and Boeckx et al. (forthcoming).

an element from the (embedded) lexical domain, re-merges it in the (embedding) lexical domain, and finally moves it to the subject position of the finite clause (2). (Unless otherwise noted, the specific labels used in the representations in this chapter are not important.)

(1)   [$_{TP}$ John [$_{VP}$ seemed [to [$_{VP}$ <John> like apples]]]

(2)   [$_{TP}$ John [$_{VP}$ <John> tried [to [$_{VP}$ <John> like apples]]]]
                                        1

The idea that the grammatical processes responsible for these two types of structure are less different than generally believed is *not* novel (see e.g. Bowers 1973). What is different is the conceptual setting of the minimalist program, most importantly the premium now placed on 'simpler' theories that eschew both theory-internal levels (like Deep Structure) or formatives (like PRO) and multiple ways of establishing grammatical dependencies (by either move-ment or construal), that is, features that do not obviously fall within the rubric of virtual conceptual necessity.

One of the most interesting things about MTC, in my view, is the fact that it is a genuine theory. A theory is a set of assumptions that, once adopted, help narrow down analytic options. The MTC does exactly that: it rests on a construct—A-movement—that is well understood, and on the supposition that movement into theta-positions is licit. It is a purely syntactic view of control that leaves little explanatory work for other components of the grammar (or mind) in accounting for the basic properties of control. This may be right or wrong (and it is easy to see what could make it wrong), but it is relatively clear.

MTC rests on the assumption that movement can target thematic positions (positions where theta-roles like 'agent-of', 'patient-of', etc. are licensed). The assumption is needed because in a control structure the moved element bears at least two theta-roles (as opposed to one theta-role in normal raising sentences), one borne by the traditional controller and the other borne by the traditional controllee.

The assumption that movement could go through theta-positions could not be made in the GB era, by definition. In GB, Deep Structure was defined as the level of representation that preceded all transformations and that expressed all thematic relations. In an approach to grammatical architecture like the one explored in the minimalist program, which does not recognize a level of representation like Deep Structure, movement into theta-positions would actually be quite natural. Thus, if in contrast to GB style theories one dispenses with Deep Structure, then it is natural to dispense with the restrictions that Deep Structure brings with it.[7] Of course, one *need* not dispense with the ban on movement into thematic positions if one discards Deep Structure (Chomsky (1995, 2000a), for one, retains the ban in a minimalist setting). But it is certainly a natural thing to consider, and it is an option that allows for different directions within minimalism.

5.3.1.2 *The virtues*   The MTC has several minimalist virtues. From an architectural point of view, as already stated, the MTC gets rid of an odd-looking element (PRO). The MTC does not need special government conditions (unlike the so-called PRO-theorem approach popular in the GB literature), or special features like Null Case to capture the fact that the controllee is not pronounced. The MTC gets rid of an entire GB module (the control module) and opens the door to the elimination of an entire class of rules (construal rules; see Hornstein 2001).

From an explanatory point of view, the MTC genuinely *explains* why PRO is always null at PF: copies left by movement are always null at PF (see below for what minimalism has to say about why this is so). The MTC also *explains* the distribution of PRO; specifically, why PRO occurs in 'porous' contexts (non-finite, temporally dependent clauses, or clauses where the main verb fails to display rich agreement with the subject): these are contexts that facilitate movement (see Boeckx 2003a, 2005a).

The MTC also *explains* the locality of control, specifically, the fact that PRO occurs only in the highest subject position in the complement clause (movement picks the highest element, on

---

    [7] I should add that nothing goes obviously wrong semantically if we assume that the same element occupies various thematic/argument positions. This, in fact, is how variables in logic are generally understood. In short, if movement between thematic positions is deemed possible, we know exactly how to interpret the resulting structure (see Hornstein 2002).

economy grounds), and also the fact that, as Rosenbaum (1970) originally observed, the controller/PRO relation generally obeys the Minimal Distance Principle. That is, PRO must be bound by the closest antecedent. For example, in (3) PRO must be controlled by the object, not the subject.

(3)   John persuaded Mary $PRO_{Mary/*John}$ to go home

The Minimal Distance Principle follows on a movement theory of control if one assumes that movement is governed by Relativized Minimality, a standard assumption. To see this, consider what the derivation of (4) would have to be like were *John* the antecedent of PRO.

(4)   John [$_{VP}$ John persuaded Mary [$_{IP}$ John to [John go home]]]

The copies of *John* mark the history of derivation. Note that in moving from the embedded Spec IP to the matrix Spec VP *John* crosses the intervening DP *Mary*. This move violates minimality and is so barred. Movement in this case did not target the closest available landing site. The only derivation not prohibited by minimality is one in which the DP in Spec IP raises to the next highest potential DP position, in this case the object. The derivation is illustrated in (5).

(5)   John [$_{VP}$ John persuaded Mary [$_{IP}$ Mary to [Mary go home]]]

So, if control is the result of A-movement, the Minimal Distance Principle follows.

The MTC also *explains* the interpretation of PRO. Specifically, as Hornstein (2001: 39–41) has shown in detail, the interpretive restrictions found in (obligatory) control contexts (obligatoriness of a (local) antecedent, ban on split antecedents, etc.) are precisely those we expect if PRO is in fact a copy left by movement.

In sum, MTC answers *why*-questions and provides a unified theory of PRO's distribution and interpretation,[8] while at the same time simplifying the theory as a whole.

---

[8] For experts: the MTC has other virtues, such as those of offering a unified analysis of standard complement and adjunct control constructions, and accounting for so-called 'PRO-gate' effects. I will not go into these here. See Hornstein (2003), Kiguchi (2002), and Boeckx et al. (forthcoming).

5.3.1.3 *The icing on the cake*   In addition to all these theoretical virtues, the MTC has offered the possibility of making sense of the phenomenon of backward control. Although backward control was observed in the 1980s, it resisted an explanation until the MTC was formulated. (One can almost say that the MTC helped linguists 'discover' backward control. Lakatos would say that backward control was a novel fact, the discovery of which indicates that the minimalist program is a progressive, fecund avenue of research.)

Polinsky and Potsdam (2002) offer the most comprehensive analysis of backward control in Tsez, a language of the Caucasus. (Backward control has also been identified in Malagasy, Brazilian Portuguese, Bezhta, Tsaxur, Kabardian, Adyghe, Korean, Japanese, and possibly Jacaltec; see Polinsky 2005 for extensive discussion.) Backward control describes cases in which the controlled PRO is higher in the structure than its antecedent. (Observe that the PRO in (6) necessarily takes *kidba* as its antecedent.)

(6)   PRO   [kidba ziya bisra] yoqsi
              girl   cow feed   began
         'The girl began to feed the cow'

Polinsky and Potsdam show in detail that the standard theories of control that involve PRO cannot easily account for backward control constructions. In fact, in most versions of the standard approach, backward control should simply be impossible. This sort of control configuration should lead, among other difficulties, to a configuration that linguists call a principle C violation: a configuration where the antecedent of the pronoun is contained within the phrase that the pronoun is merged with (antecedents are supposed to merge with a phrase that contains the pronouns they precede, not the other way around; cf. *He likes John*, which cannot mean that *John likes himself*).

By contrast, backward control can be accounted for in a movement-based theory in a rather straightforward manner, viz. as a case where the copy left by movement is pronounced, which (as we will see in the next section) is not unique to control. Backward control is one of these empirical bonuses that minimalists dream of: a phenomenon which does not fit in any framework except the one that appears more desirable from a purely conceptual point of view.

5.3.2 *Copies and linearization*

As already discussed at various points in the present work, the minimalist program sees movement as a copying operation, and not the creation of a trace, as was the case in the Extended Standard Theory and GB eras. As soon as movement is seen as copying, we expect to see several copies of an item once that item is moved. At a minimum (in case of short distance movement) we expect two copies to surface: one in the moved position and the other in the 'base' (i.e. original) position. By and large, however, only one copy (typically, the highest one in the tree) is pronounced. That is, although in the syntax *John will leave* looks like (7), at the PF-interface, one copy undergoes deletion (8).

(7)   [John will [leave John]]
(8)   [John will [leave ~~John~~]]

A minimalist would like to have an answer to why this deletion is almost always forced. GB theorists didn't have to address this question, but not for any deep reason. Traces were phonetically null, by stipulation. Stipulating copy deletion does not constitute an explanation, of course.

Nunes (1999, 2004) addresses this problem in great detail, and proposes what I take to be a deep answer.

5.3.2.1 *The basic solution*   Nunes (1999) claims that multiple copies of an item typically cannot be pronounced, due to Kayne's (1994) Linear Correspondence Axiom (LCA) (linearization procedure). The basic idea (which is all we need for present purposes) is this: according to Kayne's LCA, X precedes every element that it 'c-commands' (an element X is said to c-command an element Y if the phrase X is merged with Y). Put differently, c-command relations map onto precedence relations. Now, consider a movement situation, where an element X has moved, leaving a copy behind. A configuration like (9) obtains.

(9)   X ... Y ... X

Such a configuration is problematic for the LCA. In fact, it leads to a contradiction: X should precede Y because X c-commands Y, but at the same time Y should precede X because Y c-commands X (the copy left behind by movement). We thus face a conflicting linear-ization requirement. Nunes proposes that copy deletion (non-linearization of copies) is forced upon us to solve that conflict: deletion removes the need to linearize all copies of X, and therefore dissolves the paradox just discussed. In this way Nunes derives the fact that typically only one copy of a given element is pronounced. (Nunes (1999, 2004) proposes an answer to why typically the highest copy is pronounced, but I will not go into the details of his proposal, as it would require me to introduce technicalities that are not necessary for current purposes.) Nunes' answer to why copies undergo deletion is deep, because it appeals to a requirement (linearization) that is an inescapable demand on the grammar.

5.3.2.2 Wh-*copying* One of the interesting aspects of Nunes' proposal is that it can be extended to cases where more than one copy of an element is pronounced. One such case is the *wh*-copying construction.

Several languages, such as Afrikaans, German, Romani, Frisian, and Child English, readily allow cases of long-distance questions like (10)–(12), in which the *wh*-phrase appears to be repeated in an intermediate position. Consider the following cases, from Romani (10), Frisian (11), and Child English (12):

(10) kas   misline   kas o Demiri dikhla
      whom you-think who the Demir saw
      'Who do you think Demir saw?'
(11) wer   tinke jo   wer't   Jan wennet
      where think you   where-that Jan lives
      'Where do you think that Jan lives?'
(12) Who do you think who the cat chased?

Wh-copying languages show an interesting restriction on the construc-tion, which, as Nunes (1999, 2004) has shown, naturally follows from his analysis. For example, in Child English, as Thornton (1995) has documented, when long-distance *wh*-movement involves a morpho-logically complex *wh*-phrase, *wh*-copying is less frequent. When it happens, the *wh*-copy that is pronounced in the intermediate landing site is a 'short' *wh*-form, as shown in (13).

(13)   Which mouse do you think who/*which mouse the cat chased?

The same is true in Romani. Witness (19).

(14)   save chave mislinea *save chave/kas   o   Demiri dikhla
         which boy think-you which boy/whom the Demir saw
         'Which boy do you think that Demir saw?'

To account for these instances of multiple-copy pronunciation in a way consistent with the LCA, Nunes appeals to a suggestion made in Chomsky (1995) to the effect that the LCA cannot look into complex heads (basically, Chomsky proposes, *contra* Kayne 1994, that the LCA cannot look into the (morphological) structure of words). Specifically, Nunes proposes that more than one copy of an item can be pronounced if these copies restructure and merge with heads (so as to get 'hidden' from the LCA).

Nunes' conjecture about when multiple-copy pronunciation will be possible predicts exactly this pattern. If, in order to get pronounced, additional copies have to be 'hidden' inside complex heads, we expect the *wh*-copy to be 'minimal', or morphologically simple (head-like), for this morphological conflation to be possible. That means that when a 'big' *wh*-phrase is copied, for an additional copy to be pronounced, the copy must be reduced (*which man* → *who*) in the morphological component (an operation akin to 'impoverishment' in a framework like Distributed Morphology; see Halle (1997)).

Nunes' analysis of the *wh*-copying construction provides strong evidence for the copy theory of movement, a theory which, to repeat, provides the greatest amount of symmetry (conservation of lexical resources) in the context of displacement (/movement).[9]

---

[9] Another strong piece of evidence of the same kind for the copy-theory of movement comes from the multiple pronunciation of verbs in Verb(Phrase)-fronting constructions, as first discussed in Koopman (1984), for languages like Vata, and revisited in Nunes (2004); see also Abels (2001) on Russian, Jo (2004) on Korean, Landau (forthcoming) on Hebrew, Kandybowicz (2005) on Nupe, and Hiraiwa (2005) on Buli.

(i)   *Li* a   *li*-da   zue   saka   (Vata)
        eat we eat-past yesterday rice
        'We really did eat rice yesterday'

5.3.3 *A constraint on multiple* wh-*fronting*

Equally strong evidence for the best/minimal theory of the mechanics of movement comes from multiple *wh*-fronting constructions in Slavic, a phenomenon that has attracted a lot of attention in the minimalist literature (see Bošković 1998, 2002b, Richards 2001, Pesetsky 2000a, and Boeckx and Grohmann 2003).[10] In certain Slavic languages, such as Bulgarian or Serbo-Croatian, there is a syntactic requirement that all *wh*-words in a multiple question must front, as in (15). Failure to do so yields unacceptability. All examples are from Serbo-Croatian, from Bošković (2002b: 355).

(15)   a. Ko sta kupuje?
            who what buys
        b. *Ko kupuje sta?
            who buys what
            'Who buys what?'

As originally noted by Wayles Browne (personal communication to Željko Bošković), the requirement that all *wh*-words front appears to be relaxed just in case the fronting would yield a sequence of

---

[10] Although the basic typology of multiple *wh*-fronting was achieved in the mid-1980s in work by Rudin (1988), the theoretical interest in multiple *wh*-fronting really grew out of a series of studies in the mid-1990s that adopted a minimalist approach. I can think of at least four reasons why the minimalist program has revived the interest in multiple *wh*-fronting. Unfortunately, I can only list them here, as space limitations prevent me from providing a detailed discussion of some of the analyses proposed.

First, the latent (anti-)superiority effects discovered by Bošković (1998, 1999) has helped sharpen the economy flavor of Chomsky's original condition, in addition to offering a privileged perspective on the driving force for *wh*-movement. In addition, the investigation of multiple specifiers (Koizumi 1995, Richards 1997, 2001) appear to be tailored for multiple *wh*-fronting. Second, the data from multiple *wh*-languages have helped locate precisely the locus of featural illegitimacy giving rise to multiple *wh*-fronting, and the parameter(s) that underlie the phenomenon. Third, recent developments in the study of the structure of the left periphery of the clause (more generally, the 'cartographic' approach to clausal architecture; see Rizzi 1997) should also connect in interesting ways with the general phenomenon of multiple *wh*-fronting. This is particularly clear in cases where it has been claimed that discourse notions such as focus are the driving force for multiple (*wh*-) movement. Fourth, multiple *wh*-fronting should prove an ideal testing ground regarding the nature of constraints on the interfaces, as discussed in the main text.

homophonous *wh*-words, as in (16), a phenomenon known as haplology. In exactly this environment, the lower *wh*-word is pronounced in its base position.

(16) a. *šta šta uslovljava?
      what what conditions
   b. šta uslovljava šta?
      what conditions what
      'What conditions what?'   (Bošković 2002b: 364)

Bošković (2001, 2002b) provides a straightforward account of this relaxation using the copy theory of movement. Let me reproduce the gist of his account. In a normal clause, all *wh*-words front, creating copies. In the normal case, all but the highest of these copies are deleted as in (17a), yielding the surface order in (15b). The interpretation of (16) as a regular multiple question indicates that the representation which feeds semantic interpretation is that arising from movement. Post-syntactically, then, where highest-copy pronunciation is expected, a morphological anti-homophony filter applies (a natural PF-interface condition), blocking pronunciation of the highest copy and automatically triggering the pronunciation of the next lower copy, as in (17b).

(17) a. Ko šta kupuje ~~šta~~   [Normal case—lower copy deleted]
     who what buys what
     'Who buys what?'
   b. šta ~~šta~~ uslovljava šta?   [Anti-homophony—higher copy deleted]
     what what conditions what
     'What conditions what?'

Crucial for this analysis is the observation that in situ *wh*-words in the Slavic languages under consideration are only allowed in case the anti-homophony constraint would be violated. Bošković's explanation makes use of a key feature of the minimalist program (the copy theory of movement), which allows one to keep the syntactic requirement of multiple *wh*-fronting maximally simple (front all *wh*-phrases regardless of their phonological shape). The analysis of (16) in terms of (17) is one of the clearest and most concise examples one can give of the conceptual and empirical advantages of a technical instantiation of a central minimalist tenet.

5.3.4 *Successive cyclicity*

In addition to reaping empirical benefits such as backward control, *wh*-copying, and the constraint on multiple *wh*-fronting just discussed, much research within minimalism tries to offer a better understanding of phenomena and generalization that research of the past thirty years has firmly established as empirical data to be accounted for. One such phenomenon is successive cyclic movement.

5.3.4.1 *The basic phenomenon*   There is substantial empirical evidence for the claim that long-distance movement proceeds in short steps, cycle by cycle. For example, Sportiche (1988) has suggested that elements like *all* can be left behind in intermediate steps of movement, acting like footprints, identifying a position targeted by movement (see also McCloskey 2000). (Data in (18) are from standard English; data in (19) come from West Ulster Irish English.)

(18)   a.   All the boys seem to appear to like ice cream
      b.   The boys seem *all* to appear to like ice cream
      c.   The boys seem to appear *all* to like ice cream
      d.   The boys seem to appear to *all* like ice cream
(19)   a.   What *all* did you get for Christmas
      b.   What did you get *all* for Christmas
      c.   What *all* did John say that Peter ate for breakfast
      d.   What did John say that Peter ate *all* for breakfast

The claim that movement proceeds though successive cycles (the successive cyclic movement hypothesis) has been around ever since Chomsky (1973) proposed it. Minimalism would like to understand this feature of the language faculty.

The most principled account of successive cyclicity I know of is Takahashi's (1994) analysis, based on Chomsky and Lasnik's (1993) Minimize Chain Links Principle, which requires that each chain link be as short as possible (see also Manzini 1994, Boeckx 2003a, Bošković 2002a).

A chain is defined as a unit of syntactic computation that groups in a set all the positions that a given element occupies in the course of a derivation—in other words, all the copies of a given element.

Takahashi's core idea is that successive steps are taken due simply to the requirement that steps be local, as a matter of economy. In Takahashi's (1994) terms, each link of a chain must be as short as possible. A useful image to keep in mind here is one where someone attempts to cross a stream or river. No matter how much the person would like to jump to the other side in one go, his physical limitations will impose short steps and the use of stepping stones. The same limitation appears true of long-distance dependencies in natural languages.

5.3.4.2 *A desirable consequence*   There is one side-effect of Takahashi's proposal that until very recently has been underestimated. I wish to bring it to the fore here (see Boeckx 2005b, forthcoming for more technical discussion). As Bošković (1994) originally observed, some condition is needed to prevent the Minimize Chain Links Principle from forcing a phrase in an adjoined position to keep adjoining the same node. By 'looping' on the same node, the moving element would indeed keep chain links as short as possible, but it would not go very far.

Borrowing a key insight of Murasugi and Saito (1995), Bošković (1994) claimed that a chain link must be at least of length 1, where length can be defined in terms of phrasal category. That is, movement must target a position outside the phrase it originates from.

(20)

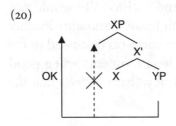

Recently, a growing number of researchers have independently argued for a condition that requires movement to be at least of length 1 (see Bissell-Doggett 2004, Ko 2005, Pesetsky and Torrego 2001, Ishii 1999, Abels 2003, Grohmann 2000, 2003, Kayne 2005, Bobaljik 2003, Boeckx 2005b, forthcoming, Lee 2004, Jeong 2006, Hornstein 2005a, Mayr and Reitbauer 2005, Rizzi and Shlonsky 2005, Ticio 2003). Grohmann (2000, 2003) in particular has argued that movement in natural language is constrained by an Anti-locality condition. The intuition behind Anti-locality is that movement cannot be too short. As Grohmann has noted, Anti-locality is the flip-side of the better-studied locality condition on movement, which rules out cases where movement has been 'too long', crossing a domain (an island) that it wasn't supposed to leave.

Anti-locality is a very nice idea. It adds symmetry to the theory (as just stated, anti-locality is the other side of the locality coin). By blocking movement that would be too short, it eliminates superfluous steps of movement, steps that wouldn't bring the moving element any closer to its ultimate landing site. So, anti-locality can be seen as an economy condition, an expression of the Last Resort condition on movement: if a movement step would be superfluous, it cannot be seen as a last resort operation, hence it is blocked.

The overall picture that emerges about movement is this. Long-distance movement cannot be too long, chain links must be kept short. In particular, a moved element must adjoin to a series of maximal projections on its way to its final landing site (this gives rise to successive cyclicity), *except* the projection it originates from (in that case movement would be too short). Without the minimalist emphasis on the last resort character of movement, and the minimalist desire to understand phenomena like successive cyclicity, such a remarkable symmetry between locality and anti-locality would not have been discovered. What is more, both locality and anti-locality appear to have desirable empirical consequences (as discussed in the papers cited above). I find that it is in these moments when good results conspire, conceptually and empirically, that one feels that the overall program is on the right track.

5.3.5 *Bare phrase structure*

Another example of work trying to offer a better understanding of phenomena and generalization that research of the past thirty years has firmly established as empirical data to be accounted for comes from the domain of phrase structure.

5.3.5.1 *Minimalist phrase structure* Most current views on phrase structure rely on Chomsky's fundamental insights expressed in 'Remarks on Nominalization' (1970). *Remarks* made three basic claims (see Fukui 2001 for detailed overview):

(21) a. Every phrase is 'headed'; i.e. it has an endocentric structure, with the head X projecting to larger phrases.
 b. UG provides the general X-bar schema of the following sort, which governs the mode of projection of a head:
 $XP \rightarrow \ldots X' \ldots$
 $X' \rightarrow \ldots X \ldots$

This gives rise to the now familiar X-bar schema:

(22)

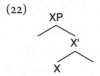

Chomsky (1994) formulated a Bare Phrase Structure theory as part of the minimalist program. In particular, he has argued against a rigid definition of the three juncture types X, X', and XP, and in favor of a more relational definition of them. Chomsky's proposal is best understood in the context of the following question (see Hornstein et al. 2006: ch. 6): how should we conceptualize the difference between X, X', and X''? The 'rigid' way of conceptualizing them would be to claim that they have different intrinsic features, the way, say, Nouns and Verbs have. Alternatively, they may differ in virtue of their relations with elements in their local environment, rather than inherently. On the first interpretation, bar-levels are categorical features; on the second, they are relational properties.

Chomsky (1994) claims that a bare phrase structure theory should treat bar-levels as relational properties.[11] Specifically, the following relations ought to be recognized:

---

[11] Recent work has extended this critique of bar-levels as features to all categorical features. Proponents of Distributed and Parallel Morphologies (see Marantz 1997, Borer 2005) have in effect proposed that lexical categories are label-less roots that acquire labels by combining with functional projections such as *v*, *n*, or *a*, yielding 'VP', 'NP', and 'AP' (for a clear expression of this idea, see Pesetsky and Torrego 2004).

(23)   a. Minimal Projection ($X^{(0)}$)
          A minimal projection is a lexical item selected from the lexicon.
      b. Maximal Projection (X'')
          A maximal projection is a syntactic object that does not project any
          further.
      c. Intermediate Projection (X')
          An intermediate projection is a syntactic object that is neither
          minimal nor maximal.

The relational view on bar-levels immediately eliminates 'spurious' or 'vacuous' projections that were standard under the rigid view. According to the latter, a bare element like *John* invariably projected as in (24).

(24)

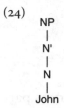

Under the relational view, an element like *John* is ambiguously minimal and maximal, its status being determined only once it enters into a syntactic relation, since bar-levels are reflexes of the position of a syntactic item with respect to others. Put differently, under a relational or 'bare' phrase structure theory, there can be no non-branching projections, since projection is a reflex of syntactic combinations, and those by definition necessitate two elements.[12]

Chomsky (2001: 7, 14) also assumes that there is no categorial feature. Baker (2003) may be read as providing further arguments against categorial features, as he tries to define [+N(oun)] and [+V(erb)] in terms of other features like [bearing the ability to refer] and [licensing a specifier], respectively. His definition of [Adjective] as neither nominal nor verbal amounts to saying that there is no categorial feature for adjective at all. Since adjectives form a major category type, it is a small step to claiming that there are no categorial features at all.

[12] Since non-branching projections were crucial for Kayne's (1994) formulation of the LCA above, Chomsky had to amend Kayne's framework. I will not discuss these technical matters here. See Hornstein et al. (2006: ch. 6).

5.2.5.2 *Empirical payoff* As Chomsky (1995: 398) observes, a potentially undesirable consequence of this assumption is that there would be no phrase-structural difference between the two types of intransitive verb that have been the focus of much research since Perlmutter's (1978) unaccusative hypothesis (see also Burzio 1986): unergatives like *laugh* and unaccusatives like *leave*. Traditionally, these were assigned the structures in (25a) and (25b), respectively:

(25)

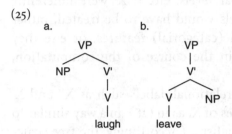

Under a relational view, both reduce to (26).

(26)

```
        VP
       /  \
      V    NP
```

Chomsky, however, notes that what appears to be a defect of bare phrase structure in this case may actually be a virtue, since as Hale and Keyser (1993, 2002) have extensively argued, unergatives appear to be a sub-species of transitive predicates (with an unpronounced object). Indeed, verbs like *laugh* can sometimes appear with an object (*John laughed a very good laugh*), which is never the case with unaccusative intransitives like *leave* (**John left a very quick leave*). Accordingly, it may be desirable to represent one species of intransitive verbs (unergatives) as regular transitives, as in (27):

(27)

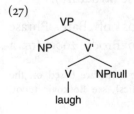

In sum, what appeared to be a problematic loss of distinction turns out to be an empirical pay-off.[13] Aside from its empirical virtues, a bare phrase structure has the advantage of conforming to the general minimalist guideline, given in the Inclusiveness Condition.

As already noted, the idea behind Inclusiveness is that narrow syntax should not create properties that are arguably not part of lexical items such as indices, bar levels, etc. If X′ were inherently different from, say, X″, bar-levels would have to be treated, rather implausibly, as intrinsic lexical (categorial) features, or else they would have to be introduced in the course of the computation, violating Inclusiveness.

By contrast, if bar-levels are relational, labels such as X″ and X′ can be treated essentially as copies of X, as in (28), in a way similar to how traces are treated in minimalism. (Accordingly, the tree structures used in this book so far are not consistent with Bare Phrase Structure assumptions, but no point I made based on them hinges on this.)

(28)

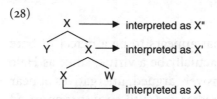

Notice that as soon as projection is seen as a copying operation, as it should be under a Bare Phrase Structure theory, the core properties of syntax reduce to Merge and Copy, with the latter subsuming traditional processes like Project and Move (see Boeckx 2005a for a systematic exploration of the parallelism between Project and Move under the copy theory of movement/Bare Phrase Structure).

5.3.5.3 Head-'movement'

An additional bonus of Bare Phrase Structure, defended in Harley (2003) (see also Brody 2000 for a

[13] For an additional argument in favor of Bare Phrase Structure based on the behavior of phonetically reduced pronouns (so-called clitics), see Bošković (2001, 2002c).

similar insight, formulated in a slightly different framework) is the fact that viewing labels as 'projected' copies of a head allows for a nice solution to the 'head-movement' conundrum within the minimalist program.

At the beginning of the 1990s, head-to-head movement of the type we used to illustrate the parametric difference between English and French in Chapter 2 was a landmark of the theory. Allowing heads to move to other heads offered a wonderful account of how verbs came to be inflected. Steps of movement added one inflectional piece at a time to the stem or bare form of the verb. The extremely elegant account of the relative positioning of verbs, auxiliaries, negation, tense, etc. in countless languages (see Cinque 1999) was a paradigm case for Principles and Parameters theory, included in essentially every modern syntax textbook.

Nonetheless, getting the structural mechanism of head-movement to interact properly with the other fundamentals of the theory was a headache even within X-bar theory (see Rizzi 1990: 117, n. 19, and Chomsky and Lasnik 1993: 47ff.) When Chomsky 1994 introduced Bare Phrase Structure as a fundamental part of the minimalist program, it became essentially impossible to represent head movement in a technically satisfactory way. Without going into the technicalities (see Harley 2003 and Brody 2000), we can say that moving a head to another head should, according to the relation definition of head in Bare Phrase Structure, turn one of them into a non-head. But this newly created non-head would then be different from the copy left behind by movement (a head). The situation clashed with Chomsky's (1995: 321) principle of Uniformity, which forced copies of one element to be uniformly head or non-head.

This technical difficulty, as well as some empirical obstacles, led Chomsky to conclude that head movement is essentially phonological—not part of the syntactic component at all (see Boeckx and Stjepanović 2001 for an independent argument in favor of Chomsky's position). Chomsky provided no suggestions as to how this conclusion could be implemented in such a way as to retain the empirical generalizations that made a syntactic treatment of head movement so attractive in the first place.

Harley (2003) argues that if labels are copies of heads, head-movement can be seen as the monotonic, strictly local (morpho-logical) conflation of a head $Y°$ and the label of its complement XP (= copy of the head $X°$).

(29)

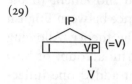

Under this view, no actual head-to-head displacement is required in the syntax, and head-movement can indeed be seen as a mor-phophonological operation. Once again, the adoption of a minim-alist guideline such as Inclusiveness/Symmetry (the copy theory of movement extended to phrasal labels) leads to conceptual and empirical refinements.

5.3.6 *Sluicing*

As is perfectly natural in the case of any conceptual shift, novel approaches lead to the revival of earlier analyses. Once put in a different theoretical setting, such analyses enjoy a new lease of plausibility. One striking example of this theoretical fact is the re-examination of Ross's (1969) seminal work on sluicing.[14]

---

[14] Another idea minimalist explorations helped revive is the notion of lexical decomposition (see Hale and Keyser 1993, 2002, Marantz 2000, and references therein). The revival of lexical decomposition has been seen by some (see Pullum 1996, Seuren 2004) as an unacknowledged return to generative semantics, a return that some take to be an indication of the conceptual bankruptcy of the generative enterprise as a whole. Such an interpretation fails to appreciate the fact that lexical decomposition in the current theory takes place within a different conceptual and theoretical setting, and does not signify a return to the model of grammar explored within generative semantics (for one thing, Generative Semantics wanted to capture all aspects of semantics at a single level of representation, Deep Structure, whereas current models that assume lexical decomposition only use it to account for lexico-conceptual regularities). I will refrain from developing the remarks just made in the main text, as lexical decompos-ition/distributed morphology does not strike me as an essential part of minimalism

Sluicing refers to examples like those in (30), which is ellipsis of the sentential complement to an interrogative complementizer hosting a *wh*-phrase:

(30)   a. Jack bought something, but I don't know what.
     b. A: Someone called. B: Really? Who?
     c. Beth was there, but you'll never guess who else.
     d. Jack called, but I don't know {when/how/why/where from}.
     e. Sally's out hunting—guess what!
     f. A car is parked on the lawn—find out whose.

Ross's take on sluicing was to assume that the *wh*-phrase has been moved from its usual position to the beginning of the clause. That movement operation is then followed by phonetic deletion of the rest of the clause (including the position from which *wh*-movement originated).

(31)

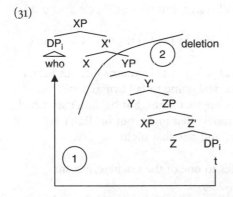

Recently, Lasnik (2001a, 2005a) and especially Merchant (2001) have offered a reappraisal of Ross's analysis in a minimalist setting.

5.3.6.1 *Island repair*   As Ross noted, one of the most puzzling properties of *wh*-movement in sluicing is that it can move *wh*-phrases out of islands. Without sluicing, the sentences sound atrocious.

(see Chomsky 2001: 44, n. 22 for a similar point of view). What is important to note is that there is nothing odd, irrational, or inconsistent about recruiting old tools for new purposes in a different theoretical context. Nature does this all the time. That's what led Jacob to call her a tinkerer.

Examples for the major kinds of syntactic island are given in (32)–(37) (examples taken from Merchant 2001).

(32) a. They want to hire someone who speaks a Balkan language, but I don't remember which.
      b. *They want to hire someone who speaks a Balkan language, but I don't remember which (*Balkan language*) *they want to hire someone* [*who speaks__*].

(33) a. She bought a big car, but I don't know how big.
      b. * She bought a big car, but I don't know how big *she bought* [*a __ car*].

(34) a. A biography of one of the Marx brothers is going to be published this year—guess which!
      b. *A biography of one of the Marx brothers is going to be published this year—Guess which (*Marx brother*) [*a biography of __*] is going to be published this year.

(35) a. It appears that someone will resign, but it's not yet clear who.
      b. *It appears that someone will resign, but it's not yet clear who it appears that will resign
      c. Sally asked if somebody was going to fail Syntax One, but I can't remember who.
      d. *Sally asked if somebody was going to fail Syntax One, but I can't remember who Sally asked if was going to fail Syntax One

(36) a. Bob ate dinner and saw a movie that night, but he didn't say which.
      b. *Bob ate dinner and saw a movie that night, but he didn't say which movie Bob ate dinner and saw that night

(37) *Adjuncts*
      a. Ben will be mad if Abby talks to one of the teachers, but she couldn't remember which.
      b. * Ben will be mad if Abby talks to one of the teachers, but she couldn't remember which (*of the teachers*) *Ben will be mad* [*if she talks to __*].

The situation we are facing is this: *wh*-movement out of islands is impossible, unless that island is not pronounced. One possibility for accounting for the fact that deletion of the island rescues the sentence from ungrammaticality is to posit, as Ross did, that the PF interface cannot parse crossed island nodes. One way of formalizing this, following in essence Chomsky (1972), is to assume that crossed island nodes are marked with some feature PF cannot tolerate, call it *. Ellipsis, of the type found in sluicing, would essentially remove the offending *-feature from the purview of PF, in effect rescuing 'bad' derivations. Lasnik (2001a, 2005a) and Merchant (2001) have proposed exactly that. Notice that under the *-deletion view islands must be construed as entities defined over PF-representations. That is, if correct, the *-deletion view forces us to say that islands are not the result of computational properties of narrow syntax that block the application of rules like *wh*-movement, for *wh*-movement does take place across an 'island.'

At this point sluicing becomes a wonderful tool to investigate the division of labor between the computational system and the kinds of condition that constrain derivations, on the one hand, and the interface systems and the kind of filters they impose on linguistic representations, on the other—exactly the type of question that a minimalist is interested in.

5.3.6.2 *Lack of repair* In this context, constraints that sluicing cannot repair are likely to be direct reflexes of properties of the computational system. To date, I know of two such constraints: the ban on preposition-stranding under *wh*-movement found in numerous languages, and superiority (see Merchant 2001 and Boeckx and Lasnik 2006). I will focus on preposition stranding here.

In languages such as English and the Scandinavian languages, which all allow regular *wh*-phrases such as *who* to strand a preposition under *wh*-movement (the (b) sentences in examples (38)–(41)), we also find the possibility of omitting a preposition that corresponds to a preposition marking the correlate of the *wh*-phrase in the antecedent to the deleted clause, as shown in the (a) sentences in (38)–(41) (examples taken from Merchant 2001).

(38) English
      a. Peter was talking with someone, but I don't know (with) who
      b. Who was he talking with?
(39) Swedish
      a. Peter har talat med någon; jag vet inte (med) vem
         Peter has talked with someone I know not with who
      b. Vem har Peter talat med?

(40) Norwegian
    a. Per har snakket med noen, men jeg vet ikke (med) hvem
       Per has talked with someone but I know not with who
    b. Hvem har Per snakket med?

In other Germanic languages, such as German, which generally do not allow preposition-stranding under *wh*-movement, retention of the preposition under sluicing is obligatory:

(41) German
    a. Anna hat mit jemandem gesprochen, aber ich weiß nicht, *(mit) wem
       Anna has with someone spoken but I know not with who
    b. * Wem hat sie mit gesprochen?

As Merchant (2001) has extensively documented, this correlation is not limited to the Germanic family, of course, though Germanic does almost seem to have a monopoly on productive preposition-stranding under *wh*-movement. In a number of non-Germanic languages (viz. Greek, Russian, Czech, Slovene, Serbo-Croatian, Bulgarian, French, Catalan, Spanish, Italian, Persian, Hindi, Hebrew, Arabic, and Basque), we find this correlation as well: they allow preposition-stranding neither in non-elliptical *wh*-questions nor under sluicing.

The correlation just illustrated finds its most natural explanation in the theory of sluicing that takes it to consist of the usual operation of *wh*-movement, subject to the usual language-particular constraints, followed by deletion of the portion of the clause out of which extraction has taken place.

Whatever prevents preposition-stranding in the languages just mentioned cannot be repaired by sluicing. A natural way of making sense of this is to take the ban on preposition-stranding to constrain syntactic derivations: derivations that would violate the ban on preposition-stranding cannot even take place, hence cannot be repaired by ellipsis. Abels (2003) has proposed that the ban on preposition-stranding is a reflex of anti-locality, combined with Chomsky's (2000a) theory of computation by phase. For present purposes, I will simplify Abels' account, and simply posit that in languages banning preposition-stranding Prepositional Phrases (PPs) have a special requirement that forces any extraction out of them to proceed through SpecPP. This ban conflicts with the requirement that movement must at least cross a full phrasal category, as it would require the complement of P to move through SpecPP. The conflict is solved if no preposition-stranding takes place, and the preposition is pied-piped under *wh*-movement. By contrast, in languages like English, which allow preposition-stranding, prepositions are complex expressions that consist of two projections: PP, and pP, say, as schematized in (42).

(42) $[_{pP} p^{\circ} [_{PP} P^{\circ}]]$

Suppose that in those languages the requirement that forces any extraction out of 'prepositional phrases' to proceed through a specifier position actually holds of pP, not PP. This time, the movement-through-spec requirement will not conflict with anti-locality, since the targeted specifier position does not belong to the same projection from which movement originates. Hence, preposition stranding is possible.

If the discussion is on the right track, the sluicing data reviewed here offers rather compelling evidence for the claim that conditions like anti-locality constrain computations in narrow syntax. The sluicing data show that consequences of economy conditions like 'form the shortest chain possible' (anti-locality) are so deeply embedded within the computational system of human language that interface operations like ellipsis cannot lessen their effects on linguistic representations. Such conclusions show how a new framework can turn an old observation into a powerful theoretical microscope.

5.3.7 *Parasitic gaps*

In this section, I would like to discuss some elements of Nunes' (1995, 2004) analysis of a phenomenon discovered in the GB era known as parasitic gap. Nunes' analysis offers some of the most compelling pieces of evidence for embracing minimalism, and—a rare fact that should not go unnoticed—it does so at both the conceptual and empirical levels.

As its starting point Nunes takes very seriously two of the core ideas underlying the minimalist program. One is the idea that displacement ought to be decomposed into the more primitive operations, Copy and Merge, as discussed at various points in this book.

On this view, a syntactic element to be moved is first copied by the computational system. Then the copy of the item is merged at the root of the tree in its appropriate place. The second idea, Form Chain, first proposed by Chomsky and Lasnik (1993), is the notion that chains are real representational syntactic objects, not just coding devices (see e.g. Brody 1995, 2003, Boeckx 2003a, 2005a, Rizzi 2006). As we saw earlier in this chapter, Form Chain allowed Takahashi to recognize the workings of economy in long-distance movement cases. On this view the derivational history of an element and its copies is irrelevant for the purposes of chain formation. As long as all of the members of a chain are in the proper relationship (c-command, uniformity, etc.) at the end of a derivation, the chain is legitimate.

Nunes' idea, arguably one of the most original ideas in the entire minimalist program so far, was to recognize that the adoption of Copy, Merge, and Form Chain as independent operations predicts that certain types of derivation that are not possible under more traditional notions of movement and chain formation should in fact be expected. In particular, there is nothing in the system to prevent movement relations between parallel, unconnected derivations as long as the conditions of chain formation are met at the end of the derivation. Such kinds of movement are what Nunes refers to as 'sideward movement'.[15] It is worth emphasizing that sideward movement is not a phenomenon that results from adding extra conditions and properties to the computational system. Rather, it is the result of taking the primitive operations of the system seriously and exploiting their full potential.

As Nunes demonstrates, sideward movement allows for a most elegant and novel account of problematic constructions such as parasitic gap constructions like (43).

(43)   Which book did you file __ [after reading __]

[15] Uriagereka (1998) calls it paracyclic movement; Bobaljik and Brown (1997) inter-arboreal movement. Citko 2005 and Svenonius (2005) call it parallel merge.

The most salient properties of parasitic gap constructions have been widely discussed in the GB era. First, (43) involves extraction from a so-called (optional) adjunct clause typically introduced by *after, before, because,* which is generally disallowed across languages. Second, this extraction is allowed only if the argument gap ('main gap') is also present:

(44)   *Which book did you file the report [after reading __]

Familiar questions arise at this point. First, why should extraction out of adjuncts ever be allowed? And second, why should it be allowed dependent upon extraction of an argument from the main clause? Nunes points out that the Copy theory of movement and Form Chain offer a natural answer that does not resort to construction-specific rules or ad hoc solutions (which previous accounts of parasitic gaps always had to resort to).

The gist of Nunes' proposal is as follows. First, the derivation of the adjunct in (43) takes place as in (45):

(45)   [after reading [which book]]

In parallel, the main clause is being constructed. The key point is that instead of merging a distinct argument as the object of the verb *file,* a copy of [*which book*] in (45) is created and merged as the argument in the main clause. The two parallel structures in (46) obtain (subscript *c* indicates copies):

(46)   a. [after reading [which book]$_c$]
       b. [you file [which book]$_c$]

Finally, *wh*-movement of the object of the verb *file* takes place and the two structures in (46) are merged. The final derivation is as in (47). It is at this point that Form Chain applies, constructing two independent chains. One is between the highest copy of *which book* and the copy of *which book* in the matrix Verb Phrase. The other chain is between the highest copy of *which book* and the copy in the adjunct clause (*after reading ___*).

(47)   [[which book]$_c$ did you file [which book]$_c$ [after reading [which book]$_c$]]

At the end of the derivation, only the highest copy of each chain is pronounced (for reasons discussed in section 5.3.2); the two lower copies are not, yielding the familiar double-gap construction.

Given the novelty, explanatory depth, empirical coverage,[16] and elegance of Nunes' analysis, the sideward movement analysis of parasitic gaps could act as a poster-child for minimalism.

5.3.8 *Existential constructions*

As a final illustration of minimalist principles at work, I would like briefly to review and comment on the various analyses of existential constructions like *There is a man in the room* within the Principles and Parameters approach.

For reasons that I detail shortly, existential constructions are 'simple'. They enable one to abstract away from the complexities involved in many other constructions found in natural language, and get to core syntactic operations for which a natural (read: minimalist) account is rather successful. So existential constructions not only will allow me to illustrate part of the empirical coverage of the minimalist program, but also, and perhaps mainly, reveal how research is conducted along minimalist desiderata. (These considerations go a long way toward explaining why existential constructions have occupied center stage in minimalism; see e.g. Chomsky (1995: ch. 4, 2000a, 2001).)

5.3.8.1 *Expletive replacement*   From a minimalist point of view, the presence of expletive *there* in (48) is puzzling.

---

[16] For experts: Nunes (2004) extends his sideward movement analysis of parasitic gaps to a host of constructions such as Across-the-Board Movement (see also Hornstein and Nunes 2002), Head-movement, and Feature-movement. In recent years, in light of Nunes' successful analysis, sideward movement has been extended to Obligatory Control in adjuncts (Hornstein 2001), anaphoric relations (see Kiguchi 2002 on PRO-gate, Boeckx 2003c on donkey anaphora, Boeckx and Hornstein 2005 on binominal *each*, Kayne 2002 on variable binding, Nunes and Uriagereka 2000 on extraction domains), and various other phenomena (see Rodrigues 2004 and Ferreira 2004 on null subjects inside adjuncts in Brazilian Portuguese, Agbayani and Zoerner 2004 on (pseudo-)gapping, and Cheng 2005 on verb-copying in Chinese).

(48)　There is a man in the garden.

The element itself does not have any obvious semantics; thus, Legibility Conditions on the LF side of the grammar under virtual conceptual necessity (the Principle of Full Interpretation) dictate that it be eliminated. To address this matter, Chomsky (1986a), building upon Burzio (1986), proposes that the associate-indefinite NP (a man in (49a)) literally replaces the expletive *there* in the covert component, as schematized in (49b).

(49)　a.　there is a man in the garden: S(urface)-Structure
　　　b.　[A man]$_i$ is [t_i in the garden]: LF-expletive replacement

The Expletive Replacement Hypothesis straightforwardly accounts for the somewhat unusual agreement configuration that obtains in existential constructions. Descriptively, the finite verb in existential constructions agrees with the associate NP to its right, not with the element in the typical subject position, which appears to be the more common agreement configuration in English (and many other languages). Contrast (50a) and (50b).

(50)　a.　There are/*is three men in the car.
　　　b.　They are/*is one and the same element.

The common agreement configuration obtains in existential constructions, albeit at LF. Aside from the agreement issue, Expletive Replacement Hypothesis is also able to explain why expletives must have associate NPs (if there is no associate, the expletive cannot be replaced, and the sentence will be LF-deviant: *There is in the garden*). More generally, this approach provides an explanation for why expletive–associate pairings pattern with movement chains, as in the contrast in (51):

(51)　a.　* A man seems [*t* has been arrested]
　　　　　(cf. 'A man seems to have been arrested')
　　　b.　* There seems [a man has been arrested]
　　　　　(cf. 'There seems to have been a man arrested')

Any version of the Last Resort Condition can account for the ungrammaticality of (51a), as *a man* receives case in the lower clause;

by essentially the same reasoning, this type of explanation should also account for the parallel (51b) involving an expletive–associate pair, if indeed the associate NP undergoes movement at LF.

But, despite its obvious virtues, the replacement analysis was criticized as soon as it was proposed. As was quickly noted, the Expletive Replacement Hypothesis makes wrong predictions. For example, as the data in (53) show, the associate NP in existential constructions is incapable of licensing reciprocals like *each other* that it does not c-command in overt syntax.

(52)   Some applicants$_i$ seem to each other$_i$ to be eligible for the job.
(53)   *There seem to each other$_i$ to be some applicants$_i$ eligible for the job.

This is unexpected under the Expletive Replacement Hypothesis since, according to the latter, (52) and (53) are the same at LF, the level of representation where semantic relations like *each other* and its antecedent are established.

5.3.8.2 *Feature-movement* Chomsky (1995) proposes a more satisfactory account of the facts, based on a conceptual argument that illustrates the minimalist logic, independent of existential constructions. Chomsky's starting point is the central tenet that movement is forced by Last Resort considerations. More precisely, movement is driven to 'check' features that would otherwise be illegitimate at the interfaces.[17] If so, it is natural to expect that 'the operation Move ... seeks to raise just F[eature]' (Chomsky 1995: 262). We therefore expect under minimalist assumptions that, if possible, the computational component can move just what is needed (features to carry out the checking operation), leaving behind any extra lexical material. This came to be known as the feature-movement (Move-F) hypothesis.[18]

[17] Much work has been devoted to trying to pinpoint the nature of the illegitimacy. No consensus has emerged at this point, so I will not go into this matter here. For valuable discussion, see Brody (1997) and Pesetsky and Torrego (2005).

[18] In (2000a), Chomsky sharpened the Move-F account technically and proposed the operation Agree. Agree amounts to a process of long-distance feature checking (or valuation) with no actual displacement. I will not go into the details of the Agree operation. Nor will I discuss its empirical advantages. For some discussion, see Boeckx (2002, 2006a), Boeckx and Niinuma (2004), Hiraiwa (2005), Rezac (2004), Bejar (2003), and many others.

Relying on the Move-F hypothesis, Chomsky proposes that in existential constructions only the features of the associate NP responsible for agreement move to the finite verb, leaving all phonological and semantic features behind. Movement of these features immediately accounts for the fact that finite agreement in existential constructions is controlled by the feature specification of the associate.

More importantly, as Lasnik 1999 has argued, the Move-F account provides a straightforward explanation for the reciprocal binding facts that were problematic for the Expletive Replacement Hypothesis if one assumes (as seems quite plausible) that more than just features responsible for agreement are needed for binding relations to be established.

The success of the Move-F account of existential constructions invites us to revisit the validity of the Y-model explicitly put forth in Chomsky and Lasnik (1977) and assumed throughout the P&P era and in the first minimalist paper (Chomsky 1993). Under the Expletive Replacement Hypothesis the relevant operation (expletive replacement) took place in a distinct covert component. Move-F opens up the possibility of doing all relevant operations overtly by letting features move (with no ancillary categorical pied-piping) in overt syntax. In other words, it opens up the possibility of dispensing with an entire component of the grammar (the 'Single Output Syntax' explored in various ways by Groat and O'Neil 1996, Bobaljik 1995, Brody 2003, Nissenbaum 2000, Pesetsky 2000a, and Chomsky 2000a, and mentioned in Chapter 3).

Feature movement also allows one to unify all instances of agreement as consisting of feature movement accompanied by an extra operation (known as 'pied-piping') that raises the rest of the element from which feature movement took place, as shown in (54).

(54)

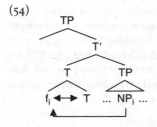

Feature valuation in existential constructions

(55)

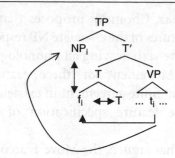

Feature valuation followed by displacement of an entire category

This unification of feature valuation strategies is highly desirable, as it allows for a greater symmetry in syntax, a major goal of minimalist research.[19]

5.4 Conclusion

In this chapter, I have examined how various phenomena like control, successive cyclic movement, and expletive constructions are treated within minimalism. I have tried to highlight two important ideas in each of these brief 'case studies'. First, I have shown how these specific phenomena interact with the three essences of the minimalist program that I have identified in Chapter 3 (virtual conceptual necessity, economy, and symmetry). Second, I have indicated how these three minimalist guidelines force certain analyses that lead to interesting empirical consequences/side effects.

---

[19] Of course, the unification under discussion raises the question of why pied-piping is required in some but not in all cases. Several authors (in particular, Lasnik 2001b, 2003b) have argued that this question is a way of making another question precise: what is the nature of the requirement that finite clauses (those clauses containing agreeing finite verbs) must have subjects, a requirement known as the Extended Projection Principle (EPP)? Ever since its introduction into the P&P approach (Chomsky 1981), the EPP has lacked an explanation. At this point I do not find the details of these proposals fully satisfactory, but it seems to me that Move-F has made the EPP problem more precise in concentrating our attention on the nature of pied-piping.

In many of these cases, I find it hard even to imagine an alternative approach to these phenomena. For empirically oriented researchers, such cases should offer a rather strong argument in favor of minimalism.

But I do not want to give the reader the impression that minimalism is anything near complete. In this sense, I agree with Lasnik (1999: 6, 2002: 436) that 'there is not yet anything close to a Minimalist theory of language'. However, I also want to stress that the case studies I have chosen do not exhaust the range of interesting minimalist analyses proposed in recent years. For example, I have said nothing about how minimalism provides us with the tools for a better understanding of why islands should emerge within derivations (see Uriagereka 1999, 2002, Nunes and Uriagereka 2000, Merchant 2001, Boeckx 2003a, Starke 2001, Abels 2003, Stepanov 2001, Rizzi 2006, Rizzi and Shlonsky 2005), and how the syntax ought to map to the interfaces (see Fox 2000, Nissenbaum 2000, Chierchia 2004, Pietroski 2005 (on the syntax–semantics interface) and Wagner 2005, Dobashi 2003, and Kahnemuyipour 2004 (on the syntax–phonology interface)). I have merely hinted in footnotes at the fact that the program leads to a questioning of poorly understood principles, such as the requirement that finite clauses must have subjects in English and many other languages (the so-called Extended Projection Principle (EPP)), which has resulted in refined hypotheses about the nature of Case and Agreement (see Alexiadou and Anagnostopoulou 1998, 2001, Boeckx 2003b, Bošković 2002a, Castillo, Drury, and Grohmann 1998, Epstein and Seely 1999, Holmberg 2000, Martin 1999, Roberts 2005, Roberts and Roussou 2002, Uriagereka forthcoming). Central P&P concepts like c-command (Epstein 1999, Hornstein 2005a) and projection (Collins 2002, Seely 2006, Hornstein 2005b, Boeckx 2005a, Koster 2003, Fukui 2005, Chametzky 2000) have also been subject to minimalist critique, not documented here. At the very least, all these attempts will lead us to determine the boundaries of optimal properties of grammar, telling us just how much language can be considered optimal, and thus to what extent other properties of this natural phenomenon have to be justified in currently unintelligible ways. In my view, minimalism is particularly significant not so much because it provides us with a set of interesting analyses of the sort just seen, but more importantly because it provides us with the *possibility* of such analyses.

6

The Minimalist Seduction

Language is no different from other objects in nature. There are many ways of studying it. Some see it in the words of Travis (1981: 1): 'weird and wonderful, the storehouse of unimaginable complexities and surprises, to be discerned very closely.' Others try to determine how fairly simple laws may give rise to such apparent complexity. Both approaches, and the countless possibilities in between, are legitimate and worth pursuing. But in systems like the language faculty, which appears so complex, the search for simplicity is not often the first one that comes to mind, even in the minds of well-trained scientists. This is why each little corner of simplicity has to be patiently investigated, cultivated, and cherished. It is to be treated as precious because it may open the door to greater simplicity.

The physicist Victor Weisskopf (1965) once distinguished between 'intensive' and 'extensive' research in science. 'Intensive research', said Weisskopf (p. 25), 'goes for the fundamental laws' while 'extensive research goes for the explanation of phenomena in terms of known fundamental laws'. He makes the point that 'there is always much less intensive research going on than extensive. Once new fundamental laws are discovered, a large and ever increasing activity begins in order to apply the discoveries to hitherto unexplained phenomena.'

This is certainly true in linguistics. Minimalism is arguably the first genuinely intensive research program in the field. I have tried in this book to outline the basic tenets of this research program, and argued that it makes sense to pursue it, on historical, philosophical, biological, and even narrowly linguistic empirical grounds.

It seems to me that failing to address the questions that minimalism asks would amount to introducing the kind of 'methodological dualism' that Chomsky has forcefully argued against for fifty years. If language is a natural object, the study of language should share the premise of natural sciences, physics included. There, one 'must start with reductionism' (Anderson 1972: 394). It is for the same reason that I think minimalism should be an integral part of linguistic sciences.

I think it is fair to say that, in linguistics, the results gathered during the GB era—the first phase of the P&P model—represent the (by nature, tentative) sum of core principles discovered by linguists. The P&P model in its GB guise led to an unprecedented explosion of extensive research in linguistics. The minimalist program is an attempt to counterbalance the amount of extensive research with intensive research. If the general outlook, the basic generative enterprise, is adopted, the worthiness of minimalism cannot be questioned. The possibility that the program may be premature is no excuse for failing to pursue it (see the papers collected in Hook 2002 for interesting reflections on prematurity in science).

For a long time linguistic principles had been tested against the range of variation found across languages. In the early 1990s Chomsky urged us to 'take the other end of the stick', as it were, and see whether the principles discovered, kept constant, could be derived from deeper principles. Consider Pollock's influential (1989) claim that morphemes like Tense and Agreement are to be treated like nouns and verbs, and as such ought to fit the X-bar projection schema discussed in Chapter 3. Pollock's article gave rise to a huge literature on so-called functional projections, with ever finer-grained structures, impressive empirical coverage, etc. Virtually every morpheme was granted a regular X-bar status. This research trend, which is now standardly referred to as the syntactic cartography project (see Rizzi 1997, Cinque 1999, Julien 2002, and many others), has detected the presence of no fewer than fifty functional projections that are supposed to constitute the structural core of sentences. Perhaps a hundred such projections will become a conservative estimate in the very near future (see Kayne 2005). But there comes a time when one wants to ponder the meaning of functional projections—not so much how many there are, but whether they fall into distinct classes, how they combine with one another, etc. These are minimalist questions, and sooner or later the urge for such questions is strong, and the drive to answer them is natural if one takes language to be an object of the world. I find this (minimalist) drive irresistible, and the prospects it offers extremely seductive.

Minimalist questions are hard, and answers are very tentative. We have to admit that many answers will be imprecise, and that it will be hard to provide concrete details immediately. Discussing the nature of minimalism, Gugielmo Cinque, a leader in the field, notes (2002: 193):

Minimalism is very demanding as an approach, more taxing, in the sense that it is a more highly theoretical approach to the study of language than GB. Minimalism is much more intransigent—in the good sense—with respect to methodology: the standard is very high. ... Minimalism certainly has a more forbidding appearance from the outside, certainly for people who are used to thinking of language as something that is close to our everyday image of language, with real sentences and so on. ... You can still do work at different levels. Some people will continue to try to contribute both empirically and theoretically, other people will be more inclined to do pure theoretical work, while others still will do descriptive work but already at a level of abstraction that is useful for theoreticians. The big difference with GB is that in minimalism, for most of us, it will be very hard to work at various levels at the same time, in particular doing descriptive and theoretical work at the same time. Most of us will have to choose, though it is not clear whether that is good. When you can combine both, like in GB, then, in moments of theoretical non-inspiration, you can always fall back on descriptive work and gathering and organizing data, which is very useful. But if you only work at the theoretical level, there is no falling back. In times of theoretical non-inspiration, there may be nothing.

We do not know in advance which of the various instantiations of the minimalist program will prove correct. In the same way that the US Supreme Court once defined pornography, we will only know what it is when we see it. We may discover that language is not an optimally designed system at all, or that it has pockets of optimality, or even that it shows pervasive signs of 'inner perfection'. There is no

way to tell in advance. One should always bear in mind the possibility, raised by Descartes, that 'we do not have intelligence enough'.
The minimalist vision may be right in principle, but the facts known
to us lead us to ask the wrong questions, just as when Kepler was
trying to deduce why there were only six planets (while in fact, there
are (and were) many more in terms of Platonic geometry), or when
Einstein tried to unify the two physical forces known to him
(whereas there are four forces, and there may be more dimensions
in the world than Einstein was willing to consider.) As Weinberg
(1993: 163–4) notes, when Kepler tried to explain the planetary orbits
using Platonic solids, the idea of applying symmetry considerations
was the right idea, but Kepler was applying it to the wrong problem.

As Wolfenstein (2003: 5002) concludes from his review of Kepler's
attempts, 'the lesson from Kepler is not that we must refrain from
asking what seem to be fundamental questions; the lesson is that we
cannot know whether there is any simple answer or where it
may come from.' The only way to find out is by carrying out the
program. As Einstein once said, 'If we knew already what it is, we
wouldn't call it research.'

As I discussed in Chapter 4, the construction of simple theories
along Galilean ideals is no easy task. And results will often be hard to
quantify because, as Weinberg (1993: 134) notes in the context of his
discussion of beautiful theories, 'simplicity is part of what I mean by
beauty, but it is a simplicity of ideas, not simplicity of a mechanical
sort that can be measured by counting equations or symbols'. As
J. K. Galbraith said, 'There is no absolute standard of beauty. That is
precisely what makes its pursuit so interesting.'

It seems to me that the results already gathered under the rubric
of the minimalist program, some of which I reviewed in Chapter 5,
give us grounds for optimism. Whatever the outcome, as Chomsky
(1995: 233–4) notes,

[t]he Minimalist Program ... has a certain therapeutic value. It is all too easy
to succumb to the temptation to offer a purported explanation for some
phenomenon on the basis of assumptions that are of roughly the order of
complexity of what is to be explained ... Minimalist demands at least have the

merit of ... sharpening the question of whether we have a genuine explanation of a problem in other terms.

This is the very least we can expect from pursuing the minimalist program. I hope that I have given the reader a sense that we can reasonably expect more.

Glossary

A-over-A principle Principle that dictates that if a given syntactic rule potentially targets either A or B, and B is contained in A, A should be targeted.

Example: in forming questions, front the question word (A) that contains the other question word (B):

Example:

  (i)   John saw (pictures (of Mary))

  (ii)   which pictures of who did John see ____

  (iii)   *who did you see which pictures of ____

[*key reference*: Chomsky 1964]

Binding Theory Theory that regulates the distribution of referentially dependent elements such as anaphors (*himself, herself*) and pronouns (*him/her*). Binding Theory contains three conditions. *Condition A* requires that the antecedent of an anaphor be in the same clause as the anaphor (*John likes himself*; **John thinks that Mary likes himself*). *Condition B* prohibits that the antecedent of a pronoun be in the same clause as the pronoun ('*John said that Mary likes him*' can mean that *him* refers back to *John*. This cannot be the case in '*Mary thinks that John likes him*.'). *Condition C* prohibits that a pronoun or an anaphor be higher in the structure than their antecedent ('*She likes Mary*' cannot mean that Mary likes herself).

[*key reference*: Chomsky 1981]

Burzio's Generalization Hypothesis that only verbs that express agency, volition, or cause can assign accusative case.

[*key reference*: Burzio 1986]

Case Filter Requirement that all nouns that relate to a verb and express notions like *agent-of, patient-of* bear some case (nominative, accusative, etc.).

[*key reference*: Chomsky 1981]

C-command An element X is said to c-command an element Y if the syntactic unit that X combines with contains Y.

[*key reference*: Epstein 1999]

Chain Unit of syntactic computation that groups in a set all the grammatical relations that a given element is involved in. For example, *who* in *Who is leaving?* is the *agent* of the action expressed by the verb, is the element that triggers *agreement* on the auxiliary verb, and is the *interrogative* word. Syntacticians assume that no element can express multiple relations in a single position. If an element A relates to several other elements B, C, and D in the structure, element A must occupy three different positions (in the vicinity of B, C, and D, respectively). A chain keeps a record of all the positions occupied by a given element within a structure.

[*key reference*: Chomsky 1981]

Control Syntactic construction where an element participates in the events expressed by different verbs. For example, in *John tried to kiss Mary*, *John* participates in the *try*-event and *kiss*-event.

[*key reference*: Rosenbaum 1967]

Copy Operation that duplicates an element A to allow A in several positions in a given syntactic structure.

[*key reference*: Chomsky 1993]

Cyclicity Hypothesis that syntactic computations are divided into domains of applicability ('cycles') which stand in a subset–superset relation with one another, such that a given syntactic process A can no longer apply in a domain D if D is already contained in a larger domain D'.

[*key reference*: Chomsky 1973]

Deep Structure Stage in the syntactic computation at which all (and only) participant-in-an-event relations like *agent-of*, *patient-of*, etc. are expressed.

[*key reference*: Chomsky 1981]

Derivation Conception of syntactic computation that crucially involves strict ordering/timing of syntactic processes/rules.

[*key reference*: Chomsky 1957]

Expletive Pleonastic, non-referential elements like *it* or *there* in sentences like *It is raining* or *There is somebody here.*

[*key reference*: Chomsky 1986a]

Empty Category Syntactic element that is not pronounced.

[*key reference*: Chomsky 1981]

Empty Category Principle (ECP) Condition that requires that a phonetically null element must be syntactically licensed either by being in the vicinity of a verb or by being close enough to an antecedent.

[*key reference*: Chomsky 1986b]

Extended Projection Principle (EPP) Requirement that clauses with a finite verb contain a subject.

[*key reference*: Chomsky 1981]

Extension Condition (a.k.a No Tampering Condition) Requirement that displacement of a syntactic element always target a higher position in the structure (i.e. expand the syntactic structure upward).

[*key reference*: Chomsky 1993]

Feature Minimal unit of syntactic computation; a word is typically seen a collection of phonetic, semantic, and syntactic features (i.e. properties).

[*key reference*: Chomsky 1995]

Finite-State Machine Computational models consisting of (i) an initial state, (ii) a finite number of states, (iii) a specification of transition from one state to another, (iv) a specification of a (finite number of) symbol(s) to be 'printed' when a particular transition obtains, and (v) a final state.

[*key reference*: Chomsky 1957]

Form Chain Syntactic process that links all the positions occupied by a given element in the course of syntactic computation, and groups them into a set that can then act as a unit of computation.

[*key reference*: Chomsky and Lasnik 1993]

Head Necessary and most important element in a syntactic group (*phrase*).

[*key reference*: Chomsky 1970]

Head-movement Displacement of the head of a phrase (necessary and most important element in a syntactic group) to another head-position.

[*key reference*: Pollock 1989]

Inclusiveness Restriction of syntactic computation that forbids syntax from adding or removing properties to lexical items in the course of a derivation.

[*key reference*: Chomsky 1995]

Index Device that codes the relation between a referentially dependent element (anaphor, pronoun, etc.) and its antecedent.

[*key reference*: Chomsky 1981]

Interface Point of contact between syntax and language-external mental systems such as the articulatory-perceptual system ('sound' or 'sign') and the conceptual-intensional systems ('meaning').

[*key reference*: Chomsky 1993]

Island Domain that once formed becomes inaccessible to subsequent syntactic computation.

[*key reference*: Ross 1967]

Last Resort Requirement that syntactic processes not apply blindly, but be driven to satisfy a given property of grammar that would not otherwise be satisfied without the application of such syntactic processes.

[*key reference*: Chomsky 1993]

Level of adequacy Benchmark to measure the success of a linguistic analysis. Standard descriptions distinguish between *observational adequacy* (accurate representation of linguistic data); *descriptive adequacy* (accurate description of a speaker's competence/knowledge of language), and *explanatory adequacy* (accurate construction of a language acquisition model).

[*key reference*: Chomsky 1965]

Level of representation Stage in a syntactic computation at which certain grammatical conditions must be met. Some levels of representation are referred to as *interface levels* when they establish a point of contact between syntax and other mental organs.

[*key reference*: Chomsky 1955]

Linear Correspondence Axiom (LCA) Specific mechanism used to convert a syntactic structure onto a linear string by assuming a one-to-one mapping between asymmetric c-command relations within syntax and asymmetric linear order, such that if A c-commands B (i.e. A syntactically combines with X which contains B), A precedes B.

[*key reference*: Kayne 1994]

Linearization Process by which syntactic structures are converted into a linear string, as required by the sensorimotor systems.

[*key reference*: Kayne 1994]

Locality Area of syntactic theory that focuses on the lower bound and upper bound imposed by universal grammar on movement of elements, and on the distance that may separate two elements that enter into a syntactic relation.

[*key reference*: Chomsky 1973]

Logical Form Stage in a syntactic derivation which connects syntax and the conceptual-intentional ('thought') systems; i.e. stage at which semantic interpretation takes place. Stage by which linguistically meaningful relations must be established.

[*key reference*: Chomsky 1993]

Merge Basic structure-building mechanism. Merge takes two elements A and B and forms a two-membered set labeled C. C can then be merged with another element. Merge is said to be *external* if A and B are previously unconnected elements. Merge is said to be *internal* if A combines with B and B contains D with which A had previously combined. Merge is said to be *parallel* if A merges with both B and D at a point in the derivation when B and D are not connected with one another.

[*key reference*: Chomsky 1993]

Minimal Binding Requirement Condition that demands that a variable receives its value from its closest antecedent, where closeness is defined over syntactic (hierarchical) structure.

[*key reference*: Aoun and Li 1990]

Minimality (Relativized) Condition that states that A and B can be related syntactically if and only if there is no C such that C is of the same syntactic category as A and B, and C combines with an element D that contains B.

[*key reference*: Rizzi 1990]

Minimize Chain Links Principle Principle that demands that the distance between the various positions occupied by a given element A during the course of a syntactic derivation be kept to a minimum.

[*key reference*: Chomsky and Lasnik 1993]

Module Subsystem of the grammar that ensures that some natural class of syntactic conditions is met (e.g. all conditions pertaining to case assignment), and ignores all other requirements of the grammar. Modules interact to yield what traditional grammars call constructions.

[*key reference*: Chomsky 1981]

Multiple dominance Situation where an element B is contained within two distinct domains A and C, which are not connected to one another.

[*key reference*: Gärtner 2001]

Parameter Open value in the statement of a principle. Source of variation across languages, and choice point for children acquiring languages.

[*key reference*: Chomsky 1981]

Parasitic gap Construction where a typically illicit configuration (movement across a domain that cannot be moved out of) is made licit of the moved element also appears to move from a domain out of which movement is licit.

Example:

(i)   *what did John file the book without reading ____

(ii) what did John file ____ without reading ____

[*key reference*: Chomsky 1986b]

Phase Recent term for *cycle*. Phases are domains of applicability which stand in a subset-superset relation with one another, such that a given syntactic process A cannot apply in a domain D if D is contained in a larger domain D′. Phases are restricted to certain syntactic categories, and they constitute points at which the syntax interfaces with the sound/sign and 'thought' systems.

[*key reference*: Chomsky 2000a]

Phonetic Form Point of contact between syntax and the sound/sign systems.

[*key reference*: Chomsky 1993]

Phrase Structure Standard term for hierarchical organization of syntactic elements.

[*key reference*: Chomsky 1957]

Phrase Structure Grammar Grammatical representation that correctly captures the set of basic syntactic relations including discontinuous dependencies that stand in a subset–superset (containment) relation.

[*key reference*: Chomsky 1957]

Poverty of Stimulus Refers to the fact that the linguistic data available to the child are not enough to infer the mature linguistic knowledge of an adult.

[*key reference*: Chomsky 1965]

Principles and Parameters (P&P) Approach to language variation and acquisition that takes Universal Grammar to consist of a complex of invariable principles with open values. In the course of language acquisition the child sets the parameters according to her input language, which assigns a value to the respective principles.

[*key reference*: Chomsky 1981]

Projection Operation which labels the set formed by the combination of two elements A and B by repeating or copying A or B, thereby designating one element as the container of the other.

[*key reference*: Chomsky 1994]

PRO-theorem Principle that regulates in which position a given element that relates to events expressed by different verbs cannot be pronounced.

[*key reference*: Chomsky 1981]

Reconstruction Situations where an element is interpreted in a position distinct from where it is pronounced; i.e. a position that the element occupied before movement. Within minimalism, reconstruction is taken to be the interpretation of a copy of a moved element.

[*key reference*: Chomsky 1993]

Representation Outcome of a syntactic derivation that can be subject so specific grammatical conditions; structure created by the application of syntactic rules.

[*key reference*: Chomsky 1970]

Sideward movement Displacement of an element B from a domain A to a domain C at a point where A and B are not connected to one another.

[*key reference*: Nunes 2004]

Single-output syntax Model of syntax where no syntactic operation applies after syntactic information is sent to the sensorimotor ('sound') systems.

[*key reference*: Groat and O'Neil 1996]

Sluicing Construction where the interrogative word is the only word pronounced in an interrogative clause (the rest of the clause is deleted and its content recovered from the preceding sentence in discourse.)

Example: John bought something, but I don't know what [meaning: 'I don't know what John bought']

[*key reference*: Ross 1969]

Spell-Out Point in the syntactic derivation at which syntactic information is transferred to the sound and meaning interfaces.

[*key reference*: Chomsky 1993]

Successive Cyclic Movement Hypothesis that long-distance dependencies are composed of shorter dependencies that are established within larger and larger syntactic domains, and ultimately combine into one.

[*key reference*: Chomsky 1973]

Superiority Condition that states that if a transformation can be applied to more than one constituent, it must be applied to the superior one, i.e. the one that is structurally higher in a given syntactic representation.

[*key reference*: Chomsky 1973]

Surface Structure Stage in a syntactic derivation at which syntactic information is transferred for purposes of pronunciation, and at which certain syntactic requirements must be met.

[*key reference*: Chomsky 1965]

Theta-role Event-relation such as 'agent-of', 'patient-of', 'goal-of'.

[*key reference*: Chomsky 1981]

Trace Coding device recording the position of an element A before movement of A.

[*key reference*: Chomsky 1973]

Transformation Grammatical device to capture crossing discontinuous dependencies (displacement; long-distance dependencies).

[*key reference*: Chomsky 1957]

Uniformity condition Condition that requires that the relations established by a given element A must be ordered in a specific way and form a natural class (i.e. be of a specific type).

[*key reference*: Chomsky 1993]

Virtual conceptual necessity Condition that demands that no assumption be built into the grammar that falls outside what current knowledge deems unavoidable.

[*key reference*: Chomsky 1993]

X-bar theory Theory of syntactic representation that assumes that all categories in all languages can be analyzed as units called *phrases* that are made of a key element (*head*) which gives the phrase its name, and modifiers, which can modify the head itself (in which case the modifier is called the *complement*), or the sub-unit formed by the head and the complement (in which case the modifier is called the *specifier*).

[*key reference*: Chomsky 1970]

Y-model Standard model of grammar that contains four levels of representation (Deep Sttructure, Surface Structure, Phonetic Form, and Logical Form)

[*key reference*: Chomsky 1981]

References

Abels, Klaus (2001). The predicate cleft construction in Russian. In *Proceedings of Formal Approaches to Slavic Linguistics* 9, 1–19. Bloomington, Ind: Michigan Slavic Publications.

—— (2003). Successive-cyclicity, anti-locality, and adposition stranding. Doctoral dissertation, University of Connecticut.

Adger, David (1994). Functional heads and interpretation. Doctoral dissertation, Edinburgh University.

—— (2003). *Core Syntax.* Oxford: Oxford University Press.

Agbayani, Brian, and Ed Zoerner (2004). Gapping, pseudogapping and sideward movement. *Studia Linguistica* 58: 185–211.

Alexiadou, Artemis, and Elena Anagnostopoulou (1998). Parametrizing AGR. *Natural Language and Linguistic Theory* 16: 491–539.

—— and —— (2001). The subject-in-situ generalization and the role of Case in driving computations. *Linguistic Inquiry* 32: 193–231.

Amundson, Ron (1998). Typology reconsidered: two doctrines on the history of evolutionary biology. *Biology and Philosophy* 13: 153–77.

Anagnostopoulou, Elena (2003). *The Syntax of Ditransitives.* Berlin: Mouton de Gruyter.

Anderson, Philip W. (1972). More is different. *Science* 177: 393–6.

Anderson, Stephen, and David Lightfoot (2002). *The Language Organ.* Cambridge: Cambridge University Press.

Aoun, Joseph, and Elabbas Benmamoun (1998). Minimality, reconstruction, and PF-movement. *Linguistic Inquiry* 29: 569–97.

—— Lina Choueiri, and Norbert Hornstein (2001). Resumption, movement, and derivational economy. *Linguistic Inquiry* 32: 371–403.

—— and Y.-H. Audrey Li (1990). Minimal disjointedness. *Linguistics* 28: 189–203.

—— and Audrey Li (1993). *Syntax of Scope.* Cambridge, Mass.: MIT Press.

—— and —— (2003). *Essays on the Representational and Derivational Nature of Grammar: The Diversity of Wh-Constructions.* Cambridge, Mass.: MIT Press.

Baker, Mark (1996). *The Polysynthesis Parameter.* Oxford: Oxford University Press.

Baker, Mark (2001). *The Atoms of Language: The Mind's Hidden Rules of Grammar*. New York: Basic Books.

—— (2003). *Lexical Categories: Verbs, Nouns, and Adjectives*. Cambridge: Cambridge University Press.

—— (2005). The creative aspect of language use and nonbiological nativism. MS, Rutgers University.

—— and Chris Collins (2006). Linkers and the internal structure of vP. *Natural Language and Linguistic Theory* 24: 307–54.

Ball, Philip (1999). *The Self-Made Tapestry*. Oxford: Oxford University Press.

Barkow, Jerome H., Leda Cosmides, and John Tooby, eds. (1992). *The Adapted Mind*. Oxford: Oxford University Press.

Bejar, Susana (2003). Phi-syntax. Doctoral dissertation, University of Toronto.

Belletti, Adriana, and Luigi Rizzi (2002). Introduction. In Chomsky (2002: 1–44).

Bellugi, Ursula, and Marie I. St. George, eds. (2001). *Journey from Cognition to Brain to Gene: Perspectives on Williams Syndrome*. Cambridge, Mass.: MIT Press.

Berlin, Isaiah (1953). *The Hedgehog and the Fox*. New York: Simon & Schuster.

Berwick, Robert (1998). Language evolution and the minimalist program: the origins of syntax. In J. Hurford, M. Studdert-Kennedy, and C. Knight (eds.), *Approaches to the Evolution of Language*. Cambridge: Cambridge University Press, 320–40.

—— and Samuel D. Epstein (1995). On the convergence of minimalist syntax and categorical grammar. In *Algebraic Methods in Language Processing 1995: Proceedings of the Twente Workshop on Language Technology 10, joint with the first algebraic methodology and software technology workshop on Language Processing*. Universiteit Twente, Enschede.

—— and Amy Weinberg (1984). *The Grammatical Basis of Linguistic Performance*. Cambridge, Mass.: MIT Press.

Bhatt, Rajesh (2002). The raising analysis of relative clauses: evidence from adjectival modification. *Natural Language Semantics* 10: 43–90.

Bissell-Doggett, Teal (2004). All things unequal: locality in movement. Doctoral dissertation, MIT.

Bobaljik, Jonathan D (1995). Morphosyntax: the syntax of verbal inflection. Doctoral dissertation, MIT.

—— (2002). A-chains at the PF-interface: copies and 'covert' movement. *Natural Language and Linguistic Theory* 20: 197–267.

—— (2003). Realizing Germanic inflection: why morphology doesn't drive syntax. *Journal of Comparative Germanic Linguistics* 6: 129–67.

—— and Samuel Brown (1997). Interarboreal operations: Head-movement and the Extension requirement. *Linguistic Inquiry* 28: 345–56.

Boeckx, Cedric (2002). Agree vs. Attract: a relativized minimality solution to a proper Binding problem. In A. Alexiadou (ed.), *Formal Approaches to Universals*. Amsterdam: Benjamins, 41–64.

—— (2003a). *Islands and Chains*. Amsterdam: Benjamins.

—— (2003b). Case matters and minimalist concerns. *Harvard Working Papers in Linguistics* 8: 159–97.

—— (2003c). Indirect binding. *Syntax* 6: 213–36.

—— (2004). Long-distance agreement in Hindi: some theoretical implications. *Studia Linguistica* 58: 23–36.

—— (2005a). Bare syntax. MS, Harvard University.

—— (2005b). Notes on Bounding. MS, Harvard University.

—— (forthcoming). *Understanding Minimalist Syntax: Lessons from locality in long-distance dependencies*. Oxford: Blackwell.

—— (2006b). Case and agreement. MS, Harvard University.

—— (2006c). Review of Postal (2003b). *Journal of Linguistics* 42: 216–21.

—— (2006a). Honorification as agreement. *Natural Language and Linguistic Theory* 24: 385–98.

—— and Kleanthes K. Grohmann, eds. (2003). *Multiple Wh-Fronting*. Amsterdam: Benjamins.

—— and —— (forthcoming). Putting phases in perspective. *Syntax*.

—— and Norbert Hornstein (2003a). The varying aims of linguistic theory. MS, University of Maryland.

—— and —— (2003b). Reply to *Control Is Not Movement*. *Linguistic Inquiry* 34: 269–80.

—— and —— (2004). Movement under control. *Linguistic Inquiry* 35: 431–52.

—— and —— (2005). The status of D-structure: the case of binominal *each*. *Syntax* 8: 23–43.

—— and —— (forthcoming a). Control in Icelandic and theories of control. *Linguistic Inquiry*.

—— and —— (forthcoming b). The varying aims of linguistic theory. In J. Franck and J. Brickmont, (eds.), *Cahier Chomsky*. Paris: L'Herne.

Boeckx, Cedric, and Norbert Hornstein (forthcoming c). Superiority, recon-struction, and islands. In R. Freidin, C. Otero, and M.-L. Zubizarreta (eds.), *Foundational Issues in Linguistic Theory.* Cambridge, Mass.: MIT Press.

—— Norbert Hornstein, and Jairo Nunes (forthcoming). Control as movement. MS, Harvard University, University of Maryland, and University of Sao Paulo.

—— and Howard Lasnik (2006). Intervention and repair. *Linguistic Inquiry* 37: 150–5.

—— and Fumikazu Niinuma (2004). Conditions on agreement in Japan-ese. *Natural Language and Linguistic Theory* 22: 453–80.

—— and Massimo Piattelli-Palmarini (2005). Language as a natural object, linguistics as a natural science. *Linguistic Review* 22: 351–70.

—— and Sandra Stjepanović (2001). Heading toward PF. *Linguistic Inquiry* 32: 345–55.

Borer, Hagit (1984). *Parametric Syntax: Case Studies in Semitic and Romance Languages.* Dordrecht: Foris.

—— (2005). *Structuring Sense.* 2 vols. Oxford: Oxford University Press.

Bošković, Željko (1994). D-structure, θ-criterion, and movement into θ-positions. *Linguistic Analysis* 24: 247–86.

—— (1998). Multiple wh-fronting and economy of derivation. In *Proceedings of the West Coast Conference on Formal Linguistics 16,* 49–63. Stanford, Calif.: CSLI.

—— (1999). On multiple feature checking: multiple wh-fronting and multiple head-movement. In S. D. Epstein and N. Hornstein (eds.), *Working Minimalism.* Cambridge, Mass.: MIT Press, 159–87.

—— (2001). *On the Nature of the Syntax–Phonology Interface: Cliticization and Related Phenomena.* London: Elsevier.

—— (2002a). A-movement and the EPP. *Syntax* 5: 167–218.

—— (2002b). On multiple wh-fronting. *Linguistic Inquiry* 33: 351–83.

—— (2002c). Clitics as non-branching elements and the Linear Corres-pondence Axiom. *Linguistic Inquiry* 33: 329–40.

—— (2005). On the locality of Move and Agree: eliminating the Activation Condition, Generalized EPP (Strength), and the Phase-Impenetrability Condition. MS, University of Connecticut.

—— and Howard Lasnik (1999). How strict is the cycle? *Linguistic Inquiry* 30: 689–97.

—— and —— eds. (2006). *Minimalist Syntax: The Essential Readings.* Oxford: Blackwell.

Bowers, John (1973). Grammatical relations. Doctoral dissertation, MIT.

Brody, Michael (1995). *Lexico-logical Form: A Radically Minimalist Theory.* Cambridge, Mass.: MIT Press.

—— (1997). Perfect chains. In L. Haegeman (ed.), *Elements of Grammar.* Dordrecht: Kluwer, 139–67.

—— (1998a). Projection and phrase structure. *Linguistic Inquiry* 29: 367–98.

—— (1998b). The minimalist program and a perfect syntax. *Mind and Language* 13: 205–14.

—— (2000). Mirror theory. *Linguistic Inquiry* 31: 29–56.

—— (2003). *Towards an Elegant Syntax.* London: Routledge.

Burtt, Edwin Arthur (1932). *The Metaphysical Foundations of Modern Science.* Mineola, NY: Dover.

Burzio, Luigi (1986). *Italian Syntax: A Government-Binding Approach.* Dordrecht: Reidel.

Butterfield, Herbert (1931). *The Whig Interpretation of History.* London: Bell.

Carey, Susan (forthcoming). *The Origin of Concepts.* Cambridge, Mass.: MIT Press.

Carroll, Sean B (2005). *Endless Forms Most Beautiful.* New York: Norton.

Castillo, Juan Carlos, John Drury, and Kleanthes K. Grohmann (1998). Merge-over-move and the EPP. In *University of Maryland Working Papers in Linguistics 8*, 63–103. University of Maryland, College Park. Repr. in part in Kleanthes Grohmann, Juan Carlos Castillo, and John Drury (1999), 'No more EPP'. In *Proceedings of WCCFL 19*, 153–66. Somerville, Mass.: Cascadilla Press.

Chametzky, Robert (2000). *Phrase Structure.* Oxford: Blackwell.

Changeux, Jean-Pierre (1980). Genetic determinism and epigenesis of the neuronal network: is there a biological compromise between Chomsky and Piaget? In M. Piattelli-Palmarini (ed.), *Language and Learning.* Cambridge, Mass.: Harvard University Press, 184–202.

Cheng, Lisa (2005). Verb copying in Mandarin Chinese. Paper presented at the workshop The Copy Theory of Movement on the PF Side, University of Utrecht, Dec. 2005.

Cherniak, Chris (forthcoming). Innateness and brain-wiring optimization: non-genomic nativism. In A. Zilhao (ed.), *Cognition, Evolution, and Rationality.* Oxford: Blackwell.

—— Zekeria Mokhtarzada, Raul Rodriguez-Esteban, and Kelly Changizi (2004). Global optimization of cerebral cortex layout. *Proceedings of the National Academy of Sciences* 101(4): 1081–6.

Chierchia, Gennaro (2004). Scalar implicatures, polarity phenomena, and the syntax/pragmatics interface. In A. Belletti (ed.), *Structures and Beyond*. Oxford: Oxford University Press, 39–103.

Chomsky, Noam (1951). Morphophonemics of modern Hebrew. MA thesis, University of Pennsylvania. Published 1979, New York: Garland.

—— (1955). The logical structure of linguistic theory. MS, Harvard/MIT. Published in part, 1975, New York: Plenum.

—— (1957). *Syntactic Structures*. The Hague: Mouton.

—— (1959). Review of B. F. Skinner, *Verbal Behavior. Language* 35: 26–58.

—— (1962). Explanatory models in linguistics. In *Logic, Methodology and Philosophy of Science: Proceedings of the 1960 International Congress*, 528–50. Stanford: Stanford University Press,

—— (1964). *Current Issues in Linguistic Theory*. The Hague: Mouton.

—— (1965). *Aspects of the Theory of Syntax*. Cambridge, Mass.: MIT Press.

—— (1968). *Language and Mind*. New York: Harcourt Brace Jovanovich.

—— (1970). Remarks on nominalization. In R. Jacobs and P. Rosenbaum (eds.), *Readings in English Transformational Grammar*. Waltham, Mass.: Blaisdell, 184–221.

—— (1972). Some empirical issues in the theory of transformational grammar. In S. Peters (ed.), *The Goals of Linguistic Theory*. Englewood Cliffs, NJ: Prentice-Hall 63–130.

—— (1973). Conditions on transformations. In S. Anderson and P. Kiparsky (eds.), *A Festschrift for Morris Halle*. New York: Holt, Rinehart, & Winston, 232–86.

—— (1975). *Reflections on Language*. New York: Pantheon.

—— (1980). *Rules and Representations*. New York: Columbia University Press.

—— (1981). *Lectures on Government and Binding*. Dordrecht: Foris.

—— (1982). *The Generative Enterprise*. Dordrecht: Foris.

Chomsky, Noam (1986a). *Knowledge of Language*. New York: Praeger.

—— (1986b). *Barriers*. Cambridge, Mass.: MIT Press.

—— (1991). Some notes on economy of derivation and representation. In R. Freidin (ed.), *Principles and Parameters in Comparative Grammar*. Cambridge, Mass.: MIT Press, 417–454. Repr. in Chomsky (1995: 129–66).

—— (1993). A minimalist program for linguistic theory. In K. Hale and S. J. Keyser (eds.), *The View from Building 20*. Cambridge, Mass.: MIT Press, 1–52.

—— (1994). Bare phrase structure. MIT Occasional Papers in Linguistics 5. Cambridge, Mass.: MIT Working Papers in Linguistics. Repr. in Gert Webelhuth (ed.), *Government and Binding and the Minimalist Program* (Oxford: Blackwell, 1995), 385–439.

—— (1995). *The Minimalist Program.* Cambridge, Mass.: MIT Press.

—— (2000a). Minimalist inquiries: the framework. In R. Martin, D. Michaels, and J. Uriagereka (eds.), *Step by Step.* Cambridge, Mass.: MIT Press, 89–155.

—— (2000b). *New Horizons in the Study of Language and Mind.* Cambridge: Cambridge University Press.

—— (2000c). Linguistics and brain science. In A. Marantz, Y. Miyashita, and W. O'Neil (eds.), *Image, Language, and Brain.* Cambridge, Mass.: MIT Press, 13–28.

—— (2001). Derivation by phase. In M. Kenstowicz (ed.), *Ken Hale: A Life in Language.* Cambridge, Mass.: MIT Press, 1–52.

—— (2002). *On Language and Nature.* Cambridge: Cambridge University Press.

—— (2004a). Beyond explanatory adequacy. In A. Belletti (ed.), *Structures and Beyond.* Oxford: Oxford University Press, 104–31.

—— (2004b). *The Generative Enterprise Reconsidered.* Berlin: Mouton de Gruyter.

—— (2004c). Language and mind: current thoughts on ancient problems. In L. Jenkins (ed.), *Variation and Universals in Biolinguistics.* London: Elsevier, 379–405.

—— (2005). Three factors in language design. *Linguistic Inquiry* 36: 1–22.

—— (forthcoming). On phases. In R. Freidin, C. Otero, and M.-L. Zubizarreta (eds.), *Foundational Issues in Linguistic Theory.* Cambridge, Mass.: MIT Press.

—— and Howard Lasnik (1977). Filters and control. *Linguistic Inquiry* 8: 425–504.

—— and —— (1993). Principles and parameters theory. In J. Jacobs, A. von Stechow, W. Sternefeld, and T. Vennemann (eds.), *Syntax: An International Handbook of Contemporary Research.* Berlin: de Gruyter, 506–69. Repr. in Chomsky (1995: 13–127).

Christiansen, Morten, and Simon Kirby, eds. (2003). *Language Evolution.* Oxford: Oxford University Press.

Cinque, Guglielmo (1999). *Adverbs and Functional Heads.* Oxford: Oxford University Press.

Cinque, Guglielmo (2002). Interview. *Glot International* 6: 190–93.

—— and Richard S. Kayne, eds. (2005). *Handbook of Comparative Syntax.* Oxford: Oxford University Press.

Citko, Barbara (2005). On the nature of merge: external merge, internal merge, and parallel merge. *Linguistic Inquiry* 36: 475–96.

Cohen, I. Bernard (1955). Einstein's last interview. *Scientific American* 193: 68–73. Repr. in A. Robinson (ed.), *Einstein: A Hundred Years of Relativity* (New York: Abrams, 2005), 212–25.

Collins, Chris (1997). *Local Economy.* Cambridge, Mass: MIT Press.

—— (2001). Economy conditions in syntax. In M. Baltin and C. Collins (eds.), *The Handbook of Contemporary Syntactic Theory.* Oxford: Blackwell, 45–61.

—— (2002). Eliminating labels. In S. D. Epstein and T. D. Seely (eds.), *Derivation and Explanation in the Minimalist Program.* Oxford: Blackwell, 42–64.

Cowie, Fiona (1999). *What's Within? Nativism Reconsidered.* Oxford: Oxford University Press.

Crain, Stephen, and Mineharu Nakayama (1987). Structure dependence in grammar formation. *Language* 63: 522–43.

—— and Paul Pietroski (2001). Nature, nurture, and Universal Grammar. *Linguistics and Philosophy* 24: 139–86.

—— and Rosalind Thornton (1998). *Investigations in Universal Grammar.* Cambridge, Mass.: MIT Press.

Crick, Francis (1998). *What Mad Pursuit: A Personal View of Scientific Discovery.* New York: Basic Books.

Culicover, Peter (1997). *Principles and Parameters.* Oxford: Oxford University Press.

—— and Ray Jackendoff (2001). Control is not movement. *Linguistic Inquiry* 32: 493–512.

—— and —— (2005). *Simpler Syntax.* Oxford: Oxford University Press.

Curtiss, Susan (1977). *Genie: A Psycholinguistic Study of a Modern-Day 'Wild Child'.* New York: Academic Press.

Darwin, Charles (1964) [1859]. *On the Origin of Species.* Cambridge, Mass.: Harvard University Press.

—— (1981) [1871]. *The Descent of Man and Selection in Relation to Sex.* Princeton, NJ: Princeton University Press.

Darwin, Sir Francis, ed. (1887). *The Life and Letters of Charles Darwin, Including an Autobiographical Chapter.* 2 vols. New York: Appleton.

Descartes, René (1965) [1637]. *Discourse on Method*. New York: Library of Liberal Arts.

Dirac, Paul (1963). The evolution of the physicist's picture of nature. *Scientific American* 208: 45–53.

—— (1968). Methods in theoretical physics. In *From a Life in Physics: Evening Lectures at the International Center for Theoretical Physics, Trieste, Italy*. A special supplement of the International Atomic Energy Agency Bulletin, Austria. Repr. in Abdus Salam (ed.), *Unification of Fundamental Forces*. Cambridge: Cambridge University Press, 125–43.

Dobashi, Yoshi (2003). Phonological phrasing and syntactic derivation. Doctoral dissertation, Cornell University.

Dyson, Freeman (1982). Manchester and Athens. In D. Curtin (ed.), *The Aesthetic Dimension of Science*. New York: Philosophical Library, 41–62.

Einstein, Albert (1949). Autobiographical notes. In P. A. Schlipp (ed.), *Albert Einstein: Philosopher-Scientist*. La Salle, Ill.: Open Court, 2–94.

—— (1954). *Ideas and Opinions*. New York: Bonanza Books.

—— (1987). *Letters to Solovine*. New York: Philosophical Library.

Emonds, Joseph (1970). Root and structure preserving transformations. Doctoral dissertation, MIT. Published as *A Transformational Approach to English Syntax* (New York: Academic Press, 1976).

—— (1978). The verbal complex V'-V in French. *Linguistic Inquiry* 9: 151–75.

Epstein, Samuel D (1999). Un-principled syntax: the derivation of syntactic relations. In S. D. Epstein and N. Hornstein (eds.), *Working Minimalism*. Cambridge, Mass.: MIT Press, 317–45.

—— (2004). On inter-modular, I-functional explanation. MS, University of Michigan.

—— Erich Groat, Ruriko Kawashima, and Hisatsugu Kitahara (1998). *The Derivation of Syntactic Relations*. Oxford: Oxford University Press.

—— and Norbert Hornstein (1999). Introduction. In S. D. Epstein and N. Hornstein (eds.), *Working Minimalism*. Cambridge, Mass.: MIT, ix–xviii.

—— and T. Daniel Seely (1999). Against the GF-notion 'subject': eliminating the EPP and Successive Cyclic A-movement. MS, Michigan University and Michigan State University.

—— and —— (2002). Rule application as cycles in a level-free syntax. In S. D. Epstein and T. D. Seely (eds.), *Explanation and Derivation in the Minimalist Program*. Oxford: Blackwell, 65–89.

Epstein, Samuel D and T. Daniel Seely (2006). *Derivations in Minimalism*. Cambridge: Cambridge University Press.

Ferreira, Marcelo (2004). Hyperraising and null subjects in Brazilian Portuguese. MS, MIT.

Feyerabend, Paul (1993). *Against Method*, 3rd edn. New York: Verso.

Feynman, Richard (1965a). *The Character of Physical Law*. Cambridge, Mass.: MIT Press.

—— (1965b). *The Feynman Lectures in Physics*. Reading, Mass.: Addison-Wesley.

Fisher, Simon E. (2005). On genes, speech, and language. *New England Journal of Medicine* 353: 1655–7.

Fitch, Tecumseh, Marc Hauser, and Noam Chomsky (2004). The evolution of the language faculty: clarifications and implications. Available at http://wjh.harvard.edu/~mnkylab/publications. Abridged version published 2005 in *Cognition* 97: 179–210.

Fodor, Jerry A (2000). *The Mind Doesn't Work That Way*. Cambridge, Mass.: MIT Press.

—— (2001). Doing without what's within: Fiona Cowie's critique of nativism. *Mind* 110: 99–148.

Fox, Danny (1995). Economy and scope. *Natural Language Semantics* 3: 283–341.

—— (1999). Reconstruction, Binding Theory, and the interpretation of chains. *Linguistic Inquiry* 30: 157–96.

—— (2000). *Economy and Semantic Interpretation*. Cambridge, Mass.: MIT Press/MITWPL.

—— (2002). Antecedent Contained Deletion and the copy theory of movement. *Linguistic Inquiry* 33: 63–96.

—— and David Pesetsky (2005). Cyclic linearization of syntactic structure. *Theoretical Linguistics* 31: 1–45.

Fox-Keller, Evelyn (2002). *Making Sense of Life*. Cambridge, Mass.: Harvard University Press.

Frampton, John, and Sam Gutmann (1999). Cyclic computation, a computationally efficient minimalist syntax. *Syntax* 2: 1–27.

—— and —— (2002). Crash-proof syntax. In S. D. Epstein and T. D. Seely (eds.), *Derivation and Explanation in the Minimalist Program*. Oxford: Blackwell, 90–105.

Freidin, Robert (1992). *Foundations of Generative Grammar*. Cambridge, Mass.: MIT Press.

—— (1999). Cyclicity and minimalism. In S. D. Epstein and N. Hornstein, *Working Minimalism*. Cambridge, Mass.: MIT Press, 95–126.

Freidin, Robert and Jean-Roger Vergnaud (2001). Exquisite connections: some remarks on the evolution of linguistic theory. *Lingua* 111: 639–66.

Fukui, Naoki (1996). On the nature of economy in language. *Cognitive Studies* 3: 51–71.

—— (2001). Phrase structure. In M. Baltin and C. Collins (eds.), *Handbook of Contemporary Syntactic Theory*. Oxford: Blackwell, 374–406.

—— (2005). Embed. MS, Sophia University.

Galilei, Galileo (1960) [1623]. *The Assayer*. Philadelphia: University of Pennsylvania Press.

—— (1962) [1632]. *Dialogue concerning the Two Chief World Systems*. Berkeley: University of California Press.

—— (1974) [1638]. *Two New Sciences*. Toronto: Wall & Thompson.

Gallistel, C. Randy (1990). *The Organization of Learning*. Cambridge, Mass.: MIT Press.

—— (1998). Brains as symbol processors: the case of insect navigation. In S. Sternberg and D. Scarborough (eds.), *Conceptual and Methodological Foundations: An Invitation to Cognitive Science*, 2nd edn., vol. 4. Cambridge, Mass.: MIT Press, 1–51.

—— (2000). The replacement of general-purpose learning models with adaptively specialized learning modules. In M. Gazzaniga (ed.), *The New Cognitive Neuroscience*, 2nd edn. Cambridge, Mass.: MIT Press, 1179–91.

—— (2001). Mental representations, psychology of. In *Encylopedia of the Behavioral and Social Sciences*. New York: Elsevier.

Gallistel, C. Randy (2005). The nature of learning and the functional architecture of the brain. In *Proceedings of the International Congress of Psychology: 2004*. London: Psychology Press.

Gärtner, Hans-Martin (2001). *Generalized Transformations and Beyond: Reflections on Minimalist Syntax*. Berlin: Akademie.

Gazzaniga, Michael (1998). *The Mind's Past*. Berkeley: University of California Press.

Gehring, Walter (1998). *Master Control Genes in Development and Evolution*. New Haven, Conn.: Yale University Press.

Gibbs, W. Wayt (2003). The unseen genome: beyond DNA. *Scientific American* 289: 107–13.

Goodwin, Brian (1994). *How the Leopard Changed its Spots*. Princeton, NJ: Princeton University Press.

Gould, Stephen Jay (1985). Geoffrey and the homeobox. *Natural History* (Nov.): 12–23.

—— (1995). 'What is life' as a problem of history. In M. Murphy and L. O'Neill (eds.), *What's Life: 50 Years After*. Cambridge: Cambridge University Press, 25–40.

—— (2002). *The Structure of Evolutionary Theory*. Cambridge, Mass.: Harvard University Press.

—— (2003). *The Hedgehog, the Fox, and the Magister's Pox*. New York: Three Rivers Press.

—— and Richard Lewontin (1979). The spandrels of San Marco and the Panglossian paradigm: a critique of the adaptationist programme. *Proceedings of the Royal Society of London* B, 205: 581–98.

Greenberg, Joseph, ed. (1966). *Universals of Language*. Cambridge, Mass.: MIT Press.

Greene, Brian (1999). *The Elegant Universe*. New York: Vintage.

Grewal, Shiv, and Danesh Moazed (2003). Heterochromatin and epigenetic control of gene expression. *Science* 301: 798–802.

Groat, Erich, and John O'Neil (1996). Spell-Out at the LF interface. In W. Abraham, S. D. Epstein, H. Thráinsson, and C. J.-W. Zwart (eds.), *Minimal Ideas*. Amsterdam: Benjamins, 113–39.

Grohmann, Kleanthes K. (2000). Prolific domains. Doctoral dissertation, University of Maryland.

—— (2003). *Prolific Peripheries*. Amsterdam: Benjamins.

—— (2005). Review of Seuren (2004). LINGUIST List 16.1890 (19 June 2005).

—— (forthcoming). The road to PF. In E. Agathopoulou, M. Dimitrika-poulkou, and D. Papadopoulou (eds.), *Proceedings of the 17th International Symposium on Theoretical and Applied Linguistics*. Thessaloniki: Aristotle University of Thessaloniki, Department of English.

Guasti, Maria Teresa (2002). *Language Acquisition: The Growth of Grammar*. Cambridge, Mass: MIT Press.

Haegeman, Liliane (1994). *Introduction to Government-Binding Theory*. Oxford: Blackwell.

—— (2005). *Thinking Syntactically*. Oxford: Blackwell.

—— and Jacqueline Guéron (1999). *English Grammar*. Oxford: Blackwell.

Hale, Kenneth (1983). Walpiri and the grammar of non-configurational languages. *Natural Language and Linguistic Theory* 1: 5–47.

—— and Samuel J. Keyser (1993). On argument structure and the lexical expression of syntactic relations. In K. Hale and S. J. Keyser (eds.), *The View from Building 20*. Cambridge, Mass.: MIT Press, 53–110.

—— and —— (2002). *Prolegomena to a Theory of Argument Structure*. Cambridge, Mass.: MIT Press.

Halle, Morris (1997). Distributed morphology: impoverishment and fission. *MIT Working Papers in Linguistics 30*, 425–49. Cambridge, Mass: MITWPL.

Harley, Heidi (2003). Merge, conflation, and head movement: the First Sister Principle revisited. *Proceedings of NELS 34*. University of Massachusetts, Amherst: GLSA.

Harris, Randy Allen (1993). *The Linguistic Wars*. Oxford: Oxford University Press.

Harrison, Ross (1937). Embryology and its relations. *Science* 85: 369–74.

Hauser, Marc D. (2006). *Moral Minds*. New York: Ecco.

—— and Susan Carey (1998). Building a cognitive creature from a set of primitives: evolutionary and development insights. In D. Dellarosa Cummins and C. Allen (eds.), *The Evolution of Mind*. Oxford: Oxford University Press, 51–106.

—— Noam Chomsky, and W. Tecumseh Fitch (2002). The faculty of language: What it is, who has it, and how did it evolve? *Science* 298: 1569–79.

Heck, Fabian, and Gereon Müller (2000). Successive cyclicity, long-distance superiority, and local optimization. In *Proceedings of WCCFL 19*, 218–31. Somerville, Mass.: Cascadilla Press.

Herschel, John (1831). *The Study of Natural Philosophy*. London: Longmans.

—— (1861). *Physical Geography of the Globe*. London: Longmans.

Heycock, Caroline (1994). *Layers of Predication*. New York: Garland.

Hiraiwa, Ken (2005). Dimensions of symmetry in syntax: agreement and clausal architecture. Doctoral dissertation, MIT.

Holmberg, Anders (2000). Scandinavian stylistic fronting: how any category can become an expletive. *Linguistic Inquiry* 31: 445–84.

Holton, Gerald (1973). *Thematic origins of scientific thought: Kepler to Einstein*. Cambridge, Mass.: Harvard University Press.

—— (1998). *Scientific Imagination*. Cambridge, Mass.: Harvard University Press.

't Hooft, Gerard (1997). *In Search of the Ultimate Building Blocks*. Cambridge: Cambridge University Press.

Hook, Hernest (2002). *Prematurity in Scientific Discovery*. Berkeley: University of California Press.

Hornstein, Norbert (1995). *Logical Form*. Oxford: Blackwell.

—— (1999). Control and movement. *Linguistic Inquiry* 30: 69–96.

—— (2001). *Move! A Minimalist Approach to Construal*. Oxford: Blackwell.

—— (2002). A grammatical argument for a Neo-Davidsonian Semantics. In G. Preyer and G. Peters (eds.), *Logical Form and Language*. Oxford: Oxford University Press, 345–64.

—— (2003). On control. In R. Hendrick (ed.), *Minimalist Syntax*. Oxford: Blackwell, 6–81.

—— (2005a). Deriving c-command. MS, University of Maryland.

—— (2005b). What do labels do? MS, University of Maryland.

—— and Jairo Nunes (2002). On asymmetries between parasitic gaps and across-the-board constructions. *Syntax* 5: 26–54.

—— —— and Kleanthes K. Grohmann (2006). *Understanding Minimalism*. Cambridge: Cambridge University Press.

Huang, C.-T. James (1982). Logical relations in Chinese and the theory of grammar. Doctoral dissertation, MIT.

Huck, Geoffrey, and John Goldsmith (1996). *Ideology and Linguistic Theory*. Chicago: Chicago University Press.

Hume, David (1948) [1779]. *Dialogues concerning Natural Religion*. New York: Hafner Press.

Hunt, Bruce (1991). *The Maxwellians*. Ithaca, NY: Cornell University Press.

Hyams, Nina (1986). *Language Acquisition and the Theory of Parameters*. Dordrecht: Reidel.

Ishii, Toru (1999). Cyclic Spell-Out and the *that-t* effects. *Proceedings of WCCFL 18*, 220–31. Somerville, Mass.: Cascadilla Press.

Jackendoff, Ray (1994). *Patterns in the Mind*. New York: Basic Books.

—— (1997). *The Architecture of the Language Faculty*. Cambridge, Mass.: MIT Press.

—— (2002). *Foundations of Language: Brain, Meaning, Grammar, Evolution*. Oxford: Oxford University Press.

—— and Steven Pinker (2005). The nature of the language faculty and its implications for evolution of language (reply to Fitch et al. (2004). *Cognition* 97: 211–25.

Jacob, François (1976). *The Logic of Life*. New York: Vintage.

—— (1982). *The Possible and the Actual*. Seattle: University of Washington Press.

Jacobson, Polly (1998). Where (if anywhere) is transderivationality located? In P. Culicover and L. McNally (eds.), *Syntax and Semantics 29: The Limits of Syntax.* New York: Academic Press, 303–36.

Jaenisch, Rudolf, and Adrian Bird (2003). Epigenetic regulation of gene expression: how the genome integrates intrinsic and environmental signals. *Nature Genetics* 33: 245–54.

Jenkins, Lyle (2000). *Biolinguistics.* Cambridge: Cambridge University Press.

—— ed. (2004). *Variations and Universals of Biolinguistics.* London: Elsevier.

Jeong, Youngmi (2006). The landscape of applicatives. Doctoral dissertation, University of Maryland.

Jerne, Niels K. (1967). Antibodies and learning: selection versus instruction. In Gardner C. Quarton, Theodore Melnechuk, and Francis O. Schmitt (eds.), *The Neurosciences: A Study Program.* New York: Rockefeller University Press, 200–05.

—— (1985). The generative grammar of the immune system. *Science* 229: 1057–9.

Jo, Jung-Min (2004). Grammatical effects of focus and topic information. Doctoral dissertation, University of Illinois, Urbana-Champaign.

Joos, Martin, ed. (1957). *Readings in Linguistics.* Washington, DC: American Council of Learner Societies.

Julien, Marit (2002). *Syntactic Heads and Word Formation.* Oxford: Oxford University Press.

Kahnemuyipour, Arsalan (2004). The syntax of sentential stress. Doctoral dissertation, University of Toronto.

Kant, Immanuel (1925) [1781]. *Kritik der reinen Vernunft.* Leipzig: Alfred Kröner.

Katz, Jerrold J., and Paul Postal (1964). *An Integrated Theory of Linguistic Descriptions.* Cambridge, Mass.: MIT Press.

Kandybowicz, Jason (2006). Conditions on multiple copy spell-out and the syntax–phonology interface. Doctoral dissertation, UCLA.

Kauffman, Stuart (1993). *The Origins of Order.* Oxford: Oxford University Press.

Kayne, Richard S. (1975). *French Syntax: The Transformational Cycle.* Cambridge, Mass.: MIT Press.

—— (1984). *Connectedness and Binary Branching.* Dordrecht: Foris.

—— (1994). *The Antisymmetry of Syntax.* Cambridge, Mass.: MIT Press.

Kayne, Richard S. (2002). Pronouns and their antecedents. In S. D. Epstein and T. D. Seely (eds.), *Derivation and Explanation in the Minimalist Program*. Oxford: Blackwell, 133–66.

—— (2005). *Movement and Silence*. Oxford: Oxford University Press.

Kepler, Johannes (1858). *Joanni Kepleri Astronomi Opera Omnia*, ed. C. Frisch. 8 vols. Frankfurt and Erlangen.

Kiguchi, Hirohisa (2002). Syntax unchained. Doctoral dissertation, University of Maryland.

Kim, Kwang-sup (1998). (Anti-)connectivity. Doctoral dissertation, University of Maryland.

Kitahara, Hisatsugu (1997). *Elementary Operations and Optimal Derivations*. Cambridge, Mass.: MIT Press.

Kitcher, Philip (1983). *The Nature of Mathematical Knowledge*. Oxford: Oxford University Press.

Ko, Heejeong (2005). Linearization and syntactic edges. Doctoral dissertation, MIT.

Koizumi, Masatoshi (1995). Phrase structure in minimalist syntax. Doctoral dissertation, MIT.

Koopman, Hilda (1984). *The Syntax of Verbs*. Dordrecht: Reidel.

—— and Dominique Sportiche (1986). A note on long extraction in Vata and the ECP. *Natural Language and Linguistic Theory* 4: 357–74.

Koster, Jan (1978). *Locality Principles in Syntax*. Dordrecht: Foris.

—— (1987). *Domains and Dynasties: The Radical Autonomy of Syntax*. Dordrecht: Foris.

—— (2003). The configurational matrix. MS, University of Groningen.

Kroch, Anthony S. (2001). Syntactic change. In M. Baltin and C. Collins (eds.), *Handbook of Contemporary Syntactic Theory*. Oxford: Blackwell, 699–729.

Kuhn, Thomas (1962). *The Structure of Scientific Revolutions*. Chicago: Chicago University Press.

Lakatos, Imre (1970). Falsifications and the methodology of scientific research programs. In I. Lakatos and A. Musgrave (eds.), *Criticism and the Growth of Knowledge*. Cambridge: Cambridge University Press, 91–195.

—— and Paul Feyerabend (1999). *For and Against Method. Including Lakatos's lectures on scientific method and the Lakatos–Feyerabend correspondence*, ed. and with introd. by Matteo Motterlini. Chicago: Chicago University Press.

Lakoff, George (1971). On generative semantics. In D. D. Steinberg and L. A. Jakobovits (eds.), *Semantics: An Interdisciplinary Reader in Philoso-*

phy, Linguistics and Psychology. Cambridge: Cambridge University Press, 232–96.

Landau, Idan (2000). *Elements of Control.* Dordrecht: Kluwer.

—— (2003). Movement out of control. *Linguistic Inquiry* 34: 471–98.

—— (forthcoming). Chain resolution in Hebrew V(P)-fronting. *Syntax.*

Lappin, Shalom, and David Johnson (1999). *Local Constraints vs. Economy.* Stanford, Calif.: CSLI.

Lappin, Shalom, Robert Levine, and David Johnson (2000a). The structure of unscientific revolutions. *Natural Language and Linguistic Theory* 18: 665–71.

——, —— and —— (2000b). The revolution confused: a response to our critics. *Natural Language and Linguistic Theory* 18: 873–90.

——, —— and —— (2001). The revolution maximally confused. *Natural Language and Linguistic Theory* 19: 901–19.

Lasnik, Howard (1999). *Minimalist Analysis.* Oxford: Blackwell.

—— (2000). *Syntactic Structures Revisited.* Cambridge, Mass.: MIT Press.

—— (2001a). When can you save a structure by destroying it? In *Proceedings of NELS 31*, 301–20. University of Massachusetts, Amherst: GLSA.

—— (2001b). A note on the EPP. *Linguistic Inquiry* 32: 356–62.

—— (2002). The minimalist program in syntax. *Trends in Cognitive Sciences* 6: 432–7.

—— (2003a). *Minimalist Investigations in Syntactic Theory.* London: Routledge.

—— (2003b). On the Extended Projection Principle. *Studies in Modern Grammar* 31: 1–23.

—— (2005a). Review of Merchant (2001). *Language* 81: 259–65.

—— (2005b). Grammar, levels, and biology. In J. McGilvray (ed.), *The Cambridge Companion to Chomsky.* Cambridge: Cambridge University Press, 60–101.

—— (2006). Conceptions of the cycle. In L. Cheng and N. Corver (eds.), *WH-movement: Moving on.* Cambridge, Mass.: MIT Press, 197–216.

—— and Juan Uriagereka (1988). *A Course in GB Syntax.* Cambridge, Mass.: MIT Press.

—— —— with Cedric Boeckx (2005). *A Course in Minimalist Syntax.* Oxford: Blackwell.

Laughlin, Robert B., and David Pines (2000). The theory of everything. *Proceedings of the National Academy of Sciences* 97: 28–31.

Lederman, Leon M., and Christopher T. Hill (2004). *Symmetry and the Beautiful Universe.* Amherst, NY: Prometheus Books.

Lee, Ju-Eun (2004). Ditransitive structures and (anti-)locality. Doctoral dissertation, Harvard University.

Lees, Robert E. (1957). Review of Chomsky (1957). *Language* 33: 375–407.

Legate, Julie, and Charles Yang (2002). Empirical re-assessment of stimulus poverty arguments. *Linguistic Review* 19: 151–62.

Le Guyader, Herve (2004). *Geoffroy Saint-Hilaire : A Visionary Naturalist.* Chicago: University of Chicago Press.

Leiber, Justin (2002). Philosophy, engineering, biology, and history: a vindication of Turing's views about the distinction between the cognitive and physical sciences. *Journal of Experimental and Theoretical Artificial Intelligence* 14: 29–37.

Lenneberg, Eric H. (1967). *Biological Foundations of Language.* New York: Wiley.

Levine, Robert (2002). Review of Uriagereka (1998). *Language* 78: 325–30.

Lewin, Kurt (1935). *A Dynamic Theory of Personality.* New York: McGraw-Hill.

Lewontin, Richard (2000). *The Triple Helix.* Cambridge, Mass.: Harvard University Press.

—— (2003). Science and simplicity. *New York Review of Books* 50: 39–42.

Lightfoot, David (1999). *The Development of Language: Acquisition, Change, and Evolution.* Oxford: Blackwell.

—— (2003). Introduction to Noam Chomsky, *Syntactic Structures,* 2nd edn. Berlin: Mouton de Gruyter, v–xviii.

Longa, Victor (2001). Sciences of complexity and language origins: an alternative to natural selection. *Journal of Literary Semantics* 30: 1–17.

Lorenzo, Guillermo, and Victor Longa (2003a). Minimizing the genes for grammar: the minimalist program as a biological framework for the study of language. *Lingua* 113: 643–57.

—— and —— (2003b). *Homo loquens: biologia y evolucion del lenguaje.* Lugo: Tris Tram.

Luria, Salvador E. (1973). *Life, the Unfinished Experiment.* New York: Scribner's.

MacWhinney, Brian, and Catherine Snow (1985). The child language data exchange system. *Journal of Child Language* 12: 271–96.

Manzini, Maria R. (1994). Locality, minimality, and parasitic gaps. *Linguistic Inquiry* 25: 481–508.

—— and Anna Roussou (2000). A minimalist theory of A-movement and control. *Lingua* 110: 409–47.

Marantz, Alec (1995). The minimalist program. In G. Webelhuth (ed.), *Government and Binding and the Minimalist Program.* Oxford: Blackwell, 349–82.

—— (1997). No escape from syntax: don't try morphological analysis in the privacy of your own lexicon. *Penn Working Papers in Linguistics* 4(2): 201–25.

—— (2000). Words. MS, MIT.

Marcus, Gary F. (2004). *The Birth of the Mind: How a Tiny Number of Genes Creates the Complexities of Human Thought.* New York: Basic Books.

Martin, Roger (1999). Case, the Extended Projection Principle, and minimalism. In S. D. Epstein and N. Hornstein (eds.), *Working Minimalism.* Cambridge, Mass.: MIT Press, 1–25.

—— and Juan Uriagereka (2000). Introduction: some possible foundations for the minimalist program. In R. Martin, D. Michaels, and J. Uriagereka (eds.), *Step by Step.* Cambridge, Mass.: MIT Press, 1–29.

Maxwell, Nicholas (2003). *The Comprehensibility of the Universe: A New Conception of Science.* Oxford: Oxford University Press.

Maynard-Smith, J., R. Burian, S. Kauffman, P. Alberch, B. Goodwin, R. Lande, D. Raup, and L. Wolpert (1985). Developmental constraints and evolution. *Quarterly Review of Biology* 60: 265–87.

Mayr, Clemens, and Martin Reitbauer (2005). Left-dislocation, agreement, and the notion of anti-locality. MS, University of Vienna.

Mayr, Ernst (2004). *What Makes Biology Unique?* Cambridge: Cambridge University Press.

McCloskey, Jim (1997). Subjecthood and subject positions. In L. Haegeman (ed.), *Elements of Grammar.* Dordrecht: Kluwer, 197–235.

—— (2000). Quantifier float and wh-movement in an Irish English. *Linguistic Inquiry* 31: 57–84.

McGhee, George (1998). *Theoretical Morphology.* New York: Columbia University Press.

McGinnis, Martha (1998). Locality in (A-)movement. Doctoral dissertation, MIT.

—— (2001). Variation in the phase structure of applicatives. *Linguistic Variation Yearbook* 1: 101–42.

McGinnis, William, and Michael Kuziora (1994). The molecular architects of body design. *Scientific American* (Feb.): 58–66.

McNeill, David (1966). Developmental psycholinguistics. In F. Smith and G. Miller (eds.), *The Genesis of Language.* Cambridge, Mass.: MIT Press, 15–84.

Merchant, Jason (2001). *The Syntax of Silence*. Oxford: Oxford University Press.

Miyagawa, Shigeru (2003). A-movement, scrambling, and options without optionality. In S. Karimi (ed.), *Word Order and Scrambling*. Oxford: Blackwell, 177–200.

Monod, Jacques (1972). From enzymatic adaptation to allosteric transitions. In *Nobel Lectures, Physiology or Medicine 1963–1970*. Amsterdam: Elsevier, 188–209.

—— (1974). *Chance and Necessity*. New York: Collins.

Moro, Andrea (2000). *Dynamic Antisymmetry*. Cambridge, Mass.: MIT Press.

Mueller, Bertha, and Charles J. Engard (1952). *Goethe's Botanical Writings*. Honolulu: University of Hawai'i Press.

Murasugi, K., and M. Saito (1995). Adjunction and cyclicity. In *Proceedings of WCCFL* 13, 302–317. Stanford, Calif.: CSLI.

Newmeyer, Frederick J. (1996). *Linguistic Theory in America*. New York: Academic Press.

—— (2003). Review article: Chomsky (2002); Anderson and Lightfoot (2002); Bichakjian, *Language in a Darwinian Perspective*. *Language* 79: 583–99.

—— (2005). On split CPs and the 'perfectness' of language. MS, University of Washington.

Newton, Isaac (1687). *Philosophiae Naturalis Principia Mathematica*. London.

Nissenbaum, Jon (2000). Investigations of covert phrase movement. Doctoral dissertation, MIT.

Nowak, Martin A. (2004). Theory is available light. *Current Biology* 14: R406–7.

Nunes, Jairo (1995). The copy theory of movement and the linearization of chains in the minimalist program. Doctoral dissertation, University of Maryland.

—— (1999). Linearization of chains and phonetic realization of chain links. In S. D. Epstein and N. Hornstein (eds.), *Working Minimalism*. Cambridge, Mass.: MIT Press, 217–49.

—— (2004). *Linearization of Chains and Sideward Movement*. Cambridge, Mass.: MIT Press.

—— and Juan Uriagereka (2000). Cyclicity and extraction domains. *Syntax* 3: 20–43.

Ouhalla, Jamal (1994). *Introducing Transformational Grammar.* London: Arnold.

Perlmutter, David (1978). Impersonal passives and the unaccusative hypothesis. In *Proceedings of BLS* 4, 157–189. University of California, Berkeley.

Pesetsky, David (1998). Some optimality principles of sentence pronunciation. In P. Barbosa, D. Fox, P. Hagstrom, M. McGinnis, and D. Pesetsky (eds.), *Is the Best Good Enough?* Cambridge, Mass.: MIT Press/MITWPL, 337–83.

—— (2000a). *Phrasal Movement and its Kin.* Cambridge, Mass.: MIT Press.

—— (2000b). The battle for language: from syntax to phonics. Handout, MIT.

—— and Esther Torrego (2001). T-to-C movement: causes and consequences. In M. Kenstowicz (ed.), *Ken Hale: A Life in Language.* Cambridge, Mass.: MIT Press, 355–426.

—— and —— (2004). Tense, case, and the nature of syntactic categories. In J. Guéron and J. Lecarme (eds.), *The Syntax of Tense.* Cambridge, Mass.: MIT Press, 495–537.

—— and —— (2005). The syntax of valuation and the interpretability of features. MS, MIT and University of Massachusetts, Boston.

Phillips, Colin (2004). Linguistics and linking problems. In M. Rice and S. Warren (eds.), *Developmental Language Disorders: From Phenotypes to Etiologies.* Mahwah, NJ: Erlbaum, 241–87.

Piattelli-Palmarini, Massimo (1980). *Language and Learning.* Cambridge, Mass.: Harvard University Press.

—— (1981). Equilibria, crystals, programs, energetic models, and organizational models. In M. L. Dalla Chiara (ed.), *Italian Studies in the Philosophy of Science.* Dordrecht: Reidel, 341–59.

—— (1986). The rise of selective theories: a case study and some lessons from immunology. In W. Demopoulos and A. Marras (eds.), *Language Learning and Concept Acquisition: Foundational Issues.* Norwood, NJ: Ablex, 117–30.

—— (1989). Evolution, selection and cognition: from 'learning' to parameter setting in biology and in the study of language. *Cognition* 31: 1–44.

—— (2005). What is language that it may have evolved, and what is evolution that it may apply to language? MS, University of Arizona.

Pietroski, Paul (2005). *Events and Semantic Architecture.* Oxford: Oxford University Press.

Pinker, Steven (1994). *The Language Instinct.* New York: HarperCollins.

—— (1997). *How the Mind Works.* New York: Norton.

—— (2002). *The Blank Slate.* New York: Viking.

—— (2005). A reply to Jerry Fodor on *How the Mind Works. Mind and Language* 20: 33–8.

—— and Paul Bloom (1990). Natural language and natural selection. *Behavioral and Brain Sciences* 13: 707–26.

—— and Ray Jackendoff (2005). The faculty of language: what's special about it? *Cognition* 95: 201–36.

Planck, Max (1949). *Scientific Autobiography and other papers.* New York: Philosophical Library.

Poeppel, David (2005). The interdisciplinary study of language and its challenges. *Jahrbuch des Wissenschaftskollegs zu Berlin.*

—— and David Embick (2005). The relation between linguistics and neuroscience. In A. Cutler (ed.), *Twenty-First Century Psycholinguistics: Four Cornerstones.* Mahwah, NJ: Erlbaum.

Poincaré, Henri (1958) [1904]. *The Value of Science.* New York: Dover.

Polinsky, Maria (2005). Expanding the scope of control and raising. MS, University of California, San Diego.

—— and Eric Potsdam (2002). Backward control. *Linguistic Inquiry* 33: 245–82.

Pollock, Jean-Yves (1989). Verb movement, universal grammar, and the structure of IP. *Linguistic Inquiry* 20: 365–424.

Poole, Geoffrey (2002). *Syntactic Theory.* New York: Palgrave.

Popper, Karl (1959). *The Logic of Scientific Discovery.* London: Hutchinson.

Postal, Paul (1972). The best theory. In S. Peters (ed.), *Goals of Linguistic Theory.* Englewood Cliffs, NJ: Prentice Hall, 131–70.

—— (1974). *On Raising.* Cambridge, Mass.: MIT Press.

Postal, Paul M. (2003a). (Virtually) conceptually necessary. *Journal of Linguistics* 39: 599–620.

—— (2003b). *Skeptical Linguistic Essays.* Oxford: Oxford University Press.

Pullum, Geoffrey (1996). Nostalgic views from Building 20. *Journal of Linguistics* 32: 137–47.

—— and Barbara Scholz (2002). Empirical assessment of stimulus poverty arguments. *Linguistic Review* 19: 9–50.

Radford, Andrew (1997). *Syntactic Theory and the Structure of English: A Minimalist Approach.* Cambridge: Cambridge University Press.

—— (2004). *English Syntax: An Introduction.* Cambridge: Cambridge University Press.

Randall, Lisa (2005). *Warped Passages: Unraveling the Mysteries of the Universe's Hidden Dimensions*. New York: HarperCollins.

Redondi, Pietro (1998). From Galileo to Augustine. In P. Machamer (ed.), *The Cambridge Companion to Galileo*. Cambridge: Cambridge University Press, 175–210.

Reinhart, Tanya (2006). *Interface strategies*. Cambridge, Mass.: MIT Press.

Reuland, Eric, ed. (2000). *Arguments and Case*. Amsterdam: Benjamins.

Rezac, Milan (2004). Elements of cyclic syntax: agree and merge. Doctoral dissertation, University of Toronto.

Richards, Norvin (1997). What moves where when in which language? Doctoral dissertation, MIT.

—— (1999). Featural cyclicity and the ordering of multiple specifiers. In S. D. Epstein and N. Hornstein (eds.), *Working Minimalism*. Cambridge, Mass.: MIT Press, 127–58.

—— (2001). *Movement in Language*. Oxford: Oxford University.

Rizzi, Luigi (1978). Violations of the wh-island constraint in Italian and the subjacency condition. *Montreal Working Papers in Linguistics 11*. University of Montreal.

—— (1990). *Relativized Minimality*. Cambridge, Mass.: MIT Press.

—— (1997). The fine structure of the left periphery. In L. Haegeman (ed.), *Elements of Grammar*. Dordrecht: Kluwer, 281–337.

—— (2001). Reconstruction, weak island sensitivity, and agreement. In C. Cecchetto, G. Chierchia, and M. T. Guasti (eds.), *Semantic Interfaces*. Stanford, Calif.: CSLI, 145–76.

—— (2004). On the study of the language faculty: results, developments, and perspectives. *Linguistic Review* 21: 323–44.

—— (2006). On the form of chains. In L. Cheng and N. Corver (eds.), *WH-movement: Moving on*. Cambridge, Mass.: MIT Press, 97–133.

—— and Ur Shlonsky (2005). Strategies of subject extraction. MS, University of Siena and University of Geneva.

Roberts, Ian (1996). *Comparative Syntax*. London: Arnold.

—— (2005). *Principles and Parameters in a VSO Language: A Case Study in Welsh*. Oxford: Oxford University Press.

—— and Anna Roussou (2002). The Extended Projection Principle as a condition on the tense dependency. In P. Svenonius (ed.), *Subjects, Expletives and the EPP*. Oxford: Oxford University Press, 125–55.

Rodrigues, Cilene (2004). Impoverished morphology and A-movement out of case domains. Doctoral dissertation, University of Maryland.

Roeper, Tom, and Edwin Williams, eds. (1987). *Parameter Setting.* Dordrecht: Reidel.

Romero, Maribel (1998). Problems for a semantic account of reconstruction. In *Proceedings of the 1997 Tübingen Workshop*, 127–154. University of Tübingen.

Rosenbaum, Peter (1967). *The Grammar of English Predicate Complement Constructions.* Cambridge, Mass.: MIT Press.

—— (1970). A principle governing deletion in English sentential complementation. In R. Jacobs and P. Rosenbaum (eds.), *Readings in English Transformational Grammar.* Waltham, Mass.: Ginn, 20–29.

Ross, John R. (1967). Constraints on variables in syntax. Doctoral dissertation, MIT. Published 1986 as *Infinite Syntax!* (Norwood, NJ: Ablex).

—— (1969). Guess who? In *Papers from the 5th Regional Meeting of the Chicago Linguistic Society*, 252–86. Chicago: Chicago Linguistic Society.

Rudin, Catherine (1988). On multiple questions and multiple *wh*-fronting. *Natural Language and Linguistic Theory* 6: 445–501.

Safir, Ken (1999). Vehicle change and reconstruction in A-bar chains. *Linguistic Inquiry* 30: 587–620.

Saito, Mamoru, and Hajime Hoji (1983). Weak Crossover and Move α in Japanese. *Natural Language and Linguistic Theory* 1: 245–59.

Sampson, Geoffrey (1999). *Educating Eve: The Language Instinct Debate.* Cassell.

Sauerland, Uli (1998). The meaning of chains. Doctoral dissertation, MIT.

—— (2004). The interpretation of chains. *Natural Language Semantics* 12: 63–127.

Saunders, Peter T., ed. (1992). *Collected Works of A. M. Turing: Morphogenesis.* London: North-Holland.

Schweber, Silvan S. (1993). Physics, community and the crisis in physical theory. *Physics Today* (Nov.): 34–40.

Seely, T. Daniel (2006). Merge, derivational c-command and subcategorization in a label-free syntax. In C. Boeckx (ed.), *Minimalist Essays.* Amsterdam: Benjamins, 182–217.

Seuren, Pieter (2004). *Chomsky's Minimalism.* Oxford: Oxford University Press.

Shea, William (1998). Galileo's Copernicanism: the silence and the rhetoric. In P. Machamer (ed.), *The Cambridge Companion to Galileo.* Cambridge: Cambridge University Press, 211–43.

Shlonsky, Ur (1992). Resumptive pronouns as a last resort. *Linguistic Inquiry* 23: 443–68.

Singh, Rajvinder (2003). Economy, scope, and computation without reference sets. MS, MIT.

Sklar, Robert (1968). Chomskyapos;s revolution in linguistics. *The Nation* (9 Sept.): 213–17.

Smith, Neil, and Ianthi-Maria Tsimpli (1995). *The Mind of a Savant: Language Learning and Modularity.* Oxford Blackwell.

Spelke, Elizabeth (2003). What makes us smart? Core knowledge and natural language. In D. Gentner and S. Goldin-Meadow (eds.), *Language in Mind.* Cambridge, Mass.: MIT Press, 277–311.

Sportiche, Dominique (1988). A theory of floating quantifiers and its corollaries for constituent structure. *Linguistic Inquiry* 19: 425–49.

—— (1998). *Partitions and Atoms of Phrase Structure.* London: Routledge.

—— (2001). Movement, binding, and reconstruction. MS, UCLA.

Sprecher, Simon G., and Heinrich Reichert (2003). The urbilateral brain: developmental insights into the evolutionary origin of the brain in insects and vertebrates. *Arthropod Structure and Development* 32: 141–56.

Starke, Michal (2001). Move dissolves into merge: a theory of locality. Doctoral dissertation, University of Geneva.

Stepanov, Arthur (2001). Cyclic domains in syntactic theory. Doctoral dissertation, University of Connecticut.

Stewart, Ian (1999). *Life's Other Secret.* New York: Wiley.

Stockwell, Robert P., Paul Schachter, and Barbara H. Partee (1973). *The Major Syntactic Structures of English.* New York: Holt, Rinehart, & Winston.

Suppe, Frederick, ed. (1977). *The Structure of Scientific Theories.* Urbana: University of Illinois Press.

Svenonius, Peter (2005). Extending the extension condition to discontinuous idioms. MS, University of Tromsø.

Takahashi, Daiko (1994). Minimality of movement. Doctoral dissertation, University of Connecticut.

Ten Hacken, Pius (2006). Review of Seuren (2004). *Journal of Linguistics* 42: 226–9.

Thom, René (1975). La théorie des catastrophes et ses applications. In *Réflexions sur de nouvelles approches dans l'étude des systèmes.* Paris: ENSTA, 9–22.

Thompson, D'Arcy (1917). *On Growth and Form.* Cambridge: Cambridge University Press.

Thompson, D'Arcy (1942). *On Growth and Form, new edn.* Cambridge: Cambridge University Press.

Thornton, Rosalind (1995). Referentiality and wh-movement in child English: juvenile delinkuency. *Language Acquisition* 4: 139–75.

Ticio, Emma (2003). On the structure of DPs. Doctoral dissertation, University of Connecticut.

Tonegawa, Susumu (1993). Somatic generation of immune diversity. In J. Lindsten (ed.), *Nobel Lectures, Physiology or Medicine 1981–1990.* Singapore: World Scientific, 381–405.

Travis, Charles (1981). *The True and the False: The Domain of the Pragmatic.* Amsterdam: Benjamins.

Ura, Hiryuki (2000). *Checking Theory and Grammatical Functions in Universal Grammar.* Oxford: Oxford University Press.

Uragereka, Juan (1998). *Rhyme and Reason.* Cambridge, Mass.: MIT Press.

—— (1999). Multiple spell-out. In S. D. Epstein and N. Hornstein (eds.), *Working Minimalism.* Cambridge, Mass.: MIT Press, 251–82.

—— (2002). *Derivations.* London: Routledge.

—— (2003). Spell-out consequences. MS, University of Maryland.

—— (forthcoming). *Syntactic Anchors.* Cambridge: Cambridge University Press.

Van der Lely, Heather K. J. (2004). Evidence for and implications of a domain-specific grammatical deficit. In L. Jenkins (ed.), *Variation and Universals in Biolinguistics.* London: Elsevier, 117–44.

—— (2005). Domain-specific cognitive systems: insight from SLI. *Trends in Cognitive Sciences* 9: 53–58.

Wagner, Michael (2005). Prosody and recursion. Doctoral dissertation, MIT.

Weinberg, Steven (1976). The forces of nature. *Bulletin of the American Academy of Arts and Sciences* 29: 13–29.

—— (1987). The laws of physics. In R. Feynman and S. Weinberg, *Elementary Particles and the Laws of Physics.* Cambridge: Cambridge University Press, 61–107.

—— (1993). *Dreams of a Final Theory.* New York: Vintage.

—— (2001). *Facing Up.* Cambridge, Mass.: Harvard University Press.

—— (2003). *The Discovery of Atomic Particles,* rev. edn. Cambridge: Cambridge University Press.

—— (2004). The making of the standard model. *European Journal of Physics* C 34: 5–13.

Weisskopf, Victor F. (1965). In defence of high energy physics. In L. C. L. Yuan (ed.), *Nature of Matter: Purposes of High Energy Physics*. Long Island, NY: Brookhaven National Laboratory, 24–7.

West, Geoffrey, James Brown, and Brian Enquist (1997). A general model for the origin of allometric scaling laws in biology. *Science* 280: 122–5.

Wexler, Ken (2004). Lenneberg's dream: learning, normal language development, and Specific Language Impairment. In L. Jenkins (ed.), *Variation and Universals in Biolinguistics*. London: Elsevier, 239–84.

Williams, Edwin (2003). *Representation Theory*. Cambridge, Mass.: MIT Press.

Wilson, Robin (2004). *Four Colors Suffice*. Princeton, NJ: Princeton University Press.

Witkoś, Jacek (2002). *Movement and Reconstruction*. Tübingen: Narr.

Wolfenstein, Lincoln (2003). Lessons from Kepler and the theory of everything. *Proceedings of the National Academy of Sciences of the USA* 100 : 5001–3.

Yang, Charles (2002). *Knowledge and Learning in Natural Language*. Oxford: Oxford University Press.

Yang, Chen Ning (1982). Beauty and theoretical physics. In D. Curtin (ed.), *The Aesthetic Dimension of Science*. New York: Philosophical Library, 25–40.

Zwart, C. Jan-Wouter (2004). The format of dependency relations. MS, University of Groningen.

Index